What they're saying about...
Backing Hard Into River History:

"I have been asking Jim for twenty years to write this book. It has proved to be fascinating to read and well worth the wait."
—Robert G. Goodwin, director, Mid-Continent Office, U.S. Maritime Administration.

"Bravo!! Jim Swift!! Backing Hard Into River History is worthy of a standing ovation! It is an enjoyably good read. His life-long love affair with the river is sensed as well as his expertise from years on The Waterways Journal, which make this book an important and definitive addition to river and riverboat history. It will be used as a reference for serious researchers and buffs as well. Besides, it's just plain fun to read."
—Sonie Liebler, river historian.

"Backing Hard Into River History," by Jim Swift is a memorable reading experience for anyone connected with mid-continent rivers. He takes the reader from the beginnings of the 'Riverman's Bible (The Waterways Journal) in 1891 up to the present day. The book is a full speed ahead, in the company notch, must-read book for whoever loves seeing a flotilla of barges pushed by a powerful towboat along the Mississippi or Ohio River. A pursuit of pleasure."
—Charles Lehman, retired vice president of public affairs
American Commercial Barge Line

"The WJ is the weekly heartbeat of America's inland waterways, and Jim has collected all the 'good stuff' into one book. I guarantee, you won't be able to put it down."
—Kathy Flippo, author, *Between The Saints: Louis and Paul*

"To anyone interested in history of commercial navigation on the inland waterways, Backing Hard... will be a fascinating account. Jim Swift, who has followed the industry for 60 years through his work with the industry's chronicle, The Waterways Journal, not only gives the reader a journalist's view of events on the river but provides sources of information for further research. It is a valuable reference work as well as an enjoyable read."
H. Nelson Spencer III, publisher, *The Waterways Journal*

Backing Hard Into River History

by

James V. Swift

Including

Materials Autobiographical in Nature

and

a

History of

The Waterways Journal

A Little River Book

Backing Hard Into River History is designated by the Publisher as Little River Books Series Vol. I.

J. R. Simpson & Associates, Inc.
Little River Books Division
2175 Huntington Dr.
Florissant, Missouri 63033-1227

First Edition

Printed in the United States of America

Endsheet illustrations by artist Lexie Palmore
Henry Miller Shreve illustration P. 98, Courtesy National Portrait Gallery, Smithsonian Institution, Washington, D.C.
Numerous articles and photographs were reproduced from the files of *The Waterways Journal*.

Special thanks to Sonie Liebler, historian; Charles Lehman, retired American Commerial Barge Line vice president of public affairs; Nelson Spencer, *Waterways Journal* publisher; Dan Owen, former editor of the *Inland River Record* and *Inland River Guide* and former associate editor of *The Waterways Journal*; Robert G. Goodwin, Jr., director, Mid-Continent Office, U.S. Maritime Administration; and Kathy Flippo, author.

Library of Congress Card Number: 00-106597

ISBN 0-9703086-0-4

To those who build and maintain the world's greatest system of navigable waterways...

To those who navigate them, carrying the Nation's goods in the most economical way...

And to the men and women who made The Waterways Journal into the "Rivermen's Bible,"

This book is respectfully dedicated.

Table of Contents

Chapter 1 — *William Henry Swift* *1*

Chapter 2 — A Different River *5*

Chapter 3 — *One of Ruth's Boys* *9*

Chapter 4 — An Excursion Boat Summer *15*

Chapter 5 — *Enter The Golden Eagle* *23*

Chapter 6 — *"The Riverman's Bible"* *33*

Chapter 7 — *Donald Thomas Wright* *65*

Chapter 8 — *One of The Crew* *73*

Chapter 9 — *Unpleasant Interlude* *77*

Chapter 10 — *The Rivers Went To War* *83*

Chapter 11 — *Helping The Rivers Work* *97*

Chapter 12 — *The Mississippi Valley Association* *113*

Chapter 13 — *Federal* *123*

Chapter 14 — *The River Grows Up* *139*

Chapter 15 — *A Boost From Technology* *163*

Chapter 16 — *Flowing With The River* *179*

Chapter 17 — *The Mark Twain Hotel* *185*

Chapter 18 — *Greenville* *193*

Chapter 19 — *The Competition* *199*

—Continued Next Page

Table of Contents Continued—

Chapter 20 — *Preserving History* *203*

Chapter 21 — *On The River Road* *207*

Chapter 22 — *The Christmas Issue* *217*

Chapter 23 — *Greater Than God?* *223*

Chapter 24 — *The Bubble Bursts* *233*

Chapter 25 — *The Agencies* *237*

Chapter 26 — *Saving The Past* *245*

Chapter 27 — *Still Fighting* *257*

Chapter 28 — *Precious Images* *263*

Chapter 29 — *The River on Canvas* *267*

Chapter 30 — *Wood, Plastic And Metal* *273*

Chapter 31 — *See The Past in River History* *279*

Chapter 32 — *Sounds of The River* *291*

Chapter 33 — *Climbing The Family Tree* *301*

Chapter 34 — *Kept on an Even Keel* *307*

Chapter 35 — *Full Ahead* *317*

Appendix I - War Vessel Construction *323*

Appendix II - Keeping Track of Tonnage *335*

Appendix III - Honors and Activities *347*

Appendix IV - From The Author's Bookshelf *353*

Appendix V - Waterway Leaders *361*

Table of Illustrations

Chapter 1

The Swift Family Houseboat 3

Author's mother, Anita Bailey Swift 4

Chapter 3

Hot Stove League on Golden Eagle 10

Hot Stove League and Friends 11

Richard Lemen 11

Ruth Ferris and Rudy Gerber on Golden Eagle 12

Capt. Donald T. Wright and Ruth Ferris in Pilothouse 12

Author Ben Lucien Burman, et al, on the Golden Eagle 13

Chapter 4

Excursion Boat Days at St. Louis (the waterfront) 16

Str. J.S. DeLUXE 18

Chapter 5

Eating on the Guards of the Golden Eagle 26

Capt. William H. "Buck" Leyhe 27

Golden Eagle at St. Paul Public Landing, June 1939 28

Golden Eagle Coming Into Chattanooga, May 1940 29

The Golden Eagle Sunk, at Chester, Illinois, June 1941 30

Chapter 6

Col. Will S. Hays 35

Capt. Abbott Veatch 38

Schoellhorn-Albrecht's Steamboat Doctor 39

Anheuser-Busch's Malt-Nutrine Advertisement 40

—Continued next page

Table of Illustrations Continued—

Typical Ads in the Journal in 1896 . . . .*41*

The Waterways Journal "Flag" in June 6, 1896, issue *42*

William Arste (Journal Publisher) *43*

Kathleen Smith (Journal Editor) *47*

Flag Pole Promoted by The Waterways Journal *49*

The Henry Sackman, Destroyed by Cyclone *59*

The Arkansas City, Destroyed by Cyclone *59*

Eads Bridge *60*

Waterways Journal Office *62*

Conventioners at Memphis, Tennessee, in 1907 . . . .*64*

Chapter 7

Donald Thomas Wright *66*

Donald T. Wright's Gravestone in Bellefontaine Cemetery *72*

Chapter 9

The Author at Camp Cooke, California *78*

Chapter 10

Submarine in Illinois Waterway Drydock *90*

LST Bound for Deep Water and Russian Vessels *90*

The Cat Fish Navy *93*

Navy Tanker Built on Rivers *94*

Destroyer Escort *96*

Chapter 11

The Snagboat John M. Macomb *98*

Henry Miller Shreve *98*

Horse-Drawn Wagons Cross Ohio During Low Water *99*

—Continued Next Page

Table of Illustrations Continued—

Waiting for Coalboat Water in Pittsburgh Harbor *100*

Col. John L. Vance *101*

Greenbrier Taking on Presidential Party at Cincinnati *103*

President Herbert Hoover, et al, on Greenbrier *103*

Tows at Blennerhassett Island on Ohio River *104*

Ohio River Mile 306 Before Dams Were Built *105*

Mile 306 After The Dams Were Built *105*

Upper Miss at Davenport in 1931 and 1953 ....*106*

President Nixon Dedicates Arkansas Waterway *108*

Chapter 12

MVA's First Annual Convention, 1918, in St. Louis *114*

MVA Welcoming Staff *116*

Herman T. Pott *118*

MVA Exhibits Layout *119*

Anoka Boat & Towing Company Welcomes MVA *120*

Chapter 13

President Theodore Roosevelt and Party on Mississippi *124*

Steamboat Parade in October 1907 ....*124*

Vessels Wait for the Parade To Start *125*

Powered Barge Tuscaloosa *126*

The General Ashburn, Patrick J. Hurley and Minnesota *128*

Mvs. Helena, Herbert Hoover and America *130*

Mv. Harry Truman in New Orleans Harbor, 1948 ....*131*

S. S. Thorpe and General Allen Arrive in St. Paul, 1927 ......*132*

The "City Boat" or "Black Boat" Natchez *133*

—Continued Next Page

Table of Illustrations Continued—

Mv. Franklin D. Roosevelt, October 23, 1946 . . . .*134*

Mv. Peter Fanchi, 5,600 hp., Built in 1977 . . . .*135*

Str. Wynoka, One of Federal's Early Boats *136*

Chapter 14

Shoving Match, D. T. Lane vs. James Rumsey *140*

SUNCO A-4 and Its "Caterpillar" Paddles *141*

Double-Width Roller Chain Operates Paddle Wheel *141*

Gas Boats on Little Kanawha River *143*

Str. Sprague With Oil Tow *145*

Str. Sprague With Oil Tow Carrying 1927 Flood Victims *146*

Southern Shipbuilding Corporation Advertisement *151*

Vessels Altair, Betsy Ann, Kansas City Socony,

   Diamond A and Kanawha *152*

Mvs. Eddie Erlbacher, James H and Ashland *153*

Havana Zephyr, Commercial Clipper and Jane Smith *154*

Sam Houston, Henry L. Hillman and A. M. Thompson *155*

Mvs. J. W. Bedford, Kansas City and J. W. Hershey *156*

Esso Tennessee, Argonaut and Jessica Brent *157*

Jim Bernhardt, Senator Stennis and Senator Eastland *158*

Mv. Austen S. Cargill and One of Cargill's Staterooms *159*

Galley and Lounge of Austen S. Cargill *160*

Pilothouse and Engineroom of Austen S. Cargill *161*

Chapter 15

Mv. Tri-State, First Western Rivers Towboat With Radar *166*

Dump Barge and Box Hopper Barge *170*

—Continued Next Page

Table of Illustrations Continued—

Hopper, Flat Deck and Dry-Cement Barges *171*

Auto Carriers and Barge Rake *172*

Integrated Tows and Berthing (Hotel) Barge *173*

Strange Barges and a Big Load Afloat *174*

Crane Barges and an Interesting Tow *175*

More Interesting Tows *176*

Missile Barge in Tow and Kort Nozzles *177*

Chapter 17

The Old Mark Twain Hotel in St. Louis *186*

Chapter 18

Lake Ferguson at Greenville, Mississippi *194*

The Marina, Port of Greenville *197*

Chapter 21

License Plate Promoting Barge Industry *214*

Chapter 23

Tow Backlog at L&D 26, April 16, 1976 . . . .*225*

Lock Wall Damage at L&D 26 . . . .*226*

Chapter 25

U.S. Engineers' Logo *238*

U.S. Coast Guard Logo *241*

Chapter 26

Capt. Fred Way and Mack Gamble on the Lady Grace *249*

The Author and Journal Publisher H. N. "Ray" Spencer *250*

Chapter 34

Picture of The Journal Family in the Mid-1960s *308*

—Continued Next Page

Table of Illustrations Continued—

Donald T. Wright, The Author and Richard Armfield 311

The Author at His Desk in 1960 312

Guy Jester and H. Nelson Spencer III

A Fleet of His Own 315

Appendix II

Iowa Department of Transportation Traffic Comparison 345

Appendix III

Ruebel Hotel, Grafton, Illinois, Honors the Author 349

Author Presents Award to John Hartford 349

Jesse Brent, River Person of the Century 350

Other River-Person-of-the-Century Finalists 351

Publisher's Note

As former editor of *The Waterways Journal* I worked with James V. Swift 22 years. It was only natural that his name was first on the list when the idea for a Little River Books series was born.

To those sadly not familiar with either the *Journal* or the author I offer a special note. In some circles Jim Swift has become known as "Mr. Waterways Journal." At 84, he has spent virtually his entire working career, except for World War II service, working for the *Journal*. No one worked there longer. Many cannot conceive of a *Journal* without James V. Swift. For that matter, who can think of the author without thinking of the *Journal* and river history? *Backing Hard Into River History* reflects those years and more.

This is the first volume in an open-ended Little River Book series. Others are in the writing stage. They will remain virtually identical in length and appearance, and will be nonfiction, thus making possible the accumulation of valuable river history, as interpreted by the authors, in one matched set.

In *If Ships Could Talk*, a collection of river and sea poetry, appears this thought:

> "What wondrous tales we'll never see
> unfold
> If we neglect to ask...when men
> Grow old."

If we neglect this commission, indeed much important river history will remain unwritten. We are grateful, therefore, to all brave souls who labor hard to write and produce books. The challenge is demanding.

A special note of appreciation to *The Waterways Journal*, for which the author still produces his "Old Boat" column; and to the owner and publisher of that 112-year-old publication, Nelson Spencer, without whose generous cooperation *Backing Hard Into River History* would have been a far more difficult task.

Jack R. Simpson

Author's Preface

Writing this book I liken to driving a troika, a Russian three-horse vehicle. One set of reins went to the river history, another to *The Waterways Journal*, and the third to myself. After all, this has been advertised as partly autobiographical. I hope I have been successful in relating all three, and have driven to a successful conclusion. I have tried to make the book interesting and informative, too.

Many people have helped me through the years with the "Old Boat" column by offering suggestions, information and pictures. I am grateful to all of them. There is a danger in using names; one is bound to forget somebody. If I have, I beg forgiveness.

Some have left us, but I will not forget them—Capt. William H. Tippitt, Hernando, Mississippi; Robert D. Burtnett, Chillicothe, Illinois; and Warren F. "Howdy" Howdeshell, Eldred, Illinois. Today there are R. Allen Coleman, Omaha, Nebraska; Carol Hugh Jones, Lincoln, Nebraska; Donald Fluetsch, Cassville, Wisconsin; Mike Giglio, Marietta, Ohio; Keith Norrington, New Albany, Indiana; Capt. Larry Geisler, Valley Boat Docks, Duffy, Ohio; Judy Patsch, Rock Island, Illinois; Herman Radloff, New Ulm, Minnesota; John J. Rous, Ashland, Kentucky; William J. Shive, Belleville, Illinois; Capt. Charles Henry Stone, Point Pleasant, West Virginia; Dave Thomson, Sun Valley, California; William Smith, Springfield, Ohio; William V. Torner, Waterloo, Iowa; Pat Welsh, Davenport, Iowa; and Capt. John Vize, East Moline, Illinois; and Virginia Bennett, Covington, Kentucky.

I thank heaven every day for Capt. Frederick Way, Jr., and his *Packet Directory, 1848-1983*, and the *Steam Towboat Directory* he did with J. W. Rutter. Ohio State University Press, Athens, Ohio, put them out. What a tremendous amount of work he did in compiling all that data! And thanks, too, to Alan L. Bates, who indexed the *S&D Reflector*, which Fred edited. (Alan has done us a great favor, too, in publishing his two encylopedias on steamboat architecture and machinery.)

I also appreciate the index Sonie Liebler did for *River Ripples*, the newsletter of the Midwest Riverboat Buffs. It is a helpful guide when tracking down history.

Lastly, thanks to publisher Jack R. Simpson for his patience while I drove through the months with this troika, and to Bette Gorden, curator of the Herman T. Pott National Inland Waterway Library, for her help in locating and supplying me with information.—JVS

Chapter 1 ——

William Henry Swift

Look back at your life and you will undoubtedly remember someone who greatly influenced your choice of a
career. It may have been a teacher, clergyman, friend, a parent
or relative.

In my case it was a paternal grandfather whom I never
knew. He died the year before I was born. William Henry Swift
was a printer and journalist, and his genes, I believe, came
down to me.

He was a native of Cayuga County, New York. He was a
printer's apprentice on the Auburn (New York) *Advertiser*
and came to St. Louis in 1850. Continuing in the printing
business, he was a journeyman printer and after a time
became foreman of the *State Journal* composing room. After
the *State Journal* ceased publication, William Swift moved
on to become a news-gatherer and became the city editor of
the St. Louis *Dispatch*. He was promoted to editor-in-chief,
but felt inclined to get into the business circle of St. Louis
and to manage the commercial and financial departments of
the *Missouri Republican*.

He moved on from this reporting to be clerk of the St.
Louis City Council and active in the business community.

1

He is quoted as saying, when he left the newspaper, "Journalism leads to anything if one quits in time."

One of William Swift's notable acts came during the Republican Party convention in Jefferson City in 1870. There was a division in the party, and it was essential for public opinion that the Liberal Republican movement, as it was called, be given a good report.

William Swift was sent to Jefferson City by the *Missouri Republican*. There were only two telegraph wires out of the place to St. Louis, and Swift preempted them. On the hook of one instrument he hung a copy of United State statutes and on the other the statutes of the state of Missouri. He then went about the business of getting news from the convention. When he got some, he would slip it into the statutes to be sent out. Other correspondents found they were barred as long as the *Missouri Republican* was paying the bill. The bill was $1,500 and Swift came back to St. Louis to turn in his expense account expecting to be fired. Instead, George Knapp, part owner of the paper, handed him an honorarium of $500!

Down To The River

William Henry Swift was to have a more tangible effect on my life than just passing on his journalistic genes. After leaving the newspapers, he got into business in the city of St. Louis and with his connections from newspaper days did quite well.

One of his enterprises was in the construction business; his biography points out that his knowledge of public affairs and diplomacy assisted him as he became associated with Jeremiah Fruin who was building public works of all kinds. Some years later Messr. Fruin, with a Mr. Bambrick and Swift formed the Fruin-Bambrick Construction Company; William H. Swift was president.

Now comes the important part of this business. As part of their construction work the company got some river work through bids with the U.S. Army Corps of Engineers.

My father was then coming of age and to him was entrusted this river work. The branch of the company that did it was called Rust, Swift and Company.

James Verdin Swift was my father, so I am actually a "junior," but because he has been dead since 1932, I do not

2

use "Jr.," although some records do show it. Verdin is from an old French family, and after I joined *The Waterways Journal* the editor, Donald T. Wright, enjoyed using it, stretching it out in introducing me. The only person who uses it now is Capt. C. W. Stoll of Louisville.

Back to Rust, Swift and Company: they had contracts for building dikes and installing shore revetment at several places on the river, including Cap Au Gris, Missouri, and Fort Gage, Illinois.

The fleet consisted of barges, pile drivers, launches, and towboats with a quarterboat for the crew. They moved from site to site, tying up in the willows where the work was going on.

There were no roads to these sites; the only way to get to the fleet was by the river. This was a big problem for my father. He now had a son, and he wanted my mother and me to be with him. The solution? A houseboat. This was not unusual along the river, for there were hundreds of people living in them all along the rivers.

This, however, was no ordinary houseboat. It was well furnished, with a big porch on one end, screened for comfort. There is no record of who built it, but we can assume that the crew of the company did it. It was about 75 feet long and 35 feet wide, on a wood hull.

My mother's maiden name was Anita Gordon Bailey, and it can well be imagined that the Bailey family (father Henry Valle Bailey, mother Evelyn Bailey, and sisters Sarah R. and Evelyn

The Swift family solution: a 75 by 35 ft. houseboat.

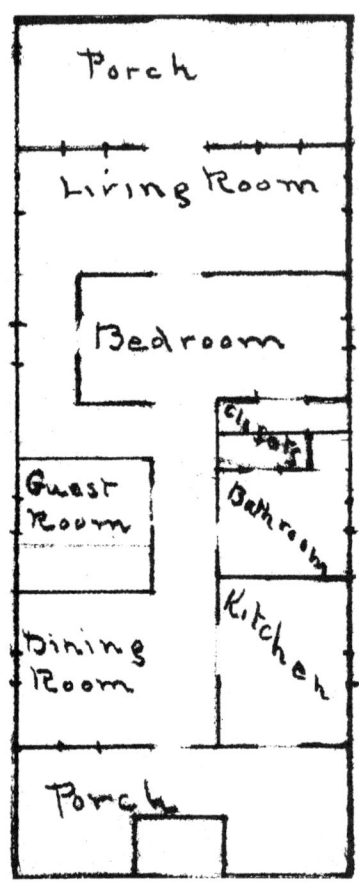

Porch

Living Room

Bedroom

Guest Room

Closets

Bathroom

Kitchen

Dining Room

Porch

The houseboat floor plan was drawn on back of boat picture.

Bailey) were not thrilled to have their daughter living on a houseboat on the Mississippi River. However there are pictures of them visiting the boat and having a good time. My father's sister, Margaret, was also there.

My mother, too, apparently enjoyed the houseboat, for she was with my father and she was learning a new way of life. One story she told was about her efforts to learn to cook. One of her cakes was a real failure; it wouldn't rise. She took it to a real friend, the cook on the quarterboat, for advice. He said, "Oh, throw the damn thing in the river!"

I arrived June 4, 1916, and shortly thereafter was taken down to the river and the houseboat. At a very early age, then, I got river air in my lungs and river water in my veins!

By the way, the fleet used the towboats G. W. Lyon, J. R. Wells and Saturn in its operations.

Early breath of river air on porch of houseboat. Held by my mother, Anita Bailey Swift.

Chapter 2 ——

A Different River

My early Mississippi River odyssey was not to last long.

World War I came and with it the terrible influenza epidemic that killed millions around the world. My father was a victim too, but he did survive. However, his health was affected, and the moist river air was not for him.

Family pictures show that a trip was made out west to the Grand Canyon, Roosevelt Dam in Arizona and other places perhaps to find a drier place to live. It was in a Model-T Ford, and I was there.

In the end, Albuquerque, New Mexico, became our new home. With a high altitude and dry climate, it had become the "tuberculosis center" for the country, with many sanitoriums for TB sufferers. My father was not in one, but it was proof of the healing power of the country.

It was about 1923 when I left the banks of the Mississippi for those of another great American river, the Rio Grande. There was one big difference—except during the spring runoffs of snow in the mountains, the Rio Grande didn't have much water in it. It was rumored that someone saw a houseboat float down one time.

It is not to say that the river was always dry; for there were some bad floods that did a lot of damage in the Albuquerque area.

We first lived in what was known as "The Heights" and then moved into the valley in what is known as "Old Albuquerque" or "Old Town," the Mexican area. The Rio Grande was only a mile or so away from our house on Old Town Road, now Rio Grande Boulevard.

One time I rode our horse to the river and onto its bed, and got pretty far across before hitting the channel, which had water in it on the west side.

When I got home my father was not pleased with my excursion.

"Did you ever hear of quicksand?" he asked.

My father liked to explore and camp out, so we visited a lot of Indian ruins and national parks. One time on the way to the Pueblo Bonito National Monument, we got caught in a sand wash and spent about a day trying to get to solid ground. During the attempt, the frame of the car broke, and my father lashed it together with rope. We got back to the highway, sold the car for junk, and rode the Yellow Way bus back to Albuquerque. I remember it especially well, because there was a fellow in the back of the bus with a guitar, and we sang all the way home.

I went to the Fourth Ward elementary school. The local school was much closer, but most of the students were Mexicans, and my mother somehow got me into a city school. I mentioned our horse; I drove him and a buggy to school; this was long before bus transportation for students.

I also recall an interesting sidelight. Our neighbors across the road, the Peffleys, got the first radio we had ever seen, and they invited us over to hear it. They picked up radio station KOA, Denver. We were amazed that we could hear it— even with the windows closed!

So I was growing up, attending Washington Junior High School and Albuquerque High School. I was a junior there when my father died in 1932.

It was during this time I wrote my first "letter to the editor." It went to the Albuquerque *Journal*; and I have no idea what it was about. But it was good enough to get a telephone response from a man who agreed with my opinion. My mother, who didn't know I had written it, was very surprised, and I think pleased.

But while I was out west, I still had a contact with the Mississippi through the albums of photographs we had, showing the houseboat, the towboats, and building revetment and dikes along the Father of Waters.

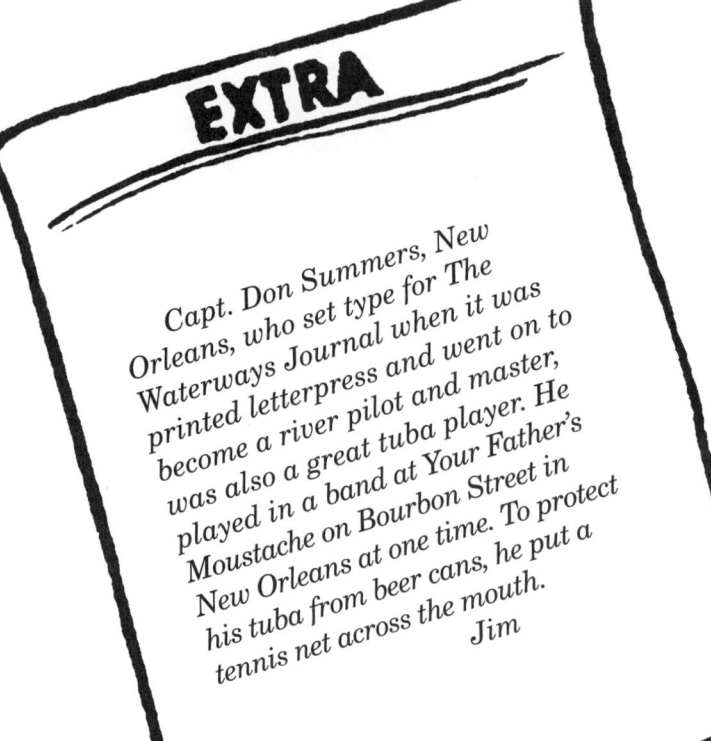

EXTRA

Capt. Don Summers, New Orleans, who set type for The Waterways Journal when it was printed letterpress and went on to become a river pilot and master, was also a great tuba player. He played in a band at Your Father's Moustache on Bourbon Street in New Orleans at one time. To protect his tuba from beer cans, he put a tennis net across the mouth.

Jim

Chapter 3 ——

One of Ruth's Boys

After my father's death we came back to St. Louis. I was in a strange and big city, with no friends of my own and no familiar places.

Of course, my relatives tried to help. My mother, knowing of my love for the river, mentioned this to one of the friends she had become reacquainted with and she said, "Yes, I know someone your son should meet, Miss Ruth Ferris. She is a teacher at the Community School, and she, too, loves the river and the boats."

I don't recall now how contact was made with Ruth Ferris, but I do know the results. Ruth invited me to take a trip with her to Boonville, Missouri, to visit the Rivercene, the home of riverman Capt. Joseph Kinney.

If I had not had an interest in the river and steamboats before this, I surely did now, because Ruth Ferris' enthusiasm for them was overwhelming. In one day I became what was known as one of "Ruth's Boys."

It is a term used for those who came under her influence in school and elsewhere, and it perked up their interest in river matters, especially history. Many prominent St. Louisans in her Community School classes bear the mark to this day. The most prominent of these is singer John Hartford. His best known

9

piece is not river-related: "Gentle On My Mind," but he has several albums of river songs and one titled "Miss Ferris," which is always a hit at his concerts.

During winter months when there were no games, baseball fans gathered for what they called the Hot Stove League to talk about baseball. Ruth Ferris reasoned that river fans should do the same when the boats laid up for the winter.

From people she knew personally and friends who rode the steamer Golden Eagle, she started the Hot Stove Navigation League of America, St. Louis Scuttle No. 1. There was even a membership card, complete with a sketch of a pot-bellied stove. This was, I believe, the first nonprofessional group of river people to be formed.

We met at each other's houses on a very informal basis to talk. The early members, as I recall, were Ruth (of course); me; Richard Lemen of East St. Louis, Illinois, who actually worked on the Golden Eagle as a watchman; Barney Rogers, who was the drummer in the Golden Eagle's three-piece orchestra; Rudy Gerber, who was in the advertising department of the Rice-Stix wholesale goods company; and Oliver C. Parmely, a chemical engineer and designer. The wives were also included.

Ruth's greatest coup was her securing of the pilothouse of the steamer Golden Eagle after the boat sank at Grand Tower

Hot Stove League on the Golden Eagle. L-R: Oliver Parmely, Jim Swift, Ruth Ferris and Rudy Gerber.

Hot Stove League members and friends on the Golden Eagle.
L-R: Oliver Parmely, unidentified, Ruth Ferris, Jim Swift and
Ed Cassady.

Island on May 18, 1947. The wreck was a menace to navigation, according to the Corps of Engineers, and had to be taken out. The pilothouse was saved, however, and it was set out on a barge; it ended up in the school yard at Community School. This

Richard Lemen

was because at an auction of the pilothouse, Ruth came with a check for $257, furnished by a friend at Community School.

Here it was a teaching tool and site of plays and programs about the river. Ruth Ferris retired from teaching in 1957 and almost immediately joined the staff of the Missouri Historical Society, which had organized a new River Room.

The center of it was the Golden Eagle pilothouse Community School had given up. In the River Room was an outstand-

—*Photo by Dick Lemen*
Ruth Ferris and Rudy Gerber on the Golden Eagle.

ing collection of river-related pictures, artifacts and models, with Ruth as curator.

She left the Historical Society in May 1965, but the pilothouse remained at the Society. Meanwhile, on the river, the former Engineer steamer Mississippi had become a restaurant boat, the Becky Thatcher. Its owner, Fred Pierson, wanted to open a museum on the first deck, and Ruth Ferris was the one who organized it. Many of the things on display came from her own collection, and it was a popular riverfront attraction at St. Louis. It was open until November 1970, when the Becky Thatcher was closed.

Ruth had her own personal museum in the basement of her home. She called it the "Steamer E. Z. Rocker." Today this tradition is carried on by another of Ruth's Boys, Keith E. Norrington, of New Albany, Indiana. He has collected many river items, including some from Ruth's artifacts, and it

—*From The Keith Norrington Collection*
Capt. Donald T. Wright and Miss Ruth Ferris in the pilothouse of the Golden Eagle in 1962.

12

makes an impressive display.

Keith first contacted Ruth Ferris at age of 13 when he wrote to the Goldenrod showboat for some information; the letter was referred to Ruth, and she, of course, replied. They met personally in 1970 when he was 16.

Author Ben Lucian Burman, left, receives membership in the Hot Stove Navigation League from Donald T. Wright on the Golden Eagle. Hostess Horty Wilder looks on.

Ruth donated her big and valuable collection to the St. Louis Mercantile Library's River Library when she grew older, and they have been busy sorting it out and cataloging it ever since.

The Library sponsored a special cruise on the President in Ruth's honor; it was attended by many of her friends and former pupils at Community School, including singer John Hartford. Of course he sang "Miss Ferris," to the delight of everyone.

Ruth Ferris died July 6, 1993, at the Memorial Home in St. Louis. She was 95. Ruth was buried in the Woodlawn Cemetery in Moberly, Missouri, wearing her favorite blouse, which had drawings of steamboats on it. A memorial service was held later at the St. Louis Mercantile Library.

EXTRA

It was goose-hunting season when I stopped at the Cairo Motel in the fall. There was a big galvanized tub on the sidewalk outside the entrance, in which muddy boots could be washed before the hunters went inside.

Jim

Chapter 4 ——

An Excursion Boat Summer

*T*hat first summer back in St. Louis with no friends and in a strange setting could have been a hard one, but I had help.

To occupy my time, and also get the river into it, the family kindly staked me to trips on the excursion boats. There were two of them running daily at St. Louis, the J.S. "DeLUXE" and the "Excursion Queen" Saint Paul. I alternated between the two. Sometimes they would go upstream to the mouth of the Illinois River, sometimes downriver to the mouth of the Meramec River.

My fellow passengers were mostly families with picnic baskets out to get some cool river air. They would come streaming down Washington Avenue and over the levee in droves. As time grew close to departure, we on the boat would hope they would make it. The captain was most accommodating, holding the boat if he saw a family running down the hill, urging the kids along; but there was usually someone left behind, to the sorrow of friends and relatives who had made it!

The J.S. and Saint Paul were big boats, both side-wheelers and coal burners. The J.S. was 264.7 by 42 by 6.8 feet, and the Saint Paul 300 by 37.4 by 6.4 feet.

Courtesy of The Waterways Journal

Excursion boat days at St. Louis. L-R: Strs. Capitol, Saint Paul and J.S.

Both had originally been in the Diamond Jo Line; the J.S. was the Quincy, and the Saint Paul was not renamed.

The Streckfus Line was run by a family which was originally from Rock Island, Illinois. Capt. John Streckfus had started with the little Freddie in 1891 and built up the packet excursion business until he could build the first J.S. in 1901. This was a stern-wheel boat that burned in 1910.

The Commodore, as he was called, had four sons who followed him into the excursion boat business; John, Joseph, Roy and Verne. Joe was the leader and a strong one.

In the 1930s, in addition to the J.S. and Saint Paul, the firm was running the Capitol, formerly the Diamond Jo's Dubuque, and the Washington, which had been the Sidney. She was in the Ohio River trade, while the Capitol tramped, that is ran at various locations on the Upper Mississippi and other rivers, and in New Orleans in the winter months.

In 1933 Streckfus bought the packet Cincinnati at Cincinnati and brought her to St. Louis to be rebuilt as an excursion boat. She was a side-wheeler. She came out as the President on July 4, 1934.

Streckfus saw the handwriting on the wall for the old-type excursion boat with wood superstructures, and the old Diamond Jo fleet began to be dismantled. The J.S. was torn down in the winter of 1938-9 at St. Louis, the Capitol in 1945, and the Washington in 1938. The Saint Paul, renamed the Senator, continued to run until 1942 when she was retired to be used by the Coast Guard as a receiving "ship" and then as the Streckfus utility and dock barge until she was towed south and sank behind a dike below St. Louis in January 1953.

When you came aboard the J.S., you found a fancy area on the main (first) deck, for she was the "DELUXE" boat. There were green and white awnings in a garden-like setting. The other excursion boats usually had games for children and machines for candy, gum, etc.

Going aft you came to the engineroom, with the big steam machinery on each side and the pitmans going in and out as they turned the wheels. There was a great smell of oil and steam, and the hiss of the steam as it issued from the engines. There was a little shudder as the pitmans turned the wheels that dug into the water.

Str. J.S. DeLUXE

When the Admiral came along in later years, the pitmans were given names Popeye and Wimpy.

Going upstairs you came on the big dance floor that was almost as long as the boat. The band stand was about in the middle. There were some very good bands, including the legendary Fate Marable; and Louis Armstrong really got his start on a Streckfus boat. The story is that he was too modest to play solo, and Capt. John Streckfus threatened to put him off the boat if he didn't.

Again, the Streckfus brothers were very concerned about the bands they used, and John Streckfus is said to have stood on the dance floor to count the beat of the bands as they played.

Another Streckfus legend, regarding music, recounts the time that a band, new and not in tune yet with the company's policies, played the then popular "Turkey Trot" when the boat (I'm not sure which one) was around Alton. The dancers responded, and their antics scandalized Capt. Streckfus, who threatened to stop the boat and throw the band off!

Getting back to our tour of the J.S. and Saint Paul, the next deck up had the picnic tables, which were at a premium and were grabbed up by the passengers who guarded them for dear life.

For those who did not bring a basket there was a cafeteria and snack bar for coffee and cold drinks. The food was very good and relatively inexpensive.

This opened out on the top deck, one of the most popular places to sit and watch the shore go by. The *Streckfus Magazine* which was issued yearly back then, had a map showing the sights to see.

Streckfus was particularly proud of their ladies' rooms, especially on the President and Admiral, which were to come in later years. The President's were named as Powder Rooms: the Plaid, Golden Petal, Copper & Jade and Black & White rooms. The Admiral's were named for celebrities, mainly, Sonja, Deanna, Glamour and Greta.

There were night trips too, or "moonlights," at which time the top deck was very popular. Undoubtedly hundreds of marriages resulted from meetings under the stars on those top decks!

On the night trips, too, the dance floor was full and the bands really did their thing. They had girl singers, too, and many were very popular at night spots on land.

It should be said that there was entertainment besides the bands on the dance floor, or ballroom, on the day trips. The dance studios often showed off their students, and there were games for the kids.

The passengers enjoyed the landings, too, lining the rails to watch the deck crew handle the lines as the master on the bridge called down instructions; and you could hear the engine bells ring as the engineer answered the pilot's instructions.

The boats landed against the wharfboat, not the levee itself; the site had been the Diamond Jo Line landing for many years, and Streckfus inherited it when they took over the line.

The big wharfboat had, in later years, given way to an office barge, which in itself was an up-to-date floating headquarters. The office barge was built in sections, each named for one of the Streckfus daughters. Altogether it was 300 feet long and 25 feet wide. At the upriver end there was a waiting room with wicker chairs and settees for those waiting for friends to board the boats. In 1998 it was sold to be used as a dock for a casino boat operation at Shreveport, Louisiana.

About 1937 Streckfus bought the big side-wheel railroad ferry Albatross and brought her to St. Louis to be converted into an excursion boat; she was not to be your ordinary river boat.

The story is that Capt. Joe Streckfus took a trip west to Seattle, Washington, and that he was impressed by the streamlined ferries on Puget Sound. The design of the new boat, to be called the Admiral, was to follow that type of construction. Nothing like it had been seen on the rivers before. It was streamlining at its ultimate. Of course, it didn't set well with many old rivermen, who called the Admiral the "overturned bathtub."

The Admiral might have been strange looking, but her enclosed form served a purpose, and a great one; she was air-conditioned, the first river passenger boat to have that comfort. Carrier, who installed the system, also did the Queen Mary's units.

But, she was to serve the St. Louis area well for many years until the Coast Guard crossed her out because of a bad hull. Before that, in 1973-4, she was dieselized with three Murray and Tregurtha units, as was the President.

Today she is a gambling casino at the foot of Washington Avenue, the old Streckfus landing, and owned by John Connally of Pittsburgh. She can't move but is very much alive as a place of entertainment. The latest plans were to move her above Eads Bridge.

Her long-time master, Capt. William F. Carroll, is also still very much alive and works with Gateway Riverboat Cruises, the successor to Streckfus Steamers. He is a great river historian and is often a speaker at group events.

The last big boat to serve St. Louis was the Belle of St. Louis, but she came out wired for slot machines, etc., and is indeed today a casino boat.

Will there ever be another big excursion boat at St. Louis? Probably not; you don't have to go down to the river to keep cool with air-conditioning; and the days of the big bands are over.

However, you can still see the harbor and enjoy a dinner on the water on boats of the Gateway Riverboat Cruises, managed by J. Thomas "Tom" Dunn. They run hourly harbor trips and dinner cruises, and charters in the evening.

The Streckfus name is also still prominent on the rivers, with both men and women descendants of the original Streckfus family on ships and river boats.

A final Streckfus story, which may or may not be true: Capt. Joe took another trip, this one out west to Denver. At the hotel he asked the desk clerk where the river was. "Well," the answer was, "we have Cherry Creek." Capt. Joe went down to it and took the next train home, indicating he didn't want to stay in a town that couldn't do better than that!

EXTRA

On my trips down the Upper Ohio River I would meet the monarch butterflies, which were migrating south. Later I would meet them in Texas.
Jim

Chapter 5 ——

Enter The Golden Eagle

I graduated from Soldan High School in 1933. My aunt Margaret Swift, who was a business woman, thought it best that I prepare for a business life, and she thought I should go to the Rubican Business School, a well-known institution.

They had courses in all the things that would be important in a business office, including typing. (Of course, computers had not even been thought of in those days.) In the end, typing was the only thing I really used, although I did employ some bookkeeping.

This was still the Great Depression, and through another aunt, Sarah Bailey, my mother's sister, I got my first job. A man whom she had helped when she was head librarian at the Crunden Branch of the St. Louis Public Library was head of the filing department at the American Automobile Insurance Company. He needed a file clerk, and he got me.

Was it fate? I don't know, but American Auto was on the 15th floor of the Pierce Building—overlooking the Mississippi River!

My fellow workers soon learned of my interest in the river. Whenever a boat came by, they let me know, and I was there. But this wasn't too often; at that time there were maybe three boats a week—Federal Barge Lines, Mississippi Valley Barge Line, and U.S. Engineers towboats.

The really important thing was that I now had money and could make some longer river trips—overnight ones. I had reservations on the Eagle Packet Company's Cape Girardeau, but they literally sold the boat from under me. She went to the Greene Line of Cincinnati and became the Gordon C. Greene. But all was not lost. They brought out the steamer Golden Eagle. She was to mean a lot to me in more ways than one. The weekend fare to Cape Girardeau was eleven dollars—and that included the berth, fare and transportation.

The winter of 1917-18 was a severe one in the Midwest. For the first time in many years the Tennessee River, which flows into the Ohio from the south, was frozen over. It was not good news for river companies that had sent their boats to the Duck's Nest at Paducah, a favorite winter quarters. They were right to be worried. On January 19, 1918, the ice went out, and with it the boats in the Duck's Nest.

The big loser was the Eagle Packet Company of St. Louis, which had the Alton, Peoria, Grey Eagle, and Spread Eagle tied up there. One of the finest fleets of steamers on the inland rivers was swept down the Ohio, crushed and sinking.

The only boats left in this proud fleet were the Bald Eagle and Piasa. The Eagle had been on the ways in Paducah, and the Piasa had wintered at St. Louis.

The Eagle Packet Company needed more boats quickly. One was available at New Orleans, the WM. Garig, and she was bought in March 1918. She was a cotton boat with wide guards for holding that commodity. She was remodeled to suit the upper river trades and was renamed the Golden Eagle.

The Wm. Garig had been built by the Howard Shipyard at Jeffersonville, Indiana, in 1904. She was 175 feet long, 35 feet in the beam and 5.2 feet deep. The engines were 14 inches in diameter with a 6-foot stroke. The two boilers were each 44 inches in diameter and 28 feet long. The machinery and boilers had first been on the packet Julian Poydras.

The Garig was built for the Baton Rouge and Bayou Sara Packet Company, but by 1908 she was running for the Carter Bros. of New Orleans. For them she was in the New Orleans-Ouachita River trade going up to Camden, Arkansas.

The Golden Eagle, when ready, was put in the Illinois River trade, leaving St. Louis on Wednesdays and Saturdays at three p.m. She left on the return trips early Monday and Friday mornings. The fare was five dollars one way, and eight dollars round-trip. The Bald Eagle was put in the Cape Girardeau, Missouri, trade.

A new boat was built by the Eagle Packet Company in 1923, the last the firm would construct. She was the Cape Girardeau, third of that name, and unlike the other two, she was a sternwheeler designed more for passengers than freight. She went to the Illinois River. The Golden Eagle was sent to the Cape Girardeau and Commerce, Missouri, trade.

However, things had changed on the rivers. Truck competition had cut into the packet business, and the Golden Eagle lasted only six months as a packet to the Cape. The Eagle Packet Company's financial condition was such that it was necessary to sell one of its two boats. (The Bald Eagle and the Piasa were no longer running, the first having been sold as a quarterboat to a construction company and the second dismantled.)

The Cape, the larger and newer boat, was sold to the Greene Line of Cincinnati. She was renamed the Gordon C. Greene.

This gave a new lease of life to the Golden Eagle, which was renovated and improved for the tourist trade. The Eagle Packet Company had a good working relationship with the Carton Travel Bureau of Chicago. They sent many hundreds of travelers to St. Louis to catch the Golden Eagle for a river cruise.

The Golden Eagle was not a luxurious boat. There was no running water in the staterooms, and of course at that time no air conditioning. To take a shower the passengers had to go back on the guards at the stern, and the same to use the bathroom. Each stateroom had a wash bowl and pitcher.

This was no cruise liner, and some passengers (after seeing the accommodations) said they were getting off at the next stop—Cape Girardeau. However, after a meal of chef Charlie Clay's cooking they changed their minds.

There is also a story of one passenger who thought the Golden Eagle was the ferry that would take him out to the main ship.

Eating on the guards.

One of Clay's specialties was fritters. Meals included corn fritters, eggplant fritters, and other kinds. Meals were served out on the guards instead of in the cabin; you had a good view of the scenery and got the river breeze—unless the boat was going with the wind.

The cabin was then open, and in the evening the three-piece band would play for dancing. The pianist, Henrietta Uxa, really hit the keys hard. The drummer, as we have mentioned before, was Barney Rogers; and there was a saxophone player whose name I cannot recall. The band would play a dinner march in the evening.

The Golden Eagle also had a hostess, Hortense Wilder, more commonly called Horty. She was a very good one and kept the passengers happy. One of her favorite songs was "Three Little Fishies," which she did with the appropriate gestures.

And there was "Way Down Yonder In The Paw Paw Patch." With the words "Come On Boys, and Let's Go Find Her," the males would all go down to the end of the cabin.

Horty would also conduct an exercise march around the upper deck after breakfast to try to remedy all of Charley Clay's food.

Coming back to St. Louis after one of the weekend trips to the Cape was a sad time, after being on the river with good friends. It meant getting back to reality again. I can still remember the smell (as I got out on deck) of the river, smoke, steam, and the Switzer Licorice plant up the hill.

The master of the Golden Eagle, Capt. William H. "Buck" Leyhe, was as much of a drawing card as the boat itself. Capt. "Buck" was a jovial host and was known for his stories. He was a good riverman and saw to it that the Golden Eagle was in good shape. The fact that in the two accidents that sank the boat no passengers were lost is a tribute to him and the crew that he assembled.

26

He was a member of a family of rivermen who started out at Warsaw, Illinois, in 1865 with the steamer Young Eagle. Henry Leyhe had come from Germany in 1846 with his family of two sons and two daughters. The sons were named Henry and William.

As business improved, so did the size and number of boats such as the Grey Eagle, Spread Eagle, Desmet, Bald Eagle, War Eagle, Alton, Peoria, Cape Girardeau, Piasa, D. H. Pike, Calhoun, and New Idlewild. (Many of the boats were renamed during their lifetimes.)

Capt. William H. "Buck" Leyhe on the Golden Eagle.

Henry and William both married and had families. William's two sons were William H. Leyhe and Henry W. Leyhe. Capt. Henry usually stayed on the bank taking care of business while William was on the river all his life.

One of the most popular of the Golden Eagle trips was to the Tennessee River and the Shiloh Battlefield. She also ran special trips to Cincinnati, and to Nashville, Tennessee, on the Cumberland.

The year 1939 was to be one of the finest in the Golden Eagle's history. It began April 22-23, when there was a race against time between the Golden Eagle and the steamers Delta Queen and Delta King on the Sacramento River in California. The Eagle ran to Cape Girardeau. It had been arranged as a feature for the World's Fair in San Francisco on Treasure Island. It resulted in a good deal of national publicity. *Life* magazine even sent a photographer.

There was doubt the Golden Eagle had much of a chance, but she did win, to the delight of her many friends. Capt. Buck was given a scroll from the City of St. Louis, and the boat flew a "Champion" pennant.

The boat's popular bartender, Harry Anderson, came up with a new drink—a "Golden Eagle Winner."

Just two months later, on June 20, 1939, she left on one of her more spectacular voyages. This was to St. Paul, the first overnight passenger boat to go on the Upper Mississippi all the way to St. Paul, Minnesota, following the completion of the lock and dam system that guaranteed a nine-foot channel all the way to the Twin Cities.

It was a triumphant trip. She was met at every lock by a large group of people, most of whom had never seen a steamboat carrying passengers before. There were a number of celebrities aboard, including the noted author of river books Ben Lucian Burman, who included mention of this trip in his book, *Blow For A Landing*.

The Golden Eagle was to be the first on the Upper Mississippi since 1923 when the Harry G. Drees tried to get to St. Paul; she grounded near Hastings, Minnesota, and never got to St. Paul.

The passengers were impressed with the beauty of the Upper Mississippi, and the almost new locks and dams were bright and shining and interesting to see and navigate.

The Golden Eagle at St. Paul public landing, June 1939.

The Golden Eagle coming into Chattanooga, Tennessee, May 1940.

The following year the Golden Eagle was off on another pioneering trip, this to the Tennessee River all the way to Chattanooga. She left St. Louis May 11. She was to navigate another set of new locks, these part of the Tennessee Valley Authority's project to revitalize the Tennessee Valley. They were big structures with high lifts.

The boat's arrival in Chattanooga was a big one, with the high school band out to serenade the passengers, and many city dignitaries out to greet the boat. She also had a big escort of pleasure craft into the city, and other steamboats in the harbor had steam up and saluted the visitor from St. Louis.

A boy's school on the bluffs let out classes so the students could see the boat, and one of the classic pictures of the trip shows the boys watching. The TVA took note of the trip and sent a photographer who photographed the Golden Eagle coming into Chattanooga from a small boat.

Unfortunately, the next years were not so pleasant. On June 14, 1941, the Golden Eagle hit a dike just above Chester, Illinois, and sank. Fortunately, when the water went down, it was found that the boat was not too badly damaged; she was repaired to run again.

The Golden Eagle, June 15, 1941, the day after sinking at Chester, Illinois.

She did two more seasons for the Eagle Packet Company, but just before her initial trip in 1944 it was found that the boilers were leaking and the trip had to be canceled. This was wartime, with materials in short supply; so the boat had to sit out the conflict.

The Eagle Packet Company sold the Golden Eagle in 1946 to Mr. and Mrs. Dewey Miller and Mr. and Mrs. E. Willers, who were enthusiastic about getting her back in service. This they did, and operated the boat in 1946.

She even made a trip to New Orleans, and coming back engaged in what was to be called a steamboat race with the Gordon C. Greene. The GCG got to Memphis first, and passengers on her gave the newspapers the news of the "great steamboat race." It was passed on to newspapers all over the country.

The Millers and Willers bowed out from operating the Golden Eagle after one year, and the boat and rights for the Eagle Packet Company were sold to St. Louis Shipbuilding and Steel Company, which chose to keep the boat in operation. The shipyard did a fine job of working on her, and when the 1947 season came around, the Golden Eagle was in beautiful condition when she left on the first trip of the year on May 17. Little did those who saw her off, or those aboard, know it was to be her last departure.

The next morning about one-thirty a.m. she took a shear to the bank on Grand Tower Island and was wrecked. Again, the passengers got off safely despite the darkness and position of the boat.

Among the passengers was Marga Sasche, who took a set of historic pictures. (Marga is now Mrs. Wilbur Finger.)

Because of the position of the boat, and the possibility she would slip into the channel and become a navigation hazard, the Corps of Engineers had the wreck removed. All that was saved was the pilothouse.

The popularity of the steamer led some of her riders to organize the Golden Eagle Club to perpetuate her memory. The group held banquets and collected river pictures and artifacts, which were displayed at several places in the St. Louis area.

The St. Louis County Parks and Recreation Department offered the group space in the beautiful Nims Mansion in Bee Tree Park in south St. Louis County, and the Golden Eagle River Museum was born. It is open from one to five p.m. Wednesday through Sunday, May 1 through Labor Day, and from one to five on weekends from Labor. Day to October 31.

I had the opportunity to ride the Golden Eagle on her two memorable trips to St. Paul and Chattanooga. I wrote them up for *The Waterways Journal*. They were long and, although I didn't realize it at the time, were to be my entry into a new career.

I got a new job at American Auto, a promotion actually, but I soon realized it was a job I didn't like and in fact couldn't handle.

What to do? I couldn't go back to the file room and admit I couldn't do the work. How about that river newspaper, *The Waterways Journal*? I visited the *Journal* office, and found I had come at an opportune time. One of the staff was getting rather feeble and needed help. I would be doing bookkeeping, not writing, but as it turned out the job lines were not strictly observed at the *Journal*; there was a chance to write too.

In the days following my leaving American Auto, the company was purchased by the Fireman's Fund of San Francisco, and the Pierce Building was remodeled into the Adams Mark Hotel.

About one river historian, a tribute of Fielding L. Wooldridge (who was a remarkable one) said: "He was preeminent in a field shrouded in confusion, inconsistencies, doubt, folklore tales and 'hear say'."

Jim

Chapter 6 ——

"The Riverman's Bible"

*I*t is time, I think, to take a closer look at the publication I joined in 1941, and with which I was to spend the rest of my working life.

We have no clue as to who conceived the idea of a newspaper for rivermen. It might have been the river fraternity itself, a good idea for businessmen, or maybe Abbott Veatch himself.

Whoever, on August 29, 1891, there was published Volume 1, Number 1, of *The River*. The masthead of that issue, with its statement about the purpose of its publication, follows:

"THE RIVER."

Published by The River Publishing Company,

A. A. SELKIRK, - - - - President.
B. J. SELKIRK, - - - Vice-President.
ABBOTT VEATCH, - Business Manager.
C. LEE CARTER, - - Sec'y and Treas.

Office, 204 North 6th Street, Telephone No. 496.

Post-Office Box 442, St. Louis, Mo.

Address all communications to

ABBOTT VEATCH, - Editor and Business Manager.

SUBSCRIPTION, - $2.00 per year.

ST. LOUIS, MO., AUGUST 29, 1891.

EDITORIAL COMMENT.

"The River" makes its bow to the Steamboatmen
of the Western and Southern rivers and announces that
it is now "on watch." This paper has been started in
the interests of the Steamboatmen and will be run in
their interests exclusively. It will be our object to furnish River news from all the principal cities on the Western and Southern rivers and we feel that we can give
good late news, as we have made arrangements with a
corps of efficient correspondents in all the cities to send
us a weekly letter of current events and authorized them
to use the telegraph when necessary to get late news.
We profess no politics and do not care who is President.
We have no axe to grind and care nothing for any kind
of news except River news. We do not claim that we
will be able to make the river change and run up stream,
but we do claim that we will be able to set the profession
in their proper sphere and to help fight the battles of the
steamboatmen whenever we can do so. All we ask is
the kind indulgence of rivermen and we will be grateful
for their assistance in any way, and especially in the
matter of news. You can all help us by sending us news
and if you will thus "press the button" we will do
the rest.

COL. WILL S. HAYS.

POET, CAPTAIN AND JOURNALIST.

The first story to be carried was about the legendary journalist poet and riverman Will S. Hays of Louisville, Kentucky. Published, too, was his most famous poem, one used at so many funerals of rivermen, beginning with that of Capt. J. M. White:

"Col. Will S. Hays was born in Louisville, Ky., July 19, 1837. He first entered the field of journalism thirty-seven years ago on the *Louisville Democrat* as river editor. He remained with that paper until it went out of existence during the close of the late war, and then spent two or three years of his life on the river as captain and clerk on various boats, the last one being the famous Jacob Strader. He finally drifted [sic] back into newspaper life, and was for a long time amanuensis to the late Geo. D. Prentice. When Prentice died Col. Hays went over to the *Courier-Journal* after they were consolidated and, with the exception, [sic] of about one year he has been with that great paper as its marine editor ever since. There are few men now living who have done more for the marine interests of the great Southwest than Will S. Hays. Always ready to do all in his power to aid in promoting the interests of river men, and the river commerce of the country; his pen never lagged in fear or force, and he never ceased to defend the weak against the strong or the right against the wrong. It was through the influence of his pen and the columns of the *Courier-Journal* that the Louisville and Portland Canal was made free, and many other evils and overburdened laws imposed upon steamboats and river men were corrected. He is a bold, prolific and poetic writer, strictly temperate in his habits, youthful in appearance, rather goodlooking withal, and one of the most popular and well known men in Louisville and the South. His reputation as a song writer is world-wide. He has written and composed more popular ballads than any man living, and bears his worldly fame and envied name with becoming modesty.

"Col. Hays has a wife, a married daughter and a son, (Sam. Brown), living. He bids fair to live a long time yet, and the marine traffic and trade of the country and the thousands of men engaged in and interested in [it] will lose a firm and fast friend, a true advocate of their interests, and a faithful, fearless and prolific writer, when the gallant colonel will lay down his pen and sing of himself as he sung of the late Capt. J. M. White:

> "Mate, get ready down on deck,
> I'm heading for the shore,
> I'll ring the bell, for I must land
> This boat, forevermore,
>
> Say, pilot, do you see that light,—
> I do—where angels stand?
> Well, hold her jack staff, hard on that,
> For there I'm going to land.
>
> That looks like Death that's hailing me,
> So ghastly grim and pale,
> I'll toll the bell,—I must go in,—
> *I never passed a hail.* [sic]
>
> Stop her! Let her Come in Slow,
> There! That will do,—no more,
> The lines are fast, and angels await,
> To welcome me ashore.
>
> Say, pilot, I am going with them,
> Up yonder, through that gate,
> I'll not come back, you ring the bell,
> And back her out—don't wait.
>
> For I have made my trip of life,
> I've found my landing place,
> I'll take my soul and anchor that,
> Fast to the Throne of Grace."

River advertisers included the St. Louis and New Orleans Anchor Line; steamer Idlewild, St. Louis to Cape Girardeau; St. Louis and Tennessee River Packet Company; Dale & Fields, steamboat contractors, St. Louis; Mississippi & Ohio River Pilots' Society, St. Louis; Wm. J. Conant and Son, general steamboat and steamship agents, St. Louis; the steamer Bald Eagle, Clarksville and way landings; and Mullen & Hoppius, steamboat painters.

Others included Evansville, Paducah & Tennessee River Packet Company, Evansville, Indiana; steamer Hudson, Pittsburgh and Cincinnati; Diamond Jo Line Steamers, Dubuque, Iowa; St. Louis, Anchor Line Stores, St. Louis; St. Louis, Naples and Peoria Packet Company; St. Louis, and the Eagle Packet Company, St. Louis.

Volume 1, Number 1 of *The Waterways Journal* was dated April 9, 1892. The masthead shows Roland Quentin as president; R. J. Groeninger, secretary and treasurer; and Abbott Veach, editor. The address is shown as wharfboat, foot of Pine Street.

The only comment about the change in name was a paragraph that states:

> *"The Waterways Journal* starts on its initial trip today. The policy of this paper will be antagonistic to nobody. Politics will not be tolerated. We do not claim to know how to improve the big Mississippi and want no special appropriation. All we want is a fair chance to make an honest living by confining ourselves to giving the news, and trust we may be successful in that line."

The masthead was plain until the August 6, 1892, issue, when a cut of the Morning Star appeared, and under it the line, "If the bends be protected from washing away, a channel will cut through the shallows." Then the Morning Star was dropped, and a St. Louis harbor scene was run from time to time.

These issues had jokes and cartoons. Advertising was not restricted to river firms; there were ads from the

American Brewing Company, Standard Lager Beer, J. W. Groeninger, Wines and Liquors; Peter Hauptmann & Company, tobacco and cigars; Burkes Corner saloon and boarding; and Anheuser-Busch Brewing Association.

A number of ads were run for the Cherokee Brewing Company and its owner Ferd Herold and his steamers Cherokee and Ferd Herold.

There was, apparently, a change in management. By February 4, 1893, R. J. Groeninger was shown as manager, and the office was at 311 Market Street.

Another person whose name appeared in the masthead from time to time in a management position was George C. Stamm. He was shown in one issue as manager of the Advertising Department.

Abbott Veatch was from an Evansville, Indiana, family, and he had a brother, John, who was also on the river. Abbott was addressed as "Colonel" by some readers. He was last shown in the masthead of the March 18, 1893, issue as editor.

Enter William Arste as editor and publisher. There apparently were some hard feelings, because a notice was published that Abbott Veatch was no longer authorized to take subscriptions to *The Waterways Journal*, and there was a sketch of a gaunt-looking "Capt." Abbott Veatch under which is the caption:

"CAPT." ABBOTT VEATCH.

"Capt. Abbott Veatch will preach to the 'poor and down-trodden.'—Post Dispatch of Wednesday, June 29."

The *Journal's* comment: "They're Off! WHAT NEXT?"

SCHOELLHORN-ALBRECHT MACHINE CO.

NEW IMPROVED
Steamboat Doctor.

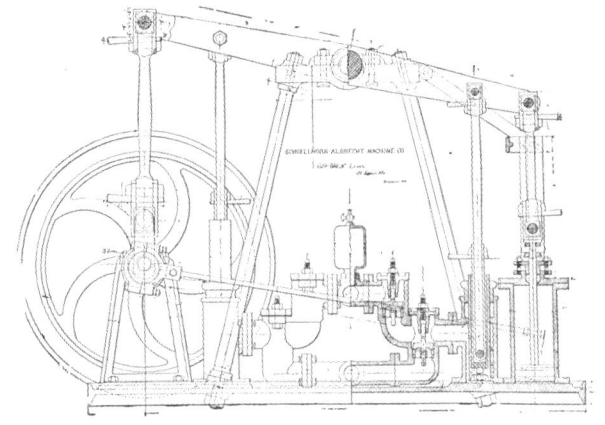

These doctors are principally built of steel, making them strong and light, as the old style doctors are made of cast-iron, which make them very heavy and is dead weight for boats.

We build them all sizes to suit.

For particulars and prices, address

Schoellhorn-Albrecht Machine Co.,

609 and 610 North Levee.
616 and 618 Commercial Street.

Telephone 307.

St. Louis, Mo.

SCHOELLHORN-ALBRECHT MACHINE CO.

Regularly scheduled full-page ad in the 1896 *Journals*.

Typical ads in the *Journal* in 1896.

THE WATERWAYS JOURNAL.

VOL. IX.

DEVOTED TO THE MARINE PROFESSION, YACHTING AND COMMERCIAL INTERESTS.

ST. LOUIS, JUNE 6, 1896.

No. 10.

In 1896 *The Journal* was devoted to the marine profession, yachting and commercial interests.

Arste was a man of some standing and is included in the biographical section of the St. Louis: History of the Fourth City books, by Stevens.

William Arste

WILLIAM ARSTE.

William Arste, who since 1892 has published the Waterways Journal in St. Louis, his native city, was born on Christmas day of 1867. He is descended from ancestry who came from Hanover, Germany. His father, Frederick W. Arste, who crossed the Atlantic in 1863, is now a retired printer. His mother, Mrs. Wilhelmina Arste, died December 22, 1907.

The son was a pupil in the Laclede and Madison public schools and completed the grammar-school course at the age of thirteen years, being thus qualified to enter the Polytechnic school, but being an only child and his father in rather limited financial circumstances, it was necessary that he earn his own living from that time and he secured a position as office boy with F. C. P. Tiedman, who was city surveyor and also secretary of the republican city central committee. For five years he remained with Mr. Tiedeman and was promoted from time to time until he became draftsman and surveyor. Having gained a good knowledge of the mechanical principles underlying this work, he secured a more profitable position with Julius Pitzman, with whom he continued for five years, eventually becoming general utility man of the business. In early life he became acquainted with the printing trade, having set type for his father when but eight years of age, his father at that time being proprietor of a newspaper in La Salle,

Illinois, the issue being called the La Salle County Volksblatt. Later Mr. Arste again took up the printers' trade and when he had mastered the business, traveled in various states of the Union, working in that line. He settled in St. Louis in 1889 and became connected with the Evening Call, owned by Rev. Ben Deering. After the failure of that paper he engaged with the St. Louis Republic, with which he remained for three years and then spent one year in the office of the St. Louis Globe-Democrat. On the expiration of that period he purchased from John A. Groeninger the Waterways Journal, which he has since successfully published.

Mr. Arste is a member of Red Cross Lodge, No. 54, K. P., and belongs to the Olympic Athletic Club, in which connections he has won several medals, being very skilled in athletic sports. He is a pronounced republican, giving to the party inflexible support.

In April, 1893, in St. Louis, Mr. Arste was married to Miss Cordelia Monger, and the same year he purchased a pleasant residence at No. 2912 Pine street. His advancement in the business world has come through the promotions which follow broad experience resulting in constantly expanding powers. Laudable ambition has prevented anything like inertia or inactivity in his career. Diligence and determination have enabled him to work his way steadily upward and he is now well known in journalistic circles.

Bill Arste's own account of his life, as published in the special 25th edition of the *Journal* on April 19, 1919, read this way:

WM. ARSTE.

Born in St. Louis December 25 (Christmas Day, 1867[sic] Attended the public schools of St. Louis, graduated from high school at the age of 14 and then entered the surveying business when St. Louis city limits ended just west of Grand avenue. He remained in the surveying business for eight years. His father being a good printer, he gradually drifted toward the printing business much against his father's wishes. At the age of 10 years he could "stick type" about as good as a fullfledged printer. At the age of 21 contracted the "wonderlust" fever and went to Omaha and Chicago, where he worked in printing offices, getting a full knowledge of the business by hard knocks for a year. Returning to St. Louis in 1889 he became a fullfledged printer by passing examination in the Printers Union and becoming a member of the union. He then "subbed" on the St. Louis Republic for four years until the linotype machines came into use and threw about 50 percent of the printers out of work. He then went on the Globe Democrat, which was the last St. Louis paper to put in linotype machines, but the Globe, also, was installing machines at that time, so he got in only six months "subbing" on the Globe Democrat. Although only "subbing" he got all the work he wanted.

On April 1, 1894, he purchased the Waterways Journal, on time (and long time at that) at a ridiculously low price, and found after running it a month, that the books had been padded; advertisers when he called upon them told him they had ordered their ads out "months ago." Names of dead men and fictitious names, etc., were on the subscription list. Everything looked blue for The Journal then, friends and his own parents advised him to discontinue publishing The Journal, but he insisted that steamboatmen should and could support a paper. Up to that time he had not known a single steamboatman, in fact, never was on a steamboat except an occasional ride, when a boy, on the Annie P. Silver, Oliver Beirne, Charles P. Chouteu, Grand Republic, etc.

He gradually gained favor among the steamboatmen by his knack of making friends of all whom he met, excepting, of course, a few he discovered whose friendship could not be coveted. At length the sun began to rise for The Journal. The task to place The Journal on a respectable basis had been a hard one, because its former owners had indulged in questionable schemes such as the "Steamboat Clerk's Association," "Public Flagpole," got it into the hands of the sheriff, etc., so that it was a hard task with no credit nor capital.

As years rolled on The Journal gradually became popular among steamboatmen and grew in strength until today, this wonderful Jubilee Edition is the answer, with each one of our advertisers and contributors replying to letters received, wrote him in the most kind and appreciative manner, and giving good wishes with loyalty of friendship until it would make even a prohibitionist intoxicated with gratitude. We venture the assertion that there is not a publication in the entire world that has the satisfied advertisers and subscribers that the Waterways Journal has—all brought about by fair dealing with all willing to correct any unintentional error or injury, but fearlessness in contending for what is right no matter whose displeasure it arouses. Mr. Arste is always, personally, trying to do his advertisers and substantial friends good, but has no time for rainbows, ingrates and leeches. That and strict attention to his own business, is the reason of his success. He extends his most heartfelt thanks to the oldtime friends that stood by him in the dark days of the 90's and to the thousands of new ones made in the interim, and hopes to be with them another 25 years and to seem them as well when making his annual trips, for they are another large factor in his success. We venture to say he knows personally, more steamboatmen than anybody else in the world. Again he thanks you, one and all of you for your most loyal support.

Bill Arste died in 1937, and his obituary of November 20 in a local paper said in part:

"Mr. Arste traveled more than 200,000 miles on steamboats on the Mississippi, Missouri and Ohio Rivers and their tributaries while he was publishing his magazine, acquaintances said. It was his custom to make an annual circuit of the waterways. In this way he became acquainted with many steamboat men on the rivers in this part of the country."

Some interesting items from those early issues show that on March 25, 1893, there was a special offer of a year's subscription for $1. Then on April 1, 1893, a notice appeared that the paper had opened a job printing plant. Single copies of the *Journal* were 10 cents, but the price was reduced to five cents in later years.

The paper had agents in many river towns to solicit subscriptions, and probably advertising.

Some other names appeared in the masthead from time to time—H. Lamoreaux, business manager, 1894; Edward Sheffield, editor, March 20, 1897, to June 16, 1900; and E. J. Picard, editor, January 11, 1902.

Then, on April 26, 1902, Kathleen Smith was shown as editor, and things were stabilized, for she was in that position until about 1919. The *Journal* story published about her follows:

KATHLIEN [sic] SMITH

Kathleen Smith

Editor of The Waterways Journal for the past fifteen years, has made of the subject of the rivers of the United States and transportation thereon a study and is as familiar with river history and the steamboat business as steamboatmen themselves, possessing a wholesome and sincere interest in behalf of same.

She was educated at Moores Hill, Ind., College, a Methodist institution in the Scientific Course and in the Business College at Valpariaso, Ind., but has made little practice use of the training received in the latter except in avocational ways because natural talent led along literary ways. Aside from a brief, and to her, unsatisfactory attempt in the stenographer's chair, she has held but two positions. The first was with a trade journal as office help, but soon the work of Associate Editor was turned over to her because she was willing to work, eager to learn and aggressive. Her employer advised her to accept the offer of The Journal, which was not as its editor at first, believing that it offered a better chance for learning and she entered its employment while still wearing short frocks. Shortly, one day in the absence of the

Manager and during a periodic attack of constitutional weakness of a fine old gentleman who was the Editor, without waiting for promotion, nonchalantly assumed editorship not so much for the sake of being editor as to prevent its failure to make its regular weekly trips to those who were expecting it.

Since that time she has been as much of a student as when she was at college, grasping every opportunity to absorb information from every available source, and has performed her duty in all sincerity and honesty with a wholesome and sincere interest in the revival of river traffic and the improvement of the rivers. In the face of some discouraging periods that The Journal has gone through one sometimes wonders whether or not she continued in its behalf or found in the work a chance to develop latent talent which sometimes requires the rough road to roundup. [sic]

She has endured some hardships, takes her own part, appreciates true friendship, but rarely asked favors. Is a Missourian by adoption, Indianan by birth, Virginian and Kentuckyan by stock and a Burton by ancestory. The line from Sir William Pennington, who was Knighted by Queen Elizabeth, contains many warriors, statesmen and lawyers. Among the first to settle in this country, these families have been among the first to defend it from the first to the last war.

The Waterways Journal did several things to get attention and, of course, subscriptions. One was a contest to pick the most popular captain and the most popular boat.

And then there was the famous flagpole. The *Journal* said every other river city had one, and St. Louis should have one too. It was "a necessity for St. Louis," as the ad for it stated.

The Board of Trustees for raising the funds was composed of many well-known and respected rivermen, including Capts. Harry M. Matson, I. P. Lusk, Henry Leyhe, I. M. Mason, John E. Massengale, P. S. Drown, and Ferd Herold. Capt. Luther M. Emerson was chairman of this board, and R. J. Groeninger was secretary.

The May 16, 1896, issue reported that:

STEAMBOATMEN AND MERCHANTS
FLAG POLE.

A NECESSITY FOR ST. LOUIS.

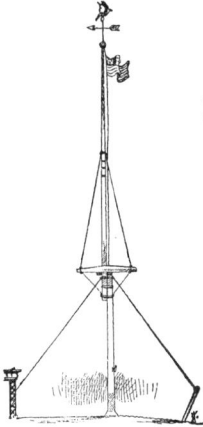

The steamboatmen of this city have at the instigation of the WATERWAYS JOURNAL began the boom to erect a pole from which to float the American Flag (Old Glory) daily, and have the same at half mast in case of death and in honor of steamboatmen, merchants or city officials. Every other city along any river point has a flag pole excepting St. Louis, the future great. The management of erecting this Flag Pole, as also disposal of the funds, are in the hands of the following Board of Trustees:

Capt. Harry M. Matson,
Capt. I. P. Lusk,
Capt. Henry Leyhe,
Capt. I. M. Mason,
Capt. John E. Massengale
Capt. P. S. Drown,
Com. Ferd Herold.

About $150.00 so far has been subscribed and mostly paid in, which is not quite enough to erect the present proposed pole, which is to cost about $400.00, including flag The pole to be 120 feet high, and the exact drawings can be seen at the offices of the Secretary of the Merchants Exchange and of the Waterways Journal, No. 311 Market street. We consider this a great credit to the city and trust that all will do something towards helping it to and early success.

CAPT. LUTHER M. EMERSON, Chairman.
R. J. GROENINGER, Secretary.

"...on last Thursday a hole about 4 x 5 feet in size and about 10 feet deep had been dug and the flagpole raised. The excavation was filled in with macadam and cement and that solidified the pole will rest, as it were, in a solid rock. It is composed of six steel tubes, joined together with bands. It rises from the surface to a height of 100 feet. At the base it is 25 inches in circumference and at the top it appears to be about the size of a baseball bat.

"It is midway between Olive and Pine Streets, just on the brow of the sloping levee."

A few days later the cyclone of 1896 hit the levee. The June 22 issue reported:

"Our Levee flagpole, though constructed of steel and imbedded deep in the earth, surrounded by a mass

49

of concrete, was twisted like a slender twig and broken
by the whirling tornado. It will soon be replaced."

There was, of course, a constant struggle to get more subscribers. The slogan was, "Help Us Grow." A poem about this
appeared in the July 2, 1921, issue.

The Steady Subscriber
How dear to our hearts is the steady subscriber,
Who pays in advance at the birth of each year;
Who lays down the money and does it quite gladly,
And casts 'round the office a halo of cheer.

He never says: "Stop it; I cannot afford it;
I'm getting more journals than now I can read."
But always say: "Send it; all readers like it—
In fact, we all think it a help and a need."

How welcome his check when it reaches our sanctum;
How it makes our pulse throb; how it makes our hearts dance.
We outwardly thank him; we inwardly bless him—
The steady subscriber who pays in advance.
—Exchange

Bill Arste had an ace in the hole in getting subscriptions. In
the back room was a barrel of whiskey, with a dipper, and the
subscriber had the opportunity to give a toast to the *Journal*.

The *Journal* was fortunate, as it is today, in having readers
contribute news from along the waterways. In those days it could
be compared to a country gossip column.

There were sections from various river cities had fetching
names like Gallipolis Gossip, Chattanooga Chatter, and
Paducah Plucks. Louisville Loops had several interesting deck
headlines, with humor, such as this one:

"If Marine Newslets, and Sintillations From
the Ohio's Broad Surface
Neat Nautical News Nuggets,
Nicely Nutshelled
For the Edification of Waterways Journal
Readers — Pithy, Pointed Paragraphs"

It was also the days when writers often used nicknames. Some appearing in the *Journal* were E. T. Plank, Coal Shovel Bill, the Duke of Paducah, Little Mike, and Huckleberry Finn and Tom Sawyer.

Editorially the editor was asking Congress for bigger appropriations for river work, and fighting low bridges, high wharfage and the railroads.

The big coup of *The Waterways Journal* was its coverage of the big St. Louis cyclone (tornado) of May 27, 1896. The *WJ* was there, in its office at Washington Avenue and the levee, and couldn't have been much closer.

Here is the *Journal's* account:

AN APPALLING CALAMITY

St. Louis and East St. Louis Visited by A Destructive Cyclone

WHARFBOATS TORN FROM THEIR MOORINGS

FIFTEEN STEAMERS LOST—TRAINS ON CARS OVER-
TURNED—HOUSES WRECKED AND WHOLE
FAMILIES BURIED BENEATH THE
RUINS—DEATH AND
DESTRUCTION

On last Wednesday afternoon, at about 4 o'clock, those who were on the lookout saw a threatening cloud gathering in the southwestern heavens, making its way directly toward the center of the city. From the river front we watched its coming closely, and, while noting the peculiar appearance of the clouds overhead, saw that they were nearly motionless. There was a slight wind blowing from the east, wafting another gathering storm from that direction, to meet the one coming from the west. Where will they come together? was the question anxiously asked by many. Watercourses are said to attract storms, and St. Louis seemed to be fated to catch the two resistless forces that were approaching each other. The blackish green masses of vapor, charged heavily with electricity, crept steadily on toward the river, and about 5 o'clock it began to rain slightly and the heavens were lighted by a continuous blaze. At 5:05 p.m. the tornado swept down upon the city, striking it a little south of the center, carrying death and destruction in its path. Coming down from the Lafayette Park district, it crossed the river to East St. Louis, leveling houses wherever it went and sweeping away a portion of the eastern approach of the Eads Bridge. Its path was wide and it moved directly up the river, striking the western bank and playing havoc with the wharfboats and steamers that were moored on the western shore of the Mississippi. Then there was a lull for about five minutes, the sky was lighted by a peculiarly lurid hue, and the great monster, seeming to have gathered new force, swept unresistingly onward, wrenching wharfboats and steamers from their moorings, sending them adrift or tearing them to pieces in its fury, and whirling many of them to the deep, storm-tossed river.

AS WE SAW IT

From THE WATERWAYS JOURNAL office we saw the top of the Diamond Jo Line's wharfboat torn away in the first dash of the cyclone, and when the second one came the great boat was wrested from its fastenings and went floating helplessly down the stream. The boats that were at the bank above the bridge came floating down under the arches, and some of them were quickly wrecked by striking the bridge piers. First came the Libbie Conger through the bridge, and then the J. J. Odil, both being dashed against the piers, the cabin of the Odil going into splinters. Then came the harborboat and the City of Quincy, both together, former having steam up and all the crew on board. Both of the harborboat's chimneys, and the pilot-house and wheel, were torn away by the wind. The City of Quincy sunk under the wheel of the harborboat, rendering her helpless. And next came the Bald Eagle, torn into splinters by the terrific storm, and the bridge finished the work. At her side was the Dolphin No. 2, which struck a pier of the bridge, then floated down and sank, turning bottom side up in the middle of the river at the foot of Olive street. As the boat struck, some of the crew, among whom was the chambermaid, crawled on to a projection of the pier and clung to it till they were rescued by a tug. She was a new boat, valued at $30,000.

The Anchor Line Company suffered severely. Their wharfboat was not torn away, but was lifted on the levee. The City of Monroe was at the wharf, ready to depart for New Orleans, when the storm came. About 40 or 50 passengers were on board, and many of their friends were present to see them off when the cyclone struck. Very naturally a panic ensued, but through the coolness of Clerk Archie Woods and the courageous actions of Engineers James Haughey and A. B. De Witt, who remained at their posts, it was soon quieted and all were saved without injury, with the exception of one lady, who was slightly hurt. The cabin of the boat was wrecked and she drifted to the East St. Louis shore, where she was secured, a few blocks below her starting point. At the foot of Chouteau avenue lay two of the company's fine steamers—the City of Cairo and the Arkansas City. The latter drifted down to Carondelet and the former crossed to the east side. Both are total wrecks. Neither of them were in commission, and consequently there were but few persons on board.

The Libbie Conger was above the bridge. She went down sidewise and missed the piers, floating on down the stream, stripped of her tops, and sank near Carondelet.

The harbor-boat struck the dumpboat and was thus kept from striking a pier. It passed through under the bridge and was driven down the stream. Both of her chimneys were blown off.

Among the many boats above the bridge was the Bald Eagle. When she broke from her moorings she struck the middle pier of the bridge, and all the crew, excepting the watchman, climbed on to a projection of the pier and were saved by ropes lowered from the bridge. The boat floated on down and sank.

The Belle of Calhoun was lying at the Tennessee River wharfboat at the foot of Locust street, and when the cyclone twisted its way up stream she broke and drifted down to the head of Arsenal Island, where she sank. The Schwartz Bros. will have her raised.

List of boats that will prove a total loss:

1. CITY OF CAIRO.
2. ARKANSAS CITY.
3. BALD EAGLE.
4. LIBBIE CONGER.
5. CITY OF QUINCY.
6. J. J. ODIL.
7. DOLPHIN NO. 2, Towboat.
8. HARVESTER, towboat.
9. H. L. CLARK, ferryboat.
10. S. B. WIGGINS, ferryboat.
11. NAPOLEON MILLIKEN, ferryboat.
12. WILLIAM CHRISTY, ferryboat.
13. GEO. A. MADILL, transferboat.
14. HENRY SACKMAN, transferboat.
15. AUSTRIA, steam pleasure yacht.

List of boats that can be saved:

1. CITY OF PROVIDENCE.
2. CITY OF VICKSBURG, almost a wreck.
3. CITY OF MONROE, part of cabin and chimneys gone.
4. PITTSBURG, cabin gone.
5. BELLE OF CALHOUN, sunk, but can be raised; water up to her cabin.
6. HARBORBOAT, pilot-house gone, part of cabin demolished and smokestacks broken off.

List of tugs that can be saved:

1. S. S. CLUBB.
2. RESCUE NO. 2.
3. BATON ROUGE BELLE.

This makes a list of 24 boats lost or injured by the storm.
The wharfboats suffered severely, but most of them will be saved. Those that broke from their moorings are:
1. DIAMOND JO LINE CO.
2. EAGLE PACKET CO.

3. TENNESSEE RIVER LINE.
4. VALLEY BARGE LINE.

The Anchor Line's wharfboat was lifted up on the levee, but it is all right.

The Alonzo Church was the only ferryboat that was saved in the district covered by the storm.

The river seems to have been more fortunate in the number of people killed than was at first supposed, only six deaths being reported, as far as can be ascertained. They are as follows:

KILLED

MORRIS FISCHER of Hardin, Ill., passenger on Odil.
MRS. GOWER of De Shirley's Landing, Ill.
SIM WOODS, clerk of Odil.
WATCHMAN on board Dolphin No. 2, name unknown.
A WHITE WOMAN, chambermaid on Odil.
SECOND COOK on Odil.

ESTIMATED LOSSES

Wiggins Ferry Company, $65,000.

Huse & Loomis Ice and Transportation Co., $10,000.

Eagle Packet Company, $10,000.

Schwartz Bros. sustained very heavy losses, the Bald Eagle being a total loss. The damage will reach $45,000.

Capts. Seaman and Jones will suffer $5000 loss for the Libbie Conger.

The City of Quincy, owned by the Ames Brothers; total loss, $6,000.

Owners of the Dolphin No. 2, $30,000.

Diamond Jo Line, $25,000.

Owners of J. J. Odil, $10,000; insured for $7,000.

The Anchor Line Company's loss is estimated at $40,000.

The St. Louis and Mississippi Valley Transportation Company estimate their loss at $100,000.

The Columbia Excursion Company's loss is placed at $30,000.

The damage to the harborboat will reach $1500.

Com. Wm. Zink, owner of pleasure boat Austria, $3000.

NOTES OF THE DISASTER.

The flagpole had a very short life. It was broken in several places.

The hull of the Harvester is all right, but her entire cabin was carried away.

The Polar Wave lost her pilot-house in the cyclone, leaving the pilot exposed to the storm's fury. She raised steam Thursday to receive some Huse-Loomis property.

The City of Vicksburg and City of Providence are both down at the ways, and the latter was pulled out yesterday. She will be ready for business in two weeks. The City of Vicksburg was very badly damaged, and it will be some time before she will be in the excursion business.

The ferryboat Alonzo Church and the Henry Lourey were the only boats that came out without a scratch. The Church was just making a crossing when the cyclone came, and it carried her up the river and whirled her around; but she met with no obstructions.

The wagon and horses which were on the Diamond Jo wharf when the storm came are still there, and the horses are alive. To Capt. Jim Boland, master of the Pittsburg, is due that no lives were lost. He was cool and collected throughout, and remained at his post of duty. The Pittsburg's cabin, from the boiler deck up, was cut off as clean as could be.

Capt. I. P. Lusk, A. W. Dawley, Wm. Albeitz, N. P. Nelson and the young lady typewriter (sic) had experiences that they will never forget. They were nearly all carried bodily from the Diamond Jo wharfboat to the steamer Pittsburg by the forces of the wind. Capt. Lusk and Mr. Nelson rendered splendid service in the work of rescue. The Pittsburg and wharfboat went down the river together.

It was reported that Capt. C. B. Zeigler of the City of Monroe was missing, and probably lost. To his many friends we are pleased to announce that he is alive and well with his boat at present. He was seen to go ashore before the worst of the storm came.

Capt. Tom Peniston [sic] and his crew were on the Eagle wharfboat when she broke loose. They had an exciting ride down the river in the hold of the boat as far as Arsenal Island, when the river pirates got in their work, charging $1 each to take them ashore.

A ferryboat drifted down as far as Twin Hollow, five miles below Jefferson Barracks, before she sank.

Dave Welsh of the harborboat was seriously injured.

The Diamond Jo Line have located their office temporarily in THE WATERWAYS JOURNAL Building.

We had just arranged with Com. Zink, owner of the handsome pleasure yacht Austria, to take out a party of Cincinnatians, headed by Wharfmaster Schmidt, during the Republican Convention, but she was lost in the cyclone.

Capt. A. P. Seaman, master of the Libbie Conger, will have another boat in a few days for the Missouri River. Capt. Seaman, with his wife and child, narrowly escaped drowning, going as far as the head of Arsenal Island with her, where she sank.

Much sorrow is expressed by the many friends of Capt. Sim Woods, the efficient and gentlemanly clerk of the steamer J. J. Odil, who met death in the terrible storm. Everybody liked the genial officer.

The most fortunate of the steamboat lines was the St. Louis & Tennessee River Packet Company, the damage sustained being very light. Their boats had all departed, and the wharfboat where they landed was owned by the Eagle Packet Company. Outside of the rough ride down the river on the wharfboat by Capt. John E. Massengale, Capt. Wm. Penniston [sic], Capt. Keiflein and Miss C. Daley, all on board escaped unhurt.

George Simon, second clerk of the Odil, had an exciting time. He was knocked off the boat when she floated against the bridge. He caught some wreckage and floated down the river to Carondelet, where he was rescued.

The Louis Houck was backing out when the storm came up. Capt. Rentfro was at the wheel. He retained his presence of mind and stayed at his post. The pilot house was torn from over his head. His partner, Joe Gibbons, pulled a man out of the river.

Much sympathy is expressed at the loss of the Dolphin No. 2 and the Libbie Conger (no insurance), as the companies who owned these steamers were almost impoverished by the loss.

Ferryboats and tugs were lifted bodily out of the river and thrown high and dry on shore.

Capt. Seaman and Charles Botsai of the steamer Libbie Conger, went down the river in a skiff to look for their boat. No one knows what became of her.

The Cyclone on the River.

The terrific storm that struck St. Louis on the afternoon of the 27th inst. [sic] was very disastrous to river interests.

Twenty-four steamers were lost or badly disabled. Fifteen will prove a total loss. As the vessels were torn from their moorings, and went floating away, many of them to sink in the troubled waters, it seemed inevitable that many lives would be sacrificed, but as far as we can ascertain, there were only six fatalities on the river—five of them on board the steamer J. J. Odil and one on the Dolphin No. 2. There may have been others, but up to the time of our going to press we had not heard of them. At this writing it is difficult to form an estimate of the money loss to the steamboat owners, as only one boat, the J. J. Odil, carried cyclone insurance, but it must be between $500,000 and $1,000,000.

The Belle of Calhoun

The new steamer Belle of Calhoun, not yet a year old, lies at the bottom of the Mississippi River, at the head of Arsenal Island, a victim of the terrible cyclone that visited this city last Wednesday. The Schwartz Bros., owners of the handsome craft, say she will be raised as soon as possible and put in running order for the accommodation of their up-river customers.

Last Sunday the Belle, under command of that prince of good fellows, Capt. Ed Young, carried an excursion party to Gilead Slough, Illinois, 73 miles up the river. A select party of gentlemen, who were out for a day's hunting and fishing, were on board, and Capt. Young, who knows every foot of the country on both banks of the mighty river, guided them safely to the best hunting grounds and to the waters where the finny tribe "most do congregate." If the gentlemen caught no fish or bagged no game, it was not the fault of the commander of the Belle. But we will venture the assertion that the disciples of Nimrod and Isaac Walton came home well supplied with the table delicacies that skilled huntsmen and fishermen can capture in forests, fields and rivers.

The Belle of Calhoun was managed in a masterly manner by the experienced commander, and made the journey of 73 miles up stream, against the strong current of a rising river, in nine hours and a half; and the down trip was made in five hours. Thus it will be seen that the swiftly gliding home built steamer made the round trip of 146 miles in 14 hours and 30 minutes. Good for Capt. Young!

Courtesy of The Missouri Historical Society
The Henry Sackman, destroyed by the 1896 cyclone.

Courtesy of The Missouri Historical Society
The Arkansas City, destroyed by the 1896 cyclone.

Courtesy of The Waterways Journal
After the cyclone of 1896, Eads Bridge was fixed temporarily.

In 1920 a young man from Oil City, Pennsylvania, Donald T. Wright, offered to buy *The Waterways Journal*. There is a story that Arste offered to sell it for two prices: one with a model of the steamer Mary Morton, which was in the front window of the *Journal* office; and another without the model. Wright took the model, paying $500 for it. It was to stay on top of his roll-top desk as long as he was alive.

Bill Arste always kept a barrel of whiskey in the office so he could offer a nip when it seemed appropriate; but Wright was a teetotaler, so Arste took the barrel with him.

The first issue of the paper under the new publisher and editor was dated January 1, 1921. The editorial was headlined "A New Year And A New Waterways Journal." It said:

The new Editor does not believe it necessary to write at length concerning the future policy of the Waterways Journal. In the past this publication has stood forth fearlessly as the champion of inland waterways, traffic and rivermen. This policy, so ably upheld by the outgoing Editor, Mr. Wm. Arste, will not only not be abandoned but will— with the continued support and co-operation of the many individuals, firms, and corporations who are so loyally standing by the incoming management—be greatly strengthened. May the Waterways Journal continue to find the hearty welcome that it has enjoyed during the past thirty years; and may it ever bind together its old and its new friends.

Waterways Journal office. L-R: Donald Wright and Sam G. Smith. Note model of Mary Morton on top of Wright's desk.

Also on the front page was Bill Arste's last contribution to the paper:

FAREWELL!

With this issue the undersigned severs his connection with the Waterways Journal after a continuous service of almost 27 years—since April 1, 1894, Mr. Donald T. Wright, of Oil City, Pa., having purchased entire control of the River Publishing and Investment Co., owners of the Waterways Journal. To Mr. Wright I extend my heartiest support and best wishes, first, because of my pride in river interests and to see the river come back; second, knowing the deplorable condition of the Waterways Journal 27 years ago, building it up, stey [sic] by step, until it is classed second to no other publication in the United States and it is my wish to see it continue to flourish. I believe Mr. Wright, who is a staunch friend of the river, can enlarge its scope of usefulness.

To my friends (which in 27 years has developed many staunch and true friends), I wish a food [sic] farewell and it is my wish that they continue to support the incoming administration as they have mine. I hope to see them purely socially on a pleasure trip I expect to make in the near future.

And to others, well, any one that knows me personally, knows they never caused me any loss of sleep.

So, once again, and thanking all for favors extended in the past, I bid all a fond farewell.   William Arste.

—From the Collections of the St. Louis Mercantile Library Association
This photograph was taken at the Memphis, Tennessee, Convention Hall in 1907 on the occasion of President Teddy Roosevelt's trip on the Mississippi. L-R: Capt. S. B. Baker, Eagle Packet Company agent at Alton, Illinois.; Capt. Saunders Fowler, Paducah, Kentucky; Capt. W. H. "Buck" Leyhe (at 34 years of age); "Clell" Tindel, banker, Caruthersville, Missouri; and William Arste, St. Louis, publisher of *The Waterways Journal* 1894-1920. Capt. Fowler is shown holding a special issue of *The Waterways Journal,* upon which can be seen a picture of Roosevelt. The men's convention badges are visible. The above picture was first run in the special issue in 1907 (during Arste's reign) and was picked up again and published in the *Journal* on July 14, 1956, by Wright.

Chapter 7 ——

Donald Thomas Wright

Donald Thomas Wright, from Oil City, Pennsylvania, had known of *The Waterways Journal* for a long time before he bought it; he had been a correspondent for it for several years. He developed a love of the river and steamboats through reading it. Why would anyone from Oil City be so interested in the subject?

Oil City, near where oil was discovered in Pennsylvania, is on the Allegheny River and saw much river traffic during the oil boom. It can be assumed that a young Donald Wright associated himself with some of the men on the boats at Oil City.

He also did so in Pittsburgh, which was down river from Oil City and a big hub of river traffic. In fact, the story goes, he did get a job on a steamboat as a clerk, probably "mud clerk." He came home very proud of having been on the river and a member of a steamboat crew. His sense of accomplishment was soon dashed; his mother had heard of bedbugs on the boats, and he had to take a bath in the basement before she would allow him to come upstairs.

There were probably some questions among his friends about sinking money in a river newspaper. The river business was in a low point then, with a declining economy and number of boats. It might not have been as evident in Pittsburgh with its big coal towing business, but on the Mississippi the big lines were gone, such as the Anchor Line and the Diamond Jo Line. The smaller, short-trade boats, were also facing competition from trucks, or would do so soon.

Capt. Russell Warner once told me in Memphis that the end of the steamboating really came when they laid the first macadam road along the river. The short-line boats couldn't meet the truck competition, and they went the way of the long-trade boats that had been lost to railroad competition.

Despite this, Donald Wright went ahead with his plans for *The Waterways Journal*. He was confident in the future of the rivers. He undoubtedly could see the future use of the waterways for the movement of bulk cargo by towboating. The Federal Barge Lines was then in the formative period, to develop the best way to use barges and towboats.

Whatever his thoughts were in this regard, Donald Wright was to play a significant role in the development of the rivers to the place they now hold in the nation's transportation picture.

Donald Wright's father, who was helping to finance the purchase of the *Journal*, came out to St. Louis to look things over. His first decision was to move the office up the hill, all the way to Eighth and Olive streets in the Chemical Building. For the first time since its inception, then, the staff of the paper could not see the river. It wasn't until Ray Spencer moved it to the Security Building in 1976, that the *Journal* windows offered a river view again.

At that time Eighth and Olive was the hub of downtown St. Louis.

Donald Thomas Wright

66

There were the Post Office, with its federal offices; other large office buildings; and two big department stores, Famous-Barr and Scruggs-Vandervort-Barney close by. The plaza in front of the Post Office was used for many civic occasions.

The Chemical Building was well-maintained, and had elevator operators on the lifts. There was also, in the basement, a big cafeteria, Miss Hullings, known for good food.

With a new editor and publisher the *Journal* became a little more business-like. The cartoons and jokes were gone, also the beer and liquor ads. The new owner did not touch intoxicating beverages and was known for this in the river circles.

He still liked river history, however, and old boat stories played a big role in the paper's bill of fare. Collecting steamboat pictures was Donald Wright's big hobby, and he was always on the lookout for them. In fact, there was a big rivalry between him and Fred Way, Jr., from Sewickley, Pennsylvania, another *Waterways Journal* person, who had written for the paper as a young man and who would be a contributor for years. There was an agreement between them that they would trade pictures if they found new ones, and we presumed this was done. (At the time of his death Donald thought all the pictures of boats had been found; how wrong he was, as Ralph DuPae, working with the University of Wisconsin-La Crosse has proved by finding thousands more, and is still uncovering them.)

Donald Wright married Pearl Burks from Pine Bluff, Arkansas, January 10, 1926. Members of her family were river-oriented, which is the likely reason they became acquainted in the first place at the Chautauqua in New York state. She was a beautiful woman, slight of build, but very strong-willed. She had a very fine speaking voice too, with a southern touch. In fact, one caught a bit of the South with her.

Mrs. Wright was a wonderful hostess, and many leaders in the river industry enjoyed the hospitality at 609 Sherwood Drive, in Webster Groves, Missouri, where the Wrights were to live.

These parties were, of course, spirits free, so the food had to be especially tasteful, which it was. There is one story about some guests who were known for their fondness for a before-dinner libation; knowing the rules of the house, they brought a bottle with them and hid it in the bushes before going in. When they came out, it was gone. They never found out what happened to it.

The decor of the Wright's house was splendid, so much so that you were afraid to touch anything. Mrs. Wright's hobby was collecting porcelain birds, and she had a wonderful collection, which today is in the Pine Bluff Public Library. The furniture was very fine, too, but there was a joke here: if you opened the drawers, you found steamboat pictures!

Mrs. Wright was also known for her beautiful garden, and when the azaleas were in bloom, there was a procession of people down Sherwood Drive to see the Wright's garden.

In a way, the house was dominated by a fluffy, orange-colored Pomeranian dog, which like the rest of the place, was well-groomed.

One of *The Waterways Journal* legends is about the day the staff heard weird noises coming from Donald Wright's office. Thinking he was having a heart attack or stroke, we rushed in to find him holding the phone; Mrs. Wright was holding the dog up to the phone at the house and he was barking through it to the office.

Webster Groves is a suburb of St. Louis on the west. The story of how Donald Wright got to the office in downtown St. Louis is an interesting one. First, it should be said that in addition to his hobby with steamboat pictures, he also had another, riding his "bycycle" as he called it; actually he had two—one being a spare.

He would leave the house and, using alleys and back streets, ride down to the train station. The Missouri Pacific ran through Webster Groves and made a stop there. He had two choices of trains in the morning, the Texas Eagle from the south or the Missouri Eagle from the west. They were both crack passenger trains. He would throw the bicycle in the baggage car and climb on the train, going to the dining car for breakfast. At St. Louis Union Station he would reclaim the bike and ride down to Eighth and Olive.

There is a story that one day a new crew on the train, not being acquainted with picking up a passenger at Webster Groves started right on through. Someone pulled the emergency cord to stop the train, and it did, flattening the wheels in the process.

At the Chemical Building the elevator operators had the freight elevator ready and up to the sixth floor (the office was there when I joined the staff; the bike went to the storage room for the day.

One of Donald's first orders of business was to enter in his bicycle book the mileage for the morning and notes about the trip. I almost got fired the first morning I was at the *Journal* when I moved the machine before he had read the odometer.

One of Donald's boasts was that he had ridden the bike across every bridge across the Mississippi River. (All of course was detailed in his bicycle books.)

When the Huey P. Long Bridge was opened in New Orleans, he started across it and had traffic backed up for miles behind him. The police got him off finally. I don't know what happened to him after that, but the next year he was back with a police escort; he knew all the officials on the bridge commission!

Let us return to the office. The bicycle is safely stored in the back room and notations made in the book for the morning's ride. It was now time for a shave. Donald would put a towel around his neck and lather up in the west-side office room. He did not stay there, for often he would dictate to the girls while moving around. If he heard someone coming down the hall, he would duck back into his own office and close the door.

Once shaved, he would go on with the business of the day— reading the mail, making phone calls, etc. Lunch was at Miss Hullings downstairs. His departure was usually about 4:30 p.m., again on the bike. At the time there were police directing traffic at the downtown street corners, and we watched sometimes as the officers would stop traffic, and here would come Donald moving at a very slow pace diagonally across Eighth and Olive to ride south on Eighth to Market.

He was not an easy man to work for. In the news department it seemed to be the little things that upset him, like a comma misplaced, or a bad abbreviation. He was most particular about using middle initials, I suppose because he was proud of his. He liked mine and often introduced me as James

VERDIN Swift, to my embarrassment, and he would drawl it out. (The only person who knew my middle name and used it prior to the printing of this book was C. W. Stoll in Louisville, and he drawls it out like Donald did.)

Although he would take off at some seemingly minor infraction, he could be tolerant of big ones. I made some big ones in the advertising department, but he would not make a big thing out of it, believing, I guess, that my having to confess my mistake to him was punishment enough.

He was particularly harsh, we thought, on Capt. Sam Smith who was up in age and forgetful. We cringed when he took off on Sam.

The office had two big vaults for storing records. We had an intern one summer, Justen Miller, who was sure Sam was going to push Donald in one of the vaults and let him suffocate.

Donald was also known for his tight control of money as it pertained to the office. For instance, he would go over the monthly phone bill with a fine tooth comb, as the saying goes, and you had better be able to explain any long distance call. I always hated to turn in my expense accounts at the end of a trip because I knew the treatment it would get.

Time was also precious in his view, and one kept busy in the office on *Journal* business. The first day I was at the office I started out to the men's room, and as I went by his office he opened the side door and put an out-of-town newspaper under my arm with a big smile. I never went to the toilet again without something to read; it did save time!

One time he bet Fred Way that he could go from Pittsburgh to Cincinnati without spending any money. It should be explained that at the time there were still packets running on the Ohio. At meal times they would visit a boat and found that a visit from *The Waterways Journal* was worth a meal, or passage on the river at night. Near the end of the trip Donald wanted some ice cream, which he loved. To Fred's embarrassment Donald told the ice cream seller that he was conducting a survey of ice cream makers and would like a sample for comparison.

In the matter of being frugal, Donald would use the backs of carbon copies of letters to type his stories. One time he forgot to cross out the copies of the letters. The printers' galleys came back with all the letters in type—not the stories.

It must be said that these accounts of Donald Wright's idiosyncrasies were strictly in-house things. He was to become a leader in the inland waterways industry, and he made *The Waterways Journal* into a leading spokesman for the industry. He knew all the men of importance in the operating end and those who built up the shipyards.

His advice was sought in matters of policy in the associations that were working towards waterways development.

One day at lunch he got in a mellow mood, and told us that he was looking forward to dying, and meeting such famous rivermen as Capt. John W. Cannon of the steamer Robt. E. Lee, and Capt. John W. Tobin of the Natchez.

He died unexpectedly on Thanksgiving Day, 1965. An entry from the *Journal* tells the story. He is buried in Bellefontaine Cemetery in the company of Capt. Isaiah Sellers and his pilot-wheel of stones.

From the December 4, 1965, *Waterways Journal*, here are the lead paragraphs of the story that ran more than a full page:

> Capt. Donald Thomas Wright, who had been at the helm of The Waterways Journal as Publisher and Editor for almost 45 years, died unexpectedly on Thanksgiving, November 25, 1965, at about 9:30 p.m. Death was attributed to a heart attack. He was 71 years old.
>
> Capt. and Mrs. Wright had just had Thanksgiving dinner at the home of Mr. and Mrs. Charles C. Rockenback in Hampton Park, Richmond Heights, Mo., a St. Louis suburb, when he was stricken. Mr. Rockenback is vice-president of the Southern States Towing Division of Triangle Refineries, Inc., St. Louis.
>
> Capt. Wright was pronounced dead about 20 minutes after he was stricken. He had not been ill and had ridden his famed 1910 bicycle more than 20 miles Thanksgiving morning and almost 50 miles two days earlier.
>
> His wife, Mrs. Pearl Burks Wright, is the sole survivor. The family home is at 609 Sherwood Drive in Webster Groves, Mo., a St. Louis suburb.

Donald T. Wright's gravestone in Bellefontaine Cemetery.

Chapter 8 ——

One Of The Crew

*M*y first contribution to the *Journal* as a news crew member, or at least the first to get a by-line (complete with my middle name), was in the November 1, 1941, issue under the heading "St. Louis Drift," a note on local events.

The masthead showed Donald T. Wright, editor and publisher; Sam G. Smith, business manager; and Andrew D. Franz, advertising manager.

The staff was still made up of river people. Sam Smith had been on the boats of the Evansville and Bowling Green Packet Company, being master of the packet Bowling Green, and also passenger agent for the excursion boat East St. Louis. He also ran the Marine Photo Company, which had rights to a number of classic steamboat pictures. (They eventually came into Donald's hands.) He was clerk on the steamer Grand when she was running on the St. Francis River in Missouri. He was clerk on the John S. Hopkins on the Green River, the Lucille Nowland on the Arkansas River, purser on the Shiloh, and was on the Ohio when she sank at Cottonwood Point, Missouri, February 17, 1894. Sam was indeed a riverman with experience in the office.

Andrew D. Franz was in the operations and business end of boats. About 1923 Capt. John F. Klein, steamboat broker, turned the Ursie Boyce into an excursion boat named City of Cairo, and Andy chartered her for a trip up the Missouri River; she got as far as Jefferson City. He and Edwin C. Koenig bought the little private pleasure boat Kabekona (in 1915) and ran charter trips with her. He was manager of the Keystone State in 1913.

He had formed the St. Louis Excursion and Packet Company which operated the steamer Belle of the Bends. He was also president of the Laclede Iron Works that made steamboat machinery.

Andy Franz also had plans to run the Harry G. Drees from St. Louis to St. Paul as a tourist boat; but as he was on the levee one day, a truck came down loaded with iron bathtubs for the boat. He gave up then and there. In fact, the Drees spent a lot of time on sandbars and may never have made it to St. Paul.

Andy was also with the Eagle Packet Company as commercial agent. He told the story about how the company cut down on his supply of free tickets for friends and customers, so he had an arrangement with the ticket taker; when Andy tipped his hat, the passenger got on board free.

Although born and reared a Catholic, Andy had fallen by the wayside and was outspoken about the church. Mary Ann Gifford, our secretary, was a very devout person, and when we heard her exclaim, "Oh, Mr. Franz!" it was very possible that he had said something irreverent.

Andy would tell how, as a boy and still working in the church, he would carry the sprinkling can of holy water down the aisle with a priest. Andy found that by elevating the can to a certain point the sprinkler would pick up a lot of water which ended up on the people in the pews.

Andy had many river friends who came to call, such as Capt. E. Nathan Smith, who came regularly after a lodge meeting. There was a lot of good river talk going on, and it was hard for me, in the next room, to keep my mind on my work.

Andy always had a roll of *Waterways Journals* under his arm, and a big cigar. He was a popular man along the river.

The *Journal* always seemed to have as secretary a woman who could hold things down if a crisis emerged. Mary Ann was such a person, and she was a big help to me in those first days when I was really green.

There was a little ditty that someone contrived about the office personnel: "Donald T. and Andy D. and Sammy G."

One unusual fact was that none of the male members of the of the staff had any children.

Someone once wrote:

Once You Ride Between Two Stacks,
    You're Doomed.

    You Will Steamboat Till
    You're Tombed.

                    Jim

Chapter 9 ——

Unpleasant Interlude

*I*was just settling into the job at the paper when, on that fateful Sunday in December 1941 while listening to the New York Philharmonic, there came that fateful news bulletin: "The Japanese Have Bombed Pearl Harbor."

It was to change the world for everyone, and of course, I was no exception. I got my letter from the President in February the following year inviting me to visit Jefferson Barracks south of St. Louis.

Donald had some ideas about this. Earlier, when J. Mack Gamble, from Clarington, Ohio, and the *Journal's* upper Ohio River correspondent, was drafted, Donald got him sent to Jefferson Barracks (or stationed there), I guess through his friends with the Army Corps of Engineers. Mack thus could do a little work for the *Journal* on the side.

With me, there was the Coast Guard. This agency had offices in the Post Office building. In fact, the commander's office could be seen from the *Journal* office, and if Donald ever wanted to know if the Admiral was in, all he had to do was look across Eighth Street.

So, I was sent across the street to see Capt. Stephen S. Yeandle. He was very pleasant and understanding, but he said, "Your eyes don't qualify you to be a Coast Guardsman. As long as you were in my district, I could watch out for you, but you would undoubtedly be sent somewhere else where I could not. Sorry, I can not help you."

Donald was naturally very disappointed, for he saw a good thing go down the tube.

I kept my date at J.B., along with hundreds of other men, and after being processed was put on a troop train for California. I was assigned to the Armored Force—the tanks.

Our destination was Camp Cooke, California (now Vandenberg Air Force Base), on the coast near Lompoc, and a little farther from Santa Barbara. We were to be part of the Fifth Armored Division, which was being formed by cadres from several existing divisions and induction centers.

A few days before our arrival, a Japanese submarine had shelled an oil refinery at Santa Barbara, and the men who pre-ceeded us to Camp Cooke were painting the windows of the barracks, which overlooked the Pacific Ocean, olive green.

As all other units did, we were toughened up for action by a series of maneuvers that took us from west to east and from hot to cold climates. In those first days of training, all the action was focused on North Africa, where the British and Germans were pushing each other back and forth. We, being in the tanks, figured that would be our destination.

Here I am at Camp Cooke, California, on the coast near Lompoc.

We went to the Mohave Desert to Desert Center for maneuvers and a taste of life in that hot, dry region. Water was rationed, we had to take salt pills, and in a violent sand storm lost some equipment.

Due to a reversal of the British, I guess, we had to ship our tanks out by train to resupply them.

When we got back to Camp Cooke we got a new commander, Maj. Gen. Lunceford E. Oliver. The most interesting part of this was that he came from the Corps of Engineers and had been the District Engineer at St. Louis and Vicksburg. I always thought we made such good time in Europe because, as an engineer, he knew about roads and bridges and how to repair them.

Gen. Oliver was just the opposite of Gen. George Patton. He didn't look for publicity, and the Fifth Armored didn't get too much, although we were right up with the leading units in Europe.

For the militarily minded I should say that an armored division has three fighting units called combat commands, A B, and R (reserve) supported by infantry, artillery, antiaircraft units, medics, signal units, and supply companies all unified in one mobile outfit.

During the Battle of Midway one of our combat commands was sent down to Los Angeles, where they camped in a city park. At Camp Cooke we were on full alert, carrying our gas masks and side arms with us wherever we went. We didn't know what was going on, but it had to be something important.

We said goodbye to Camp Cooke and headed east to Tennessee for more maneuvers. We were around McMinnville. We had woods and ravines to contend with instead of sand.

Then, on to Indiantown Gap, Pennsylvania, and finally Pine Camp, New York, in the real woods. It was here one day that we were issued winter clothing, parkas, boots, thermal underwear, all the good things. This really started the rumors flying. Were we going to Russia, or Alaska? But immediately it was all called back. We had orders to go overseas.

We embarked on the transport Edmund B. Alexander at Staten Island, New York, on February 10, 1944. (We were to come home on the same ship when the war was over.) It is said we went over in one of the largest convoys ever up to that time—with no enemy attack. We landed at Liverpool, England, on February 21.

Our destination was the Salisbury Plains in southern England in about the middle. It was good tank country for further maneuvers. I had the chance to go to London on pass, and we went to Bath and Bristol on business for the company.

Then came June 6, 1944. The sky was full of planes coming back from the invasion of France. It was an awe-inspiring sight, and we knew we would see action soon.

We had not been in the invasion, of course, for in the Allies strategic plan for liberating France, the Fifth was not needed until it was time to break through and move fast. It was called "Cobra" by Gen. Omar Bradley.

We moved across the English Channel on July 26 to join other armored units. A big air bombardment and artillery barrage hit the Germans around St. Lo on July 25, and the way was open.

The Fifth was at Coutances on August 2, and we swung to the north with other units of the Third Army of Gen. Patton to close the noose on the retreating Germans at the Falaise Gap. The officers wanted to keep going north and close the Gap but were held back. Many Germans escaped, but they took a terrific beating.

On the road again, we were through Paris August 30, with our advance units fighting in the suburbs, while the main body was in the city. The Second French Armored had taken Paris earlier. Their tanks were still along the streets, and I recall seeing some girls crawling in and out of the tank turrets.

The journey through France was something to remember. As liberators we got the good treatment, including bottles of wine. Some of it was calvados, a very potent apple-jack liquid that had a wallop. One bottle was thrown into the Chief of Staff's half-track, hitting him in the head and knocking him out.

Later we turned north into Belgium and became part of First Army.

We were in a little town in eastern Belgium on December 16. My unit was on the second floor of a building by a river, when there was a roar of a plane and an explosion. The Germans were trying to take out a bridge. It was the start of the Battle of the Bulge.

Of course, we didn't know that was going on at first, but it was a wild time. It was learned that the Germans had captured and were using vehicles, especially Jeeps (we called them peeps in the Fifth Armored) with Fifth Armored markings and manned by English-speaking Germans to change roadsigns, give confusing signals, etc. Passwords were changed to use words with the letter "V" which are hard for Germans to use, and people were also asked: "What team did Babe Ruth play for?"

Paratroops were rumored to have been dropped in the area, and the next morning we were out in the forest looking for them. It was a scary time.

The Fifth had been beaten up in the Hurtgen Forest and was in a regrouping stage when the Battle of the Bulge started, so the Division was deployed in a holding pattern around Aachen. We ate Christmas dinner there, and while in line for chow, a German plane tried to strafe us.

The Battle of the Bulge over, we started east again, and crossed the Rhine River at Wesel, Germany, on March 31. We were amazed at the autobahns which fit our tanks just right. I am sure a lot of people recognized then how far behind the U.S. was on highways, and got the idea for the interstate system.

By April 12, we were on the Elbe River, ready to put bridges across and head for Berlin. But it was not to be. The Russians were to take the city. Germany surrendered May 7. On the Elbe we got word of President Roosevelt's death, and there was a feeling of let-down. Who ever heard of Harry Truman?

We played the part of occupation troops for a while. We were in a village down in the valley, and the Russians were in a castle up on the hill.

Now dubbed the Victory Division, the Fifth had the distinction of liberating the Grand Duchy of Luxemborg in one day, with Crown Prince Felix riding into his capitol of Luxemborg City on a Fifth Armored Jeep.

Units of the Fifth were the first American troops to enter Germany on September 11, 1944, around Bitburg. Earlier the Fifth was the first to cross the Meuse River, September 7.

Action over, the Fifth was deactivated along the banks of the Seine in western France. It was a trying time, because there was the possibility of being sent to the Pacific, where the war was still in full force.

The point system was set up, with those having the most points being up for discharge. It was a complicated thing with the amount of service, battle stars and other things figured in. Counting points was the big game.

But then came the A-Bomb and V-J Day. On September 10, we were on our way home.

I have been remiss in not saying something about my job with the Fifth. I was not driving a tank. I was in the supply room of Headquarters Company of the division and came out as a technical sergeant. The best thing was I had a typewriter, and I became an overseas correspondent for *The Waterways Journal*. As I recall, I did three articles, all of which, I discovered later, were titled "One More River to Cross—the Thames, Seine and Rhine." All, of course, had to get by the censor.

Chapter 10 ——

The Rivers Went To War

Meanwhile, back at the ranch—or on the rivers. What was going on? Plenty!

The issue of *The Waterways Journal* for the week following Pearl Harbor had a prophetic editorial:

Now That War Has Come

As this editorial is being written on Monday, December 8, loud speakers outside the offices of The Waterways Journal are blaring out the man-to-man vote in the House of Representatives on a resolution declaring war on Japan. The bombs that fell in Pearl Harbor have sent repercussions that have thrown the United States into another world conflict.

The Pacific Ocean is a long way from the inland waterways of the Midwest. It is so far that the people of the Mississippi Valley and all its tributary valleys may feel secure and safe. They must remember that this is to be a conflict that will eventually bring sorrow and deprivation to everyone in every part of this country. It will be when one part of this nation suffers, every other section will suffer with it.

What has this to do with the inland waterways? We must remember [how] important their part is in this time of crisis. Even without traffic from War Department plants they are carrying a tremendous volume of vital materials, are carrying metal for tanks, armour plate, merchant ship construction, coal, gasoline to power machines making vital products, chemicals for making powder and an endless number of other items. Now the railroads will be loaded with troop trains and freight that must be moved with speed. The waterways will have an increased burden.

The inland rivers and the carriers on them now have a new importance. The vital importance of speed and efficiency with which they deliver the essentials of war may well mean victory or defeat. At the least, it will mean a short or a long war, with the accompanying difference in loss of life and materials. The successful operation of every engine, every lock, and the efficiency of every man in the crew of every boat is all-important. Now we do not have to supply Russia, Britain, China, and Free France only with products for war; we must repair our own damaged fleet and build up our own services. It is a vast program, a staggering one, one which must be fulfilled successfully if this country is to survive.

There may be readers who think this importance of the rivers is an exaggeration. They have only to take a broad look at this war to see that America is in it until the end, and that the waterways are as vital a link in the supply line as the railroads. Any supply line must be in A-1 shape if a military force is to survive.

There is a great contrast on the rivers today in 1941 compared with 1917. Then there were no great year-around channels, no barge lines, no great fleets of modern barges and boats. In this one factor the United States is indeed lucky. The barge lines are ready and able to assist, and there can be no question of how they will function. We know their officers and the crew members of their boats well enough to know also that nothing will be left undone to move cargo swiftly, efficiently, well. It will be "full speed ahead" on every river. It will be "heads up" with a quick eye for sabotage. It will be "all out" work on every boat and in every waterway office for the United States of America.

Another article in that issue was titled "The Rivers Are Ready"; it emphasized the ability of the waterways to carry cargo, as indeed they did.

One way they proved their worth was providing a safe way to move petroleum products from the Gulf to the East Coast—around the submarine menace. The U-boats were taking a terrible toll on tankers off the Atlantic Coast.

The oil could move over the mountains by pipeline or truck. The article said:

> The problem was, where was the equipment to move this product? Also, there was the general increase in need to move many other basic products. One solution was a crash program to build the needed equipment and this was done through the Defense Plant Corporation.
>
> ### The DPC Towboats
>
> Twenty-one steam powered, screw-propelled towboats were commissioned by the Defense Plant Corporation. They were built out of one mold, so to speak, because time and energy were vital commodities. The hulls were 180 feet, $10\frac{1}{2}$ inches by 52 by 11 feet and the twin engines were 2,000 hp. at 185 rpm. Built by Fulton, they were 4-cycle triple expansion, 16 by 26 by 32 by 32, with a 2-foot stroke. The boats had Foster-Wheeler boilers developing 275 psi. The twin propellers were nine feet in diameter.
>
> When it came to naming the boats, it was decided to use the names of battles in which the United States had been engaged. That early in the war there weren't too many big ones; we were not in Europe; and that is the reason so many boats on the Mississippi had strange sounding names out of the South Pacific, the Aleutian Islands and North Africa. It was a lessen [sic] in geography for a lot of rivermen.
>
> Here is a list of the DPC towboats, where they were built, who first ran them, and after they were declared surplus at the end of World War II, who bought or acquired them.

Cargill, Inc., Savage, Minn., shipyard: Bataan, Federal Barge Lines, Sohio Petroleum Company (Sohio Latonia); Bou Arada, Sohio, later the Sohio Fleetwing; Coral Sea, begun at Savage, finished by Pidgeon-Thomas Iron Works at Memphis, Federal Barge Lines; Milne Bay, also completed at Memphis, Mississippi Valley Barge Line, Martin Oil Company (Allen B. Wood).

Dubuque Boat & Boiler Company, Dubuque, Iowa: Tenaru River, Federal Barge Lines, American Barge Line.

Jeffersonville Boat & Machine Company, Inc., Jeffersonville, Ind.: Attu, American Barge Line, New Orleans Engineers; Corregidor, American Barge Line, Memphis District Engineers; Guadalcanal, Mississippi Valley Barge Line, American Barge Line; Java Sea, American Barge Line; Tulagi, Union Barge Line, Vicksburg District Engineers; Wake Island, Federal Barge Lines, John I. Hay, Ashland Oil & Refining Company and back to Federal.

Marietta Manufacturing Company, Point Pleasant, W. Va.: Guam, Mississippi Valley Barge Line, Jones & Laughlin Steel Company (H. E. Lewis); Kiska, Mississippi Valley Barge Line, J&L, (W. J. Creighton).

Mount Vernon Bridge Company, Ironton, Ohio: Lunga Point, Butcher-Arthur, Inc., Ore Steamship Corporation; Midway Islands, Ashland Oil, Sohio (Sohio Southern).

St. Louis Shipbuilding & Steel Company, St. Louis: Buna, Butcher-Arthur, Ore Steamship Corporation and then Federal Barge Lines; Casablanca, American Barge Line; Kokoda, Lake Tankers Corporation, Federal; Gona, Globe Oil Barge Company, Hennepin Towing Company; Mateur, Federal Barge Lines, Vicksburg District Engineers; Tunis, Butcher-Arthur, Ore Steamship Corporation, Federal.

Beginning and End

The Wake Island was the first of the DPCs to go into operation. She was accepted at Cairo, Ill., by the government in mid-October, 1943. She then went south to meet the Herbert Hoover, upbound with an oil tow.

86

The Defense Plant Corporation also augmented the inland waterways fleet with barges, some even made of wood. There were 221 DPC barges.

> The war over, the Defense Plant Corporation assembled its equipment in the East Pearl River near Madisonville, La. On November 17, 1945, there were five miles of barges, tugs and towboats laid up there, with more coming in. There were 65 steel barges 230 by 45 by 11, with 113 more due; twenty-eight 175 by 26 by 10; sixty-five 195 by 35 by 10, with 60 due; and four 175 by 36, with 1 due. There were also 32 DPC tugs, with 13 more to come.
>
> For safety the vessels were laid up in fleets, labeled red, green, yellow and blue, with fire lanes in between. Donald T., Wright, then editor and publisher of The Waterways Journal, cruised by the assembled armada, and wrote that it was the largest fleet of steamboats in federal service assembled since the boats gathered during the Civil War to take Union troops up the Tennessee River in 1862.

What had not been foreseen when the war started was how the inland waterways would help the war effort through construction of vessels. With the coastal shipyards working at full capacity for ocean-going shipping, the government turned to the waterways to build smaller, and shallow-water vessels.

Between January 1, 1942, and September 30, 1945, The American Waterways Operators figures that 3,943 crafts of many types were built on the rivers and sent down to the Gulf.

There was a great variety, but the ones that were more spectacular and caught the public eye were the LCTs and LSTs—landing craft and ship, tank.

In his book *Citizen Soldiers*, Stephen E. Ambrose called them "the Allies' secret weapon, far more practical and effective than the secret weapons Hitler put into operation a week after D-Day." They kept the Allied armies supplied when there were no ports, and put the troops ashore to begin with.

Seven hundred and four of them were built on the inland waterways. The yards that constructed the LSTs, were Dravo, at Neville Island, Pittsburgh; American Bridge Company, Ambridge, Pennsylvania; Jeffersonville Boat and Machine Company,

Jeffersonville, Indiana; Missouri Valley Steel Company, Evansville, Indiana, and the Seneca Shipyard, Seneca, Illinois, Chicago Bridge and Iron Company.

Jeffboat built 123 LSTs, and Evansville 171. The Pennsylvania yards did 286.

Also spectacular was the movement of submarines down from the Great Lakes. They were built at Manitowoc, and because of their depth had to be put on drydocks for passage down the Illinois and Mississippi rivers. The Federal Barge Lines towboat Minnesota did much of this work. Movements were often made at night to avoid observation, and bridges were closed when the subs passed under them. Twenty-eight submarines were sent down the rivers in this fashion.

The river pilots most used for this work included Capts. Lowell L. Sorrells, Gordon Cooper and Louis De Long.

Other large vessels built on the rivers included 29 destroyer escorts, many by Dravo.

Smaller craft like LCIs came out of yards on the Missouri River (86) and also LCTs, 135.

Small Navy tankers were built at Savage, Minnesota, on the Minnesota River. After the war, *The Waterways Journal* received some interesting facts about these vessels.

> The Navy also received supply-type vessels over the inland waterways. Cargill, Inc., activated a shipyard in the cornfields at Savage, Minnesota, on the Minnesota River, half an hour from downtown Minneapolis. The "Meadowland Shipyard" (Port Cargill) turned out 18 AOG (auxiliary oil and gas tankers) in addition to 3 DPC's, the Bataan, Bou Arada and Coral Sea. (The latter boat was completed at Memphis by the Pidgeon-Thomas Iron Works.) The tankers were named for small American rivers.
>
> Donald Fluetsch, Cassville, Wisconsin, has some interesting material on the project at Savage. We have him to thank for the picture of one of the AOGs built at Savage.
>
> They were well-built, as evidenced by a run-down on the vessels from the Navy Bureau of Ships in July 1966. Two of them, the Kishwaukee and Noxubee, were then being reactivated from the mothball fleets

in Portland, Oregon, and Baltimore, respectively; the Elkhorn, Genesee and Tombigbee were on active duty in the Pacific; the Chewaucan, Mattabesset and Newpelen were on active duty in the Atlantic; and the Namakakon was on loan to New Zealand.

The Natchaug was on loan to Greece; the Pecatonica was on loan to Nationalist China at Formosa; the Pinebog was being held by the Air Force for Dew Line supply in the Artic; the reserve fleets and the Agawam (first one launched in Savage, May 6, 1943), Chestabee and Wacissa at Olympia, Washington; the Nemasket was at Astoria, Oregon; and the Maquoketa was at Suisan Bay, San Francisco. The Chehalis sank in October 1949 at Tutuila, American Samoa, after the war was over.

It was indeed a source of pride to Cargill that the craftsmanship of elevator men, farmers, house painters and others in the "Meadowland Shipyard" of the 1940s still is seaworthy and capable of important jobs.

According to the stories Mr. Fluetsch sent, the Namakakon, launched at Savage October 28, 1944, delivered fuel oil to Pearl Harbor and shuttled oil and gas to central Pacific island naval bases. The Mattabesset, launched November 11, 1944, made fuel runs to Pacific islands before being transferred to the Atlantic Fleet to become part of the Mediterranean Sixth Fleet; in 1955 she weathered two hurricanes and participated in the first experiment of fueling operations between a submarine and an AOG.

In 1951, a Cdr. Stolz, who was in charge of building the AOGs for the Navy, spotted the Mattabesset only 800 miles from the North Pole and in 1963 the Queen of England saluted the Tombigbee in the harbor of Nelson, New Zealand. The Elkhorn was supplying bases in the Central Pacific as late as 1964.

In his book, *Lore and Lure of the Upper Mississippi River*, the late Capt. Frank J. Fugina recalls that the tankers were 319 feet long and weighed 4,000 tons. Federal Barge Line boats took them down to the Mississippi where other FBL vessels moved them south. The Demopolis worked on the Minnesota, with Capts. Ray Prichard, David Stein, Fed Thoreen and John Bishop in command. The fleets

From the Files of The Waterways Journal

Submarine built at Manitowoc, coming down the Illinois Waterway in dry-dock.

Courtesy of Dravo Corporation

LST bound for deep water—ships at the bottom of the picture are Russian vessels on the ways at Dravo.

were in charge of Capt. Roy Wethern, while Capts. James E. Simmons and Carl Cutting, superintendents of vessels for Federal, had the general supervision of bringing the tankers out.

How were all these war craft sent from the rivers to the sea—or Gulf? They had to be guided by people who knew the rivers. Enter what had become know as the "Cat Fish Navy." After the war the *Journal* received some recollections of this service and these are printed here.

> The Navy crews that were to sail the vessels usually came on board at the yards and were "salted down" while the river ferry crews piloted them down the river. Some interesting things happened between these regular Navy people and the rivermen. A few LSTs ended up in the willows and river docks, but not because of pilot error.
>
> An interesting account of such a trip was written by Herbert G. Telsey for the United States Naval Institute Proceedings of December 1951. It was titled "LST Ferry Crew One." During the war Mr. Telsey's crew made 42 delivery trips covering 71,000 statute miles.
>
> The crew traveled approximately the same mileage by railroad (mostly in coaches) between New Orleans and the various shipyards via St. Louis for orders.
>
> Mr. Telsey reminds us that at the time the river operations were controlled by the Ninth Naval District under the immediate command of the district Coast Guard office at St. Louis. He also points out that the ferry crews, in addition to having a pilot and assistant pilot, had a radioman, the latter a Coast Guard regular.

Capt. Lowell Sorrels, who we have mentioned before, sent *The Waterways Journal* some interesting pictures of World War II activities, and Capt. William H. Tippitt wrote asking for names of fellow ferry pilots. The author checked back in the files and found an item in the June 23, 1945, *Waterways Journal* that named 16 pilots who were released from duty (or who were to be released July 1), and they included Chief

Boatswains Clyde W. Curd, Ralph K. Raise, Lt. (jg) Davenport I. Day, and Lts. A. A. Dittlimger, N. C. Duclos, H. S. Russell, Lynne J. Gordon, S. H. Henson, Jr., R. W. Holland, Lance E. Keplinger, V. G. Leadicker, F. L. Martin, H. C. Morrow, E. M. Rodgers, Kenneth Templeton and W. H. Tippitt.

However, 22 pilots were to remain on active duty. Three were on the Ohio River run from Pittsburgh to Louisville: Ens. William B. Fenton, Boatswain Joseph L. McKee and Chief Boatswain Bert Shearer. Six on the Louisville to Memphis run were Lt. Harold E. Hanle, Boatswain Ralph H. Eggleston, Lt. (jg.) Richard J. Lynch, Lt. (TR) Edward C. Nickell, Lt. (TR) Fred F. McCandless and Lt. Harris D. Underwood. Capt. Beckwith Jordan was in command of the Coast Guard at St. Louis.

There were, of course, other rivermen who went to work for their country at this time, as Capt. Tippitt recalls them, including C. W. Stoll, Roy L. Barkhau, W. L. Fegan, E. K. Henson, Frank Hollinghead, Edward Heckman, William M. McNeely, F. Federson, Donald Gordon, Alva E. Kirk, Eugene Multhaupt, Dalys Hide, Vernon C. Smith, Robert Zang and John Graham. At headquarters there were Capt. Morey Brady in St. Louis and Ben I. Pattison in Cincinnati, as we recall. Undoubtedly there were more pilots.

All told these men took some 2,115 vessels of many types from the river yards to the sea—distinguished service, indeed. Is there little doubt that the inland waterways served the country well in time of emergency?

Capt. Tippitt also wrote:

I am very proud of being one of the pilots who rendered yeoman service to their country in World War II; in fact, if it had not been for the Cat Fish Navy, the Coast Guard would not have been able to fulfill its assigned task.

From the Files of The Waterways Journal

In this rare picture of the part of the Cat Fish Navy, which Capt. Tippitt sent, Lt. Cdr. Morey Brady, assistant to the ship movement officer, addresses the ferry pilots in St. Louis in 1944. In the front row, L-R, are Lt. E. L. Multhaupt, Lt. F. L. Martin, Lt. K. Templeton, CBS R. S. Jacobs, Lt. William H. Tippitt and Lt. N. C. Duclos; second row, Lt. (j.g.) E. C. Nickell, BS J. L. McKee, Lt. F. F. McCandless, Lt. H. D. Underwood, BS R. H. Eggleston, Lt. E. M. Rodgers and Lt. D. J. Gordon; third row, Lt. E. Heckman, CBS B. Shearer, Lt. H. E. Hanle, Lt. A. E. Kirk, Lt. V. G. Leadicker and Lt. J. H. Graham; and fourth row, Ens. W. B. Fenton, CBS V. C. Smith, Lt. L. J. Gordon, Lt. E. W. Holland and Lt. D. I. Day.

When the shipyards on the inland rivers began to turn out the LSTs, LCIs and many other vessels, the Navy had assigned six CBMs to the Federal Barge Lines to learn the rivers from Pittsburgh, St. Paul, etc., to New Orleans. The Memphis District was called upon to supply pilots for the vessels brought down out of the Great Lakes and from various points on the Ohio and Mississippi where naval reserve units had sub chasers of World War I to pilot these craft to New Orleans. I was one of those pilots.

These Navy men were later assigned as commanders of the ferry crews to take the vessels then being built from shipyards to the New Orleans Naval Base. Also, the crew that was to man these vessels in naval units were also being indoctrinated in their operation from shipyard to New Orleans, where the vessels were turned over to them after outfitting was completed.

The Coast Guard was assigned the task of providing the pilots. Fortunate for them, the draft boards were ignoring the previous regulation that exempted river pilots from their jurisdiction, and there was a rush of eligible, experienced pilots to join the Cat Fish Navy. I was just 10 days ahead of my draft board in joining the Coast Guard.

There was quite a bit of confusion in their recruitment and assigning pilots to various routes, until Capt. Morey Brady of the U.S. (St. Louis District) Engineers was shanghaied to take over this assignment. Capt. Brady organized the pilots into groups averaging about eight and assigned them to specific routes or sections of the river. In so doing he assigned men to routes on which they held license and would be posted at all stages of the river. Needless to say, there were only a few minor mishaps after he took charge of assigning the pilots, and he also assigned a steersman to accompany each pilot, so in reality he had men ready to replace any that might have dropped by the wayside.

We were strictly rivermen, doing a job for which we had spent years training. As for the indoctrination into the Coast Guard 'bible' or rules and regulations, we never had the time nor the inclination to abide by them.

From the Files of The Waterways Journal

Navy tanker built on rivers.

In fact, I don't think they wanted us to, for we knew no hours of duty, on and off. We often exceeded 15 to 18 hours at a stretch, sometimes running through the full 24 hours in the Memphis to New Orleans run, counting on the four-hour fueling stop at Baton Rouge to catch up on our sleep. Why not? Well, we got $10 per day when we were off the boats. Yep, they knew how to get the most out of the pilots of the Cat Fish Navy. Nuff said—the Cat Fish Navy delivered the Goods! In 1943 I made 57 trips from Memphis to New Orleans.

Capt. Tippitt also wrote some notes in addition to his story that the alumni of the Cat Fish Navy would probably enjoy. For example"

One Saturday morning Roy Barkhau and myself were called at 4:30 a.m., expecting to make a fast run; we ran from 14 to 18 hours per day. Breakfast was regular Navy fare, and the first encounter with Navy beans. I balked, went up and looked around and then told the captain it was a little hazy, so we would lay up till the sun came out.

Of course, the ferry crew was in a hurry to get to New Orleans and back to St. Louis. The 'old man' caught on right quick and asked me what I would like for breakfast. 'Bacon and eggs and toast.' Well, cook was there and all the officers, and before a cat could scratch his back, up came our eggs! We were underway at 5:30 a.m., haze or no haze!

Now, on real good stages some of the fellows who lived in Memphis with their families would run straight through, the cumshaw being a can of that bacon or hamburger to take home. My racket was cigarets; while I did not use them, preferring a pipe, I quickly found out in a chain drug store a carton of cigarets in my pocket would get me all the film I wanted for my camera, as it was also rationed. At a chain drug store on Canal Street a little blond would hold back the 120 film they received twice a month until I arrived (we were in New Orleans three or four times a month) and from a ship's store on Lower Canal I could always get a carton of cigarets. I had plenty of film!

By the way, the reason I am in khakis in the group picture of ferry pilots is that in New Orleans the CO had ordered a change in uniform khaki from

From the Files of The Waterways Journal
Destroyer escort.

blues, and being jacked up on arrival there for not being in uniform I changed when I got back to Memphis and was the last of the contingent to get to St. Louis; they were still in blues.

As I wrote before, when Capt. Morey Brady took over, he took out the confusion, and he also got us 'dog houses' for the con to keep us out of the weather and also searchlights in 1943. Give credit where credit is due!

Chapter 11 ——

Helping The Rivers Work

*I*t was providential that the rivers were ready to help in the war effort.

It did not just happen in a short time.

It took a lot of hard work and advocating to get the money that went into the work to create good channels and stable water. This was done with government money, and the advocates of river improvements had to prove that the money would be well spent.

The projects had to be approved by the House and Senate subcommittees on rivers and harbors, then the committees on public works, and the full House and Senate, with differences being smoothed out in conferences between the two legislative bodies. Finally, the Rivers and Harbors Bill had to be approved by the president. One can see it was a long process, one fraught with dangers of non-acceptance, and not getting all the money requested. (The names of these congressional committees may not be exactly accurate, but the purpose they served can be understood.)

One of the biggest days of the year among river advocates was that day upon which the budget for rivers and harbors was announced in Washington, D. C.

From the Files of The Waterways Journal

The snagboat John M. Macomb.

In the early days of river transportation it was the removal of snags that concerned rivermen most. They were serious menaces to life and property, and resulted in a high loss of life and steamboats and cargo. The advent of steam on the Western Rivers increased the need of snag removal, with calls for the work increasing as people moved west and commerce increased. An example was the Red River Raft which seriously deterred navigation on that important water-

National Portrait Galley, Smithsonian Institution, Washington D.C.

Henry Miller Shreve

way to northern Louisiana and Texas. It was a plea by settlers in the region that finally got Congress to appropriate money for its removal and a Western Rivers improvement program. Henry Miller Shreve was named superintendent.

The Great River Raft extended about 150 miles from 25 miles above Natchitoches; it was not solid all the way, occupying about a third of the distance. The Raft was made up of timber and debris carried down stream and lodged together. It grew up to two miles a year.

Money did not come regularly from Washington, and sometimes Shreve ran out of money. Henry M. Shreve developed the snagboat, an ingenious vessel with a split hull that could straddle a snag and lift it out of the water so it could be cut up and destroyed. His early snaggers were named Archimedes and Heliopolis. (The design was later used by James B. Eads for his salvage fleet named the "Submarines.")

Stable and deeper water became more important on the waterways as barge tows grew in size. It is hard to believe today what conditions were like on the rivers as late as the 1900s. There were actually only inches of water over the bars in many places, including the Ohio. Only shallow-draft packets could run.

Courtesy of The Waterways Journal

The water was so low on the Ohio River at St. Marys, West Virginia, that horses and wagons could be driven across.

Capt. Bill Pollock Collection

Waiting for coalboat water in Pittsburgh harbor.

In Pittsburgh the huge fleets of coal barges would be moored waiting for a rise; when it came, all the towboats would pick up their tows and head south. What a sight it must have been!

It might have been interesting to watch, but it was certainly not an economically sound situation to be able to navigate at only certain times of the year with barges loaded sometimes to less than capacity.

Ohio River interests knew that they had to have deeper and stabler water and that dams were the answer. Smaller rivers like the Monongahela had been canalized with locks and dams, but doing this with the Ohio, for 981 miles, was a different proposition.

Congress was invited to come West and see what was needed firsthand. In 1911, Pittsburgh interests raised $15,000 to entertain the entire Rivers and Harbor Committee of the House and about 40 other members of the House during a 10-day junket. The members of the House left Washington on a special train to Warren, Pennsylvania, on the Allegheny River, and thence to Pittsburgh, with a study of the proposed Lake Erie and Ohio River Ship Canal. After two days in Pittsburgh, they boarded the steamer Kanawha for Cairo, Illinois.

For the purpose of showing the visitors what navigating in low water was like, the trip couldn't have been better. The boat grounded every day but one, and from Tell City, Indiana, to Owensboro, Kentucky., a pilot in a rowboat had to go ahead of the Kanawha to find enough water to get through.

In unity there is strength, and river interests often banded together to present their request for appropriations from Congress. One of the most effective and strongest organizations was the Ohio Valley Improvement Association with headquarters in Cincinnati. It had the interests of coal, steel and later oil shippers behind it.

The OVIA was formed in Cincinnati in 1895 for the purpose of getting the Ohio River made navigable with a nine-foot channel through the construction of locks and dams. Elected president of the organization was Col. John L. Vance, of Gallipolis, Ohio. He was editor and publisher for 30 years of the Gallipolis Bulletin.

Col. Vance was re-elected president of the OVIA year after year, and in 1917 was elected president for life. He died in 1921 at the age of 82. Presidents that come after him included O. Slack Barrett and Harry Mack, of Neare, Gibbs and Company, Cincinnati. A leader of OVIA who was great in economics and law was William Hull, who wrote many papers on the good things the Ohio River could do for industry. Betty Justice was the secretary.

Col. John L. Vance

The first attempt at damming the Ohio River was the Davis Island Dam near Pittsburgh. It was dedicated October 7, 1885. There was a big boat parade down from Pittsburgh.

Some noted that the boats were not grouped as they might have been by affiliation. The reason probably was because not all Pittsburgh towing operators liked the idea of locks and dams. They probably could see those big coal tows having to be broken up at each lock, with a great waste of time and effort.

In fact, not everyone in the Corps of Engineers liked the idea either. They wanted an alternate; construction of dams on the tributaries that could hold water back until it was needed in the main river.

The Corps came up with what might be called a compromise. They built wicket dams that could be lowered when the river was at a good stage and the boats could pass through without locking. When the stage got low, the wickets were raised and the water held back to form a nine-foot channel.

The series of 50 dams were finished by 1929, and in October of that year the canalization of the Ohio River was celebrated. President Herbert Hoover came out for the celebration and rode the lighthouse tender Greenbrier from Cincinnati to Louisville. There was quite a parade of vessels between Pittsburgh and Cairo.

Unfortunately there was an anticlimax to the event. The stock market crashed, to mark the beginning of the Great Depression!

But the OVIA was not through. Modern river traffic found the small original 600-foot locks unsuited for the bigger tows and barges, and the OVIA lobbied for new locks.

It was successful again.

Meanwhile, in Pittsburgh another waterways development group had formed with the acronym DINAMO, which stood for Association for the Development of Interstate Navigability on the Allegheny, Monongahela and Ohio. The organizational meeting was held in March 1981.

The inland waterways industry was in recession then, and the OVIA was not getting its previous support; in 1983 it merged with DINAMO which changed its name to the Association for the Development of Inland Navigation in America's Ohio Valley.

It followed the OVIA's efforts in getting congressional approval of bigger locks. In 1986 money was appropriated for four new locks on the upper Ohio, and in 1988 funds to build a replacement for Locks 52 and 53 on the lower Ohio. DINAMO still functions.

It should be said that the annual OVIA conventions in October in Cincinnati were considered by *The Waterways Journal* to be the second most important of the organizational meetings, and I attended many of them. The *Journal* had a special OVIA Issue.

On the Upper Mississippi River the packet trade had stopped. The Diamond Jo Line that once ran a large fleet of big

Courtesy of The Waterways Journal

The Greenbrier taking on presidential party at Cincinnati for the Ohio River canalization parade in October 1929. Steamer Cincinnati is at right.

President Herbert Hoover, left, and party on the steamer Greenbrier at Cincinnati.

G. W. *"Jerry" Sutphin Collection*

Tows tied up at Blennerhassett Island on the Ohio River, waiting for more water (circa 1900).

G. W. "Jerry" Sutphin Collection

Mile 306 on the Ohio River before the dams were built.

Huntington District, U.S. Engineers

Mile 306 on the Ohio River after the dams were completed in 1929.

boats had sold them to the Streckfus Line, which turned them into excursion boats.

The Interstate Commerce Commission ruled that there was no longer water competition on the Upper Mississippi River. The railroads immediately raised their rates, which was something they should not have done—at least they should not have put them so high. The businessmen on the Upper River got mad and saw that they had to get water competition back. To do so they built their own fleet of boats by soliciting money in every Upper Mississippi River town.

The Upper Mississippi River Barge Line had several sternwheel steam towboats built by the Dubuque Boat and Boiler Works, such as the C. C. Webber, General Ashburn, S. S. Thorpe and John W. Weeks. They were owned by the Upper Mississippi Barge Line Company, of which S. S. Thorpe was the first president, and C. C. Webber second president.

In January 1916, the Upper Mississippi Barge Line signed a contract with the government's Inland Waterways Corporation (IWC) to lease the equipment and operate it. The IWC had been formed to try to bring barge transportation back to the Mississippi and Warrior rivers. On June 1, 1928, the Federal Barge Line, as the Inland Waterways Corporation was better known, bought the fleet built by the Upper Mississippi Barge Line, and all efforts of the officers and directors of the group turned to getting money for the Corps of Engineers to

May 1931

October 1953

Courtesy of The Waterways Journal

Upper Mississippi River at Davenport, Iowa, before and after the locks and dams were built. The amount of water flowing in the river is approximately the same in both views.

develop a nine-foot channel from St. Paul to St. Louis. The Engineers were then working on a six-foot channel by building wing dams and revetments.

Their efforts were successful, and a series of locks and dams finally provided a nine-foot channel. It was just in time; the last structure was completed in 1939 at LeClaire, Iowa.

The organization continues to function as Upper Mississippi Waterway Association, with a goal of improving the locks on the Upper River with the addition of auxiliary locks and new and larger main locks. The locks and dams are now more than 50 years old.

On the Gulf Coast, farsighted men saw the need for a protected barge channel from the Gulf of Mexico waters, so they organized the Gulf Intracoastal Canal Association. The original purpose was to build the waterway from the Mexican border to New Orleans where it would connect with the Mississippi River System. Later the organization moved east to take the canal through Mississippi to Alabama and Florida.

The need for this protected route became more apparent with the rise of the oil and chemical industries in Texas and Lousiana, and it was vital when World War II came. For years Dale Miller was president of the Association, followed by Vernon Behrhorst. Ora Mae Rohan was secretary. The group held conventions at various cities along the Gulf Coast, and they were among those *The Waterways Journal* attended regularly, mostly by me. The *Journal* put out a special issue for the Gulf Canal meeting.

The Arkansas Basin Development Association, working out of Tulsa, Oklahoma, focused on damming the Arkansas. Many people thought of it as a pipe dream, but they did not recognize the power of Sens. John McClellan, of Arkansas and Robert S. Kerr, of Oklahoma. (Members of the St. Louis Propeller Club thought it ridiculous, and I got some slides from the U.S. Engineers and showed them one night; I attended the Tulsa meetings and knew how dedicated the men were to the project.)

The McClellan-Kerr Arkansas River Navigation System, the real name of the waterway, was dedicated June 5, 1971, with President Richard Nixon in attendance. The Verdigris River is used as the upper end of the project, at Tulsa-Port of Catoosa.

Courtesy of The Waterways Journal

President Richard M. Nixon dedicates the McClellan-Kerr Arkansas River Navigation System June 8, 1971.

Also successful in getting their project done were members of the Red River Valley Association of Shreveport, Louisiana. The locks and dams on that river are well underway and are being used now to Alexandria and above. In 1998, the steamer Delta Queen made a pioneering trip on the Red. She did not get above Alexandria because of low water, but she is scheduled to go back up the Red in 1999.

Another success story is that of the Tennessee-Tombigbee Waterway Development Authority of Columbia, Mississippi, guided by Glover Wilkins. The cut-off to allow traffic to avoid the current of the lower Mississippi River is in use and is proving popular with recreational boaters as well as commercial boats.

The Kaskaskia Regional Port District was able to get a lock built to open up the Kaskaskia for coal and grain towing and is still working on developing commerce. Stanley L. Reeble was long the general manager of the organization.

The interests of the Illinois Waterway are overseen by the Illinois River Carriers' Association, Joliet, Illinois.

On the Missouri, the Missouri River Basin Association, with James A. McPherson, vice president, gave way to Mo-Ark, Association. Today the Missouri is under attack by the environmentalists who have apparently chosen it as one of their next targets. We will have more to say about this later.

The Ouachita River Valley Association, of Camden, Arkansas, was successful in getting the river improved, but the high hopes for a successful port at Camden have not materialized. The organization itself fell into disarray, but it is being revived today and may get the trend reversed.

The leader of the Ouachita River organization was H. K. Thatcher, a very dignified, rather large man who to me was an example of Southern manners and personality. When the port of Camden was dedicated, a group of us flew there from Tulsa in a small commuter plane. Someone said that if it crashed, the waterways organizations would be in a bad way; as I recall the passengers included Harry Cook, who was first executive secretary of the National Waterways Conference and then became its president; Mike Cassady, president of the Mississippi Valley Association; and others.

The big surprise was to find H. K. Thatcher barbequeing in apron and tall chef's hat, with the words "Big Daddy" on the apron.

The Tri-Rivers Waterway Development Association, of Dothan, Alabama, looks out for the Apalachicola, Chattahoochee and Flint rivers and at one time had ideas of extending this series of waterways to Atlanta. There is a problem with low water on the lower reaches, but the Georgia Port Authority has facilities at Bainbridge and Columbus.

Also in the South, the Warrior-Tombigbee Development Association, Birmingham, Alabama, meets regularly to discuss problems on those rivers.

The Tennessee River got dammed by the Tennessee Valley Authority as part of its project to rejuvenate the area, with the U.S. Engineers operating the locks and dams. On the upper reaches of the Tennessee, power companies put in the dams with locks to allow navigation.

Its companion river, the Cumberland, was one of the earliest streams to be dammed, beginning in 1832. Now, the slack water extends to Nashville.

Another river improved early was the Monongahela, because of its coal fields. A private company, the Monongahela Navigation Company, started out building locks and dams in 1838-9 and charged tolls for using them. When the federal government took over the operation of the system years later there was a big steamboat parade at Pittsburgh celebrating the lifting of the tolls. Work continues even today on the lock system.

The Kanawha, another Ohio tributary, got the backing of the OVIA and other Ohio valley river-oriented groups, and its locks are being enlarged today.

Not so fortunate was the Allegheny Valley Improvement Association of Oil City, Pennsylvania. The plan of this group was to unite the Allegheny River with Lake Erie via French Creek. It was a very active organization, and Donald T. Wright, being from Oil City, was one of its leaders. When I started making my Ohio River trips, I first went to the Allegheny meetings to represent him. After his death, I was named vice-president, which was a bit weird, being in St. Louis. The mayor of Oil City, Guy Mammolite, became president of the AVIA, and tried hard to promote the organization. One of the features of the meetings would be his presentation of young ladies from the Oil City High School chosen to represent the city in such roles as "Miss Beautification." Also active in the group was George Needle. I lost touch with the organization when I stopped traveling, and as far as I know, it is no longer active.

Also not succeeding was the Trinity Improvement Association of Irving, Texas. They wanted to improve the Trinity River to Dallas, and might have done so if it were not for the environmental movement that threw many obstacles in the way.

One of the big social events connected with the Trinity was the annual White Heron Fish Fry held at Liberty, Texas. It was a fun thing and well attended. I would go there on my way from Houston to Port Arthur on my Texas trips.

110

The Wabash Valley Association, Terre Haute, Indiana, was not successful either in its efforts to develop the Wabash for barge navigation.

There was also another attempt to join the Great Lakes with the Ohio River farther west; in fact there is still an interest in this.

The Big Sandy Valley Association, too, failed in its promotion of that stream.

Many of the papers and programs of these water-oriented organizations are in the collection of the Herman T. Pott National Inland Waterways Library of the St. Louis Mercantile Library at the University of Missouri-St. Louis.

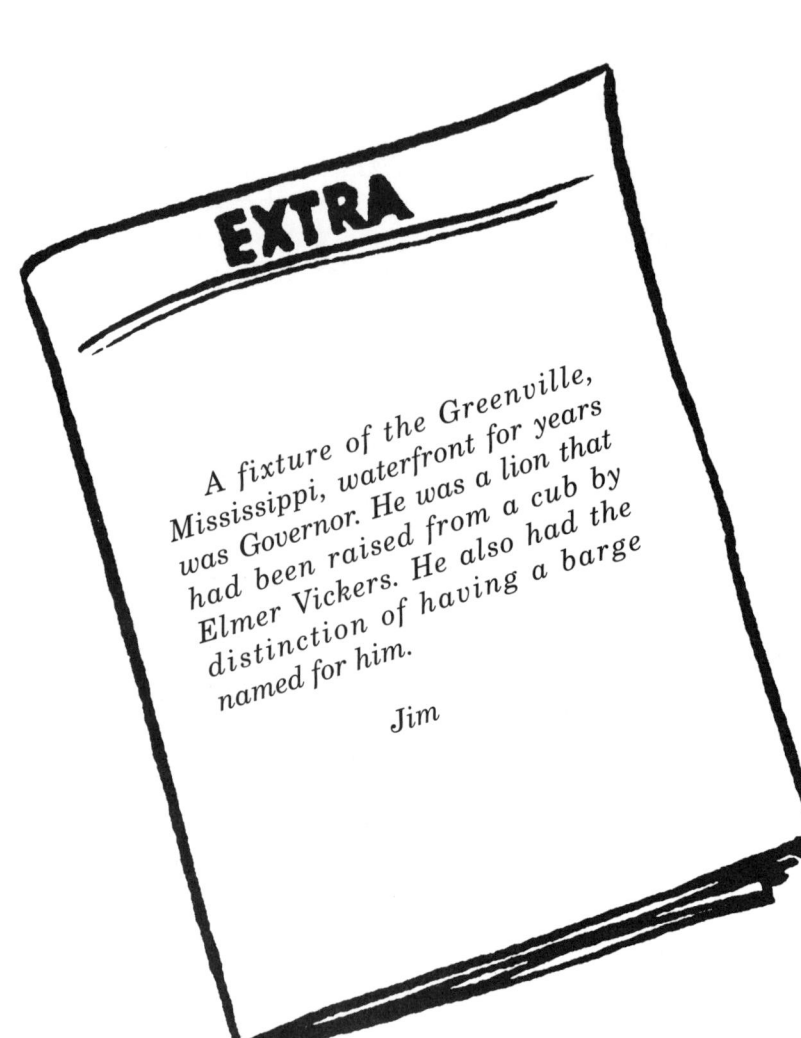

EXTRA

A fixture of the Greenville, Mississippi, waterfront for years was Governor. He was a lion that had been raised from a cub by Elmer Vickers. He also had the distinction of having a barge named for him.

Jim

Chapter 12—

The Mississippi Valley Association

You might say that the "Mother" of these rivers organizations was the Mississippi Valley Association (MVA) of St.
Louis. It helped shape the budgets for waterways work in
Congress, and assisted in arranging the appearance of river advocates before the congressional committees.

The Waterways Journal's lead article in the May 11, 1918
issue read:

CALL FOR CONVENTION

Co-ordination of Railways and Water-
ways Necessary as a War
Measure.

The first annual convention of the Mississippi
Valley Waterways Association will be held in St.
Louis at the Statler Hotel May 14 and 15, 1918, the
first session to convene at 10 o'clock, Tuesday
morning.

The official call has been sent out to the
Governors of all of the States of the Mississippi

Photo by A. W. Sanders

The first annual convention of the Mississippi Valley Association was held at the Statler Hotel in St. Louis, Missouri, in March 1918. This general session picture was taken on the 14th.

Valley, to the Chambers of Commerce, Boards of Trade, Traffic Bureaus, Commercial Clubs, Merchants' Exchanges and all other commercial organizations; to the Mayors, City Councils and other public officials who may be interested. All to whom have sent the call are earnestly urged and are authorized to appoint and accredit delegates....

The article does not say who sent out this call for convention, but it came because of World War I and the problems the railroads were having in taking care of the freight.

At a conference in St. Louis in May 1917, Brig Gen. William M. Black, Chief of the Army Corps of Engineers, sounded an alarm, saying in part: "The waterfronts of our river cities must be freed from their incumbrances and restored for use as water terminal, factory and elevator sites....Water-carrying lines must be organized, financed and operated with the same thoughtful care as is given the railways."

The *Journal* article mentions that this was the result of work by the Mississippi Valley Waterways Association since May 1917. On May 14, 1918, the association held a convention at the Hotel Statler in St. Louis.

On January 14, 1919, twenty men met in New Orleans and formed the Mississippi Valley Association. The Mississippi Valley Waterways Association held its second convention in St. Louis in April 1919, and at that time merged into the Mississippi Valley Association. The MVA was chartered in New Orleans in January 1919.

The early leader of the association was Lachlan Macleay. His work was detailed in a history of the MVA on its 50th anniversary in the *Journal* of February 1, 1969, as written by Charles C. Clayton:

> In World War I, the transportation monopoly of the railroads and the North Atlantic shipping lines proved unequal to the task of mobilizing America's resources for war. In desperation, the government was forced to take over the railroads and to turn to the rivers to bridge the transportation gap. It was this emergency action that undoubtedly was a factor in inspiring that first meeting in New Orleans. The men who attended that meeting recognized that low-

Courtesy of The Waterways Journal

Typically, convention goers were welcomed by MVA staff, which, in this instance, were: Everett T. Winter, executive vice-president (lower left); and other staff members (clockwise) James R. Smith of Omaha, vice-president; Lew Paramore, Kansas City; E. Michael Cassady, St. Louis; Robert R. Shortle, New Orleans; and Miss G. Bier, of St. Louis, MVA secretary.

cost water transportation held the key that could unlock the rail stranglehold on the midwest.

But private enterprise, understandably, was not interested in attempting to revive river services in competition with the railroads. The only solution was to persuade Congress to finance a pioneer barge line to demonstrate the soundness of the idea. From that modest beginning, there has flowed relentlessly in the ensuing years the program which has revitalized the whole economy of the Mississippi basin, broken the rail freight rate barriers, developed the Gulf ports, and launched the whole modern concept of water conservation and use.

The 308 Reports

The first real breakthrough came in the form of the historic 308 Reports, which provided the fundamental data upon which all progress since that time has been based. The 308 Reports were the brain child of the late Lachlan Macleay, who for many years guided the destiny of the MVA. The vigorous support of the association persuaded Congress to authorize the study proposed by Mr. Macleay, and provide funds for its preparation. The results provided the basis for every navigation, flood control and water conservation project authorized by Congress since.

The MVA did not bring all its business to St. Louis. To better serve the waterways it had offices in other cities. In New Orleans Robert I. Shortle was in charge, and on the Missouri River two offices were established—at Kansas City with Lew Paramore, and Omaha with James R. Smith. In St. Louis there were Robert G. Goodwin, Jr., and Anthony Kucera. Holding everything together was Miss G. Bier, secretary, a person who won great respect from waterways people.

Following Lachlan Macleay's presidency, Everett T. Winter was executive vice-president. E. Michael Cassady was in St. Louis, also, and was to become president of MVA in later years.

In the spring of 1971 there was a merger of MVA, which had become Water Resources Associated, with the National Rivers and Harbors Congress, which had been in existence since 1901. The latter had yearly urged Congress to pass adequate bills to fund river improvements.

The first convention of the new Water Resources Congress was at the Chase-Park Plaza Hotel February 5-7, 1972. *The Waterways Journal* pointed out in its editorial of January 29, 1972, that it was a "year of decision," with the Administration contemplating new legislation that would hamper the waterways, and continuing efforts of the environmentalists to stop river and canal work.

After many years at the Statler Hotel, Ninth and Washington, the MVA moved to a bigger hotel, the Jefferson, at Locust and 12th Street (now Tucker Boulevard.) There were more rooms, conference space, and the Gold Room was more suited to the final event of the convention—the banquet.

This was the big social event of the year for many, with the ladies getting a chance to meet people they had heard their

Courtesy of "St. Louis Commerce"

Herman T. Pott, president of the St. Louis Shipbuilding and Steel Company and chairman of the executive committee of the Federal Barge Lines, Inc., presided over the former company's hospitality room during the February 1936 convention.

husbands talk about through the year, and to renew friendships.

One year, the Fabick Tractor Company put a big yellow Caterpillar engine in the lobby of the Jefferson, and then the Radiomarine Corporation of America had an exhibit of marine communications equipment on the balcony. It was the start of what was to become to marine operators the real MVA Convention.

These exhibits grew in size until they were occupying a good part of the hotel, and when the MVA moved again, west to the Chase Hotel, they took up a full floor, actually an exhibit hall. The latest items of marine propulsion, communications, cordage, paint, hardware, anything for use on a barge or towboat could be found at the MVA show.

Along with the exhibit booths many firms had a hospitality room for more customer contact. There were so many (40) that it was a problem for the *Journal* staff to visit all of them and stay sober, not referring to me, of course. It would have been noticed if a *Waterways Journal* staff member did not make an appearance, especially with our advertisers. To refuse their hospitality would have been inappropriate.

One of the better known sites of the conventions was St. Louis Shipbuilding and Steel's "Temple of Culture." It was centered around a piano, with Arthur Parsons often singing in his fine tenor voice. There were also hostesses to serve the friends of St. Louis Ship.

Another firm specialized in showing movies. One year I invited a well-known and rather distinguished eastern marine

How to Find MVA Waterway Exhibit:

Courtesy of The Waterways Journal

Typical exhibit layout for an MVA Convention.

boat broker to come out for the MVA. Unfortunately his room was close to the movies, and he didn't get any sleep because the folks lined up all night near his door to see the show.

There were really two MVAs, then—the working one for the waterways and one for those who used them. It was often an annoyance to the organization when the action in the hospitality room sometimes got out of hand. But the MVA needed the support of the towing industry and the added attendance that resulted.

The most famous incident was at the Chase when a fight broke out in a room, resulting in the breakage of every piece of furniture. There was also a report of someone hanging out the window by their fingernails. There were various reasons given for the scuffle, but one most acceptable was an argument over which was the best state—Arkansas or Louisiana. Anyway,

Hello M V A
From
ANOKA BOAT & TOWING CO.
MEMPHIS, TENNESSEE

Courtesy of The Waterways Journal

This welcome-MVA advertisement was among those appearing in the February 6, 1965, issue of *The Waterways Journal*.

when the man who rented the room came back to the hotel after being out, he was greeted by the hotel management with a huge bill for damages.

Later, the association decided it was best to move around the country with the convention. It was, of course, not a popular decision with *The Waterways Journal* after being at the home base of the action for so long. In 1955 the MVA was in Chicago. It was a memorable event because it was one of the coldest days they had in the Windy City for a long time. You stepped outside the hotel and the cold took your breath away We got off the plane, and the hat of Ben Wilkins of the *Journal* took off down the apron with Ben in pursuit. (He was baldheaded, by the way.) The guys from the South had never seen weather like that, and if I recall correctly the Greenville, Mississippi, contingent didn't even have overcoats.

The conventions had such an effect on the towing industry that Carole Brent, of Greenville, Mississippi, even wrote a song about it!

The MVA Issue of *The Waterways Journal* was the second most important of the year after the Annual Review (Christmas Issue.) About two weeks after the MVA Issue the *Journal* carried the registration list, as it did for the OVIA and Gulf Intracoastal Canal Association. Even now, if one wants to know what firm people were associated with (and the spelling of their names) they can find them in the issue of the *Journal* for a number of years. The St. Louis Mercantile Library has them in the Herman T. Pott National Inland Waterways Library. Many papers from the MVA and WRC are also in the Pott Library.

The Water Resources Conference moved its offices to Washington, D.C., about 1970. The rise of the operating-oriented associations eclipsed its importance and support, and WRC gradually withered away.

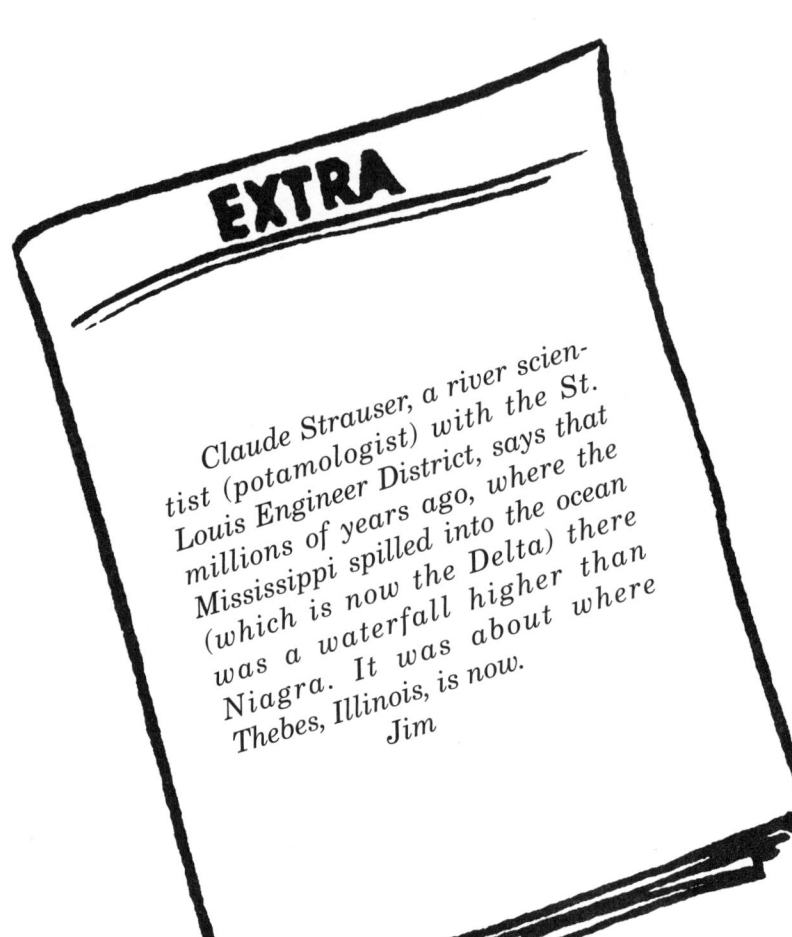

EXTRA

Claude Strauser, a river scientist (potamologist) with the St. Louis Engineer District, says that millions of years ago, where the Mississippi spilled into the ocean (which is now the Delta) there was a waterfall higher than Niagra. It was about where Thebes, Illinois, is now.

Jim

Chapter 13 ——

Federal

The reader will understand from previous chapters that the principal event that led to the revitalization of the rivers was World War I; the railroads could not handle the traffic alone.

However, the move to bring the rivers back had begun before this.

President Theodore Roosevelt appointed an Inland Waterways Commission (IWC) in March 1907, and its report of January 3, 1908, was sent to Congress on February 26 with the President's endorsement. He said in part: "The development of our waterways and the conservation of our forests are the two most pressing physical needs of our country...and they should be vigorously met together and at once."

However, the report called for only a four- to six-foot channel on the Upper Mississippi.

Roosevelt was to have some first-hand exposure to the river during a trip he made from Keokuk, Iowa, to Memphis in October 1907 as a guest of the Lakes to the Gulf Deep Waterways Association. He rode the Corps of Engineers' vessel Mississippi, which was joined in the trip by a number of boats in the "Roosevelt Parade." (The vessel Mississippi at that time was actually used by the Mississippi River Commission.)

From the Files of The Waterways Journal

President Theodore Roosevelt and party on the stage of the steamer Mississippi.

Steamboat parade in October 1907. The U.S. Engineers' Mississippi flies the presidential flag for Theodore Roosevelt.

Courtesy of Ralph DuPae, Murphy Library, University of Wisconsin-LaCrosse

St. Louis in October 1907. Waiting for the parade to start with President Theodore Roosevelt.

Two years later Pres. William Howard Taft was on the river on the lighthouse boat Oleander from St. Louis to New Orleans.

Back to World War I. The Federal Control Act of 1916 was passed, giving control of the railroads to the federal government. W. G. McAdoo, Director General of the Railroad, also commandeered all privately owned floating equipment on the Mississippi and Warrior rivers in 1918. He also purchased new equipment and started a weekly service between St. Louis and New Orleans.

Coal movements were begun from Birmingham, Alabama, and New Orleans; they started in 1919.

Federal control of the railroads ended in 1920, but the Secretary of War kept an interest in the waterways, established the Inland and Coastwise Water Service to operate the barge lines. In 1924 Congress established the Inland Waterways Corporation, which was more commonly known as the Federal Barge Lines.

The goal was to show once again the value of water transportation, via experiments in equipment.

Since access to the rivers had become a problem in a railroad-dominated world. Federal was aided by river terminals built by cities located along the rivers; these cities saw the need for river transportation. There were such facilities at St. Paul; Minneapolis; Dubuque; Rock Island (Three City Terminal, also serving Davenport and Moline, Burlington, Iowa (a floating dock)); St. Louis (North Market Street); East St. Louis, Illinois; Cairo, Illinois (an incline); Memphis (an incline); Helena, Arkansas; Greenville, Mississippi; Vicksburg, Mississippi; Baton Rouge; New Orleans; Houston; Mobile; Birmingham, Alabama (Port Birmingham); Omaha, Nebraska;

Courtesy of The Waterways Journal

Powered barge Tuscaloosa in Warrior River service.

Kansas City, Missouri; Peoria, Illinois; Chicago (Western Avenue); and Stillwater, Minnesota.

At the start, because of government status, Federal had to accept for shipment anything offered it, and this included less than barge loads, just as the packet boats had done. This was not the modern barge line concept, and it was not a profitable operation by any means.

Federal started with many traditional sternwheel, steam-powered boats. Even the big state boats came out with stern-wheels. Those acquired from the Upper Mississippi River Barge Line were of that type.

There was at the time a controversy about using screw propellers on the rivers; Federal was using propeller-power on the "City boats" and self-propelled barges on the Warrior River system.

The fleet at the start included the following:

The Choctaw came from the Memphis District of the U.S. Engineers, the Nokomis from the St. Louis District, and the Wynoka from the Memphis District. All had been built origi-nally for the Mississippi River Commission and were stern-wheel boats. Federal also had the Advance on the Mississippi, and the Clio (185 hp.) and Darling (350 hp.) on the Warrior.

Also used was the New Orleans (formerly the Louis Houck and Barrett), Advance, and Slack Barrett. On the Warrior River they had the Volcano, which was to handle the first Federal tow on that river in January 1919. The Altair was also used.

The IWC took over the Kansas City and Missouri River Navigation Company and its boats, the A. M. Scott and Chester (which had been converted to propeller).

Federal also bought the fleet that had been built by Upper Mississippi River interests (as described in a previous chapter) and this included the C. C. Webber, General Ashburn, S. S. Thorpe and John W. Weeks. These were stern-wheel boats 130 by 35.1 by 5.1. Also coming from the Upper Mississippi were the James W. Good and Patrick J. Hurley, larger sternwheelers, 158.1 by 42 by 6.1 feet.

The IWC (or General Ashburn) commandeered four boats of the Goltra Barge Line: the "state" boats Illinois, Iowa, Minnesota and Missouri. (The Goltras sued the government,

Courtesy of The Waterways Journal

The General Ashburn, one of the Upper Mississippi boats.

Wm. J. Torner Photo —Murphy Library, University of Wisconsin-LaCrosse

The Patrick J. Hurley, a larger Upper Mississippi River boat.

Courtesy of The Waterways Journal

Federal "state" boat Minnesota. Her stacks were cut down to let her get to Lockport, Illinois, to bring submarines down in World War II. She sank on the Missouri River June 21, 1951.

and the litigation went on for years.) These were stern-wheel boats to start with, 230 by 58 by 8. (They were converted to propellers around 1937.)

Rivermen were still arguing about whether sternwheels or propellers were better at the time, but Federal took the deep plunge and built a fleet of what were to be called the "City" or "black boats" that included the Baton Rouge, Cairo, Memphis, Natchez, St. Louis and Vicksburg, with propellers. They were 200 by 40 by 10.

General Ashburn also had a business boat, like a yacht, the North Star.

For the Warrior River service Federal tried a different type of vessel, a self-propelled barge. These included the Birmingham, Gulfport, Mobile, and Tuscaloosa. Ordinary Federal towboats on the Warrior system included the Cordova, Demopolis, and Dwight F. Davis. The Montgomery was also first used on the Warrior but later came over to the Mississippi system and was an Illinois River boat.

Federal also built the Mark Twain, a steam-powered stern-wheeler; she was 157 by 42 by 6. This was to be their last stern-wheel boat. Also steam power was giving way to diesel, although the Helena, Tom Sawyer, Huck Finn and Kansas City were steam and propeller driven; they were dieselized in 1947 and 1948.

When Federal went to diesel power, it was done in a big way. The towboat Herbert Hoover was built in 1931 at the Dubuque Boat and Boiler Works in Dubuque, Iowa, to be the largest and most powerful diesel towboat of her time. She was 215 by 43.6 by 10.1 and had 2,200 hp. She was a talking point for river people at the time of her building. (She was later the New Orleans of the Mississippi Valley Barge Line.)

Federal's most unusual creation was the Harry Truman. She was really a powered unit, pushing a set of integrated barges designed to be dropped off at river terminals along the way. To prove how fast she was, Federal planned a time race for her against that of the steamer Robt. E. Lee, which had set the record in 1870. The Lee made the run from New Orleans to St. Louis in three days, 18 hours and 14 minutes. The Truman only missed this record by an hour and 16 minutes.

Photo from Capt. Lowell Sorrells

Mv. Helena underway with tow.

From Harold Pierson in Waterways Journal Collection

Mv. Herbert Hoover, the biggest and most powerful towboat when built in 1931.

Courtesy of The Waterways Journal

One of the giants, the America.

The power unit of the Truman was 135 by 54 feet, with 3,200 hp. She had a bow piece, and nine barges—five large ones, a medium-sized one, and three small units.

Federal built two other notable boats known for their size and power. The twins, America and United States, came out of St. Louis Ship in 1960; they were 184 by 58 by 10.3 and had four diesel engines each, with a horsepower of 9,000. With four stacks and a yellow paint job, they were a prominent sight along the Mississippi.

While experimenting with equipment, Federal tried some things that were to be helpful to future towing operations, and some that weren't. On the Illinois, for instance, while still using a sternwheel, they tried a new paddle design patented by Tom Dunbar. The vessel was also given equipment to burn pulverized coal, but it did not work out.

The most important thing that Federal did was to prove that a four- or six-foot channel was not enough for economic and efficient barge line use; there had to be at least nine feet of stable water to run on.

Courtesy New Orleans District, U.S. Engineers

The Mv. Harry Truman with its unit tow in New Orleans Harbor July 21, 1948.

131

Some of the highlights of Federal's early movements included the trip of the S. S. Thorpe, when she left St. Louis for St. Paul with three loaded barges drawing 4 feet. Aboard were General Ashburn and the designer of the Upper Mississippi River sternwheelers, T. R. Tarn. The trip began on August 15, 1927.

A year earlier, the Wynoka had made a trial run with five barges loaded with water ballast; she grounded at Island 17, and the General Ashburn had to finish the trip. General Ashburn himself had come on the Wynoka.

These two boats teamed up again for the opening of the Peoria, Illinois, Federal Terminal in June 1931; General Ashburn and his wife rode the Ashburn.

The General Ashburn was along when the Mark Twain took the first Federal tow into Kansas City June 27, 1932. The Secretary of War Patrick J. Hurley was on the Mark Twain.

The Franklin D. Roosevelt took the first Federal tow into Omaha, Nebraska, on October 23, 1946.

Federal suffered its greatest loss on March 4, 1948, when the Natchez hit the Greenville, Mississippi, bridge, rolled over

S. S. Thorpe arrives in St. Paul with the first commercial tow for Federal Barge Lines, August 24, 1927. U.S. Engineers' General Allen follows with part of her tow.

Courtesy of The Waterways Journal

Courtesy of The Waterways Journal

Federal's "city boat" or "black boat" Natchez. She sank against the Greenville Bridge.

and sank. Fourteen people were lost, including Capt. James F. Browinski; chief engineer Keith A. Montgomery; and second engineer Charles Jarvis. Capt. Walter I. Hass, pilot off watch, saved himself by clambering up the hull as the boat turned over. The fuel tanks ruptured on impact; the oil stains are still visible on the bridge pier.

Federal boats began life (at first) in a coat of dark green paint with black trim, but later this olive drab appearance changed to a more colorful yellow. They ended up white with black trim.

With the rise of private carriers that could do the job efficiently on the inland waterways, there was a constant effort underway to get the government out of the river business.

Finally, in 1953, Federal was sold to Herman T. Pott, and it became a subsidiary of St. Louis Shipbuilding and Steel Company. In 1959 Federal acquired the Gulf Canal Lines, Inc., of Houston, and in 1968 the United Barge Company, of Minneapolis, Minnesota.

In 1977, Pott Industries merged with the Houston Natural Gas Corporation of Texas. Eight years later Houston sold Federal to The Ohio River Company, of Cincinnati. Rivermen appreciated the fact that the boats kept their old names.

Federal trained many men who went on to be leaders in the private sector. Some that come to mind are Glen Taylor, Fred F. Pearson, Capt. C. E. Patton, John Patrick Higgins, R. R. Odell, Harry E. Rudiman, L. E Barry, D. C. Newlon, J. S. Brodie, Elmer H. Cordes, and John Clark Berry.

Courtesy of U.S. Engineers, Omaha

Mv. Franklin D. Roosevelt with first tow into Omaha, Nebraska, October 23, 1946.

The presidents who guided Federal were Maj. Gen. Thomas Q. Ashburn, Chester C. Thompson, John S. Powell, Capt. A. C. Ingersoll, Jr. (with the government and later with St. Louis Ship), William Oliphant (interim), Noble Parsonage, Peter Fanchi, Jr., Robert Kyle, and Jack Lynch.

Many of Federal Barge Lines' papers are in the Herman T. Pott National Inland Waterways Library at the St. Louis Mercantile Library. There are so many, in fact, that there is a special inventory of them in book form.

Included in this collection are the files of Robert A. Labdon, FBL's marine superintendent, with many blueprints, including many of the DPC towboats of World War II. One could almost build a boat from them.

Other papers deal with traffic, operations, finances, machinery history, engineering and maintenance.

Business papers of the barge line are not included in the collection; many are in the National Archives in Washington, D. C. Others are in *The Waterways Journal* collection of the Pott Library under separate files.

I had a certain affinity with Federal Barge Lines. It probably started when I first went with the *Journal*, and one of my weekly tasks was to go down to the Federal offices in the Boatmen's Bank Building at Broadway and Olive in downtown St. Louis, and pick up the FBL boat movements for the week. The *Journal* carried them for a long time.

I was indebted to them, too, for two of my best river trips. My wife and I rode the steamer Coral Sea from St. Louis to New Orleans one year. Leonard McArthur was master, and Fred Sheldon was pilot. Capt. Sheldon did not like the coffee from the galley (he was from New Orleans or somewhere in the South), and he had his own coffee machine in the pilothouse to make the stronger chicory variety. He also had a rack of bananas hanging in the back of the pilothouse, and he would reach back every so often and pull one off. It was a very enjoyable trip.

The other major voyage with Federal, with my wife along, was on the Missouri River on the big Minnesota. Capt. Leonard Thompson was master. When we got to Kansas City to catch the boat she wasn't ready, so we were told to go to a hotel, and they could call us when to come. John Welch, Federal's agent at Kansas City, took good care of us and got us down to the Minnesota and safely aboard.

But the Minnesota's barges were still not ready, so we had many hours to wait before the trip could begin. However, it was by no means dull, because with us in the pilothouse was a

Courtesy of Boat Photo Museum

Modern 5,600 hp. Federal towboat Peter Fanchi, built in 1977.

135

Courtesy Murphy Library, University of Wisconsin-LaCrosse

Str. Wynoka, one of Federal Barge Lines early towboats, acquired from the U.S. Army Corps of Engineers.

noted Missouri River story-teller, Cecil E. Griffith, contact pilot for the Kansas City District of the U.S. Engineers. He had some great tales (including some about "floaters"), which I could see were making my wife a little queasy.

We finally got underway, and it was to be a rocky trip; the tow broke up several times on bars and had to be reassembled. When it happened at night it was a colorful affair, with the breaking wires sparking like fireworks.

When we got to Jefferson City, Missouri, the river was so low over a bar that the Minnesota could go no further and had to wait for a dredge to come up from Gasconade to open up a channel. My time had run out, and we had to be taken ashore in the motorboat to catch a train back to St. Louis.

I was invited to ride the new towboat Lachlan Macleay on her maiden voyage in 1955. I was to meet her in St. Charles, Missouri, and I was out on the bridge a long time waiting when I got the word (I don't recall how) to go to the hotel and wait there. Word came that she was coming in, and I went to the east end where the motorboat came in. Out stepped Capt. A. C. Ingersoll, Jr., President of Federal; and Donald Steele, operating manager. We got as far as South Point, Missouri, where I had to get off.

Even my mother, Anita Bailey Swift, got into the act. A female journalist wanted to do a story on the river and ride a boat from St. Louis to New Orleans. She had to have a chaperone. Donald Wright found out about it and asked me if I thought my mother would like to go. Well, she jumped at the chance. We went down to the North Market Street Terminal to get on the Illinois. The women friends who had taken us down to the terminal almost fainted when my mother, baggage and companion were put on a platform that swung out over the river to lower them down on the boat.

Back on the river after so many years, my mother really had a good time. Her companion, however, threw the crew into a tizzy by sunbathing on the barge covers. The Illinois' captain—and I am sorry I don't recall his name— finally asked my mother, "Mrs. Swift, do you think you could persuade your companion to stay off the barges in that bathing suit?"

At New Orleans, my mother had the highest praise for how nice Capt. John Skidmore was to help in getting her off the Illinois and up to the train.

As far as the lady writer was concerned, I don't believe she was heard from again, nor was there a story.

EXTRA

During my river trips, I used to take my marine radio into the motel at nights and turn to Channel 4, the party line on which rivermen called home. It made for interesting listening. I recall one night that a wife explained how she let a contractor put a load of rock on top of a wet driveway. It disappeared in the mud. The captain, as I recall, was not happy.

Jim

Chapter 14 ———

The River Grows Up

While the federal government was experimenting with river equipment, the private sector was not idle.

In St. Louis, the Mississippi Valley Barge Line started business with Carl J. Baer developing some new ideas for river equipment, including a barge with pointed bow and stern so they would fit together as a unit, perhaps the first unit tow.

Valley also had their own "state" boats, the Ohio, Indiana, Tennessee, and Louisiana. They were propeller-driven, and steam-powered. The Indiana and Louisiana were built by the Charles Ward Engineering Works at Charleston, West Virginia. The company was a pioneer in building propeller-driven vessels.

Ward had made history in 1903 when one of the boats the company built, the screw-propelled James Rumsey, had a shoving match with the stern-wheel D. T. Lane. The Rumsey bested the Lane, proving the worth of a tunnel hull, propeller-driven boat. But many rivermen were not convinced.

Ward went on to build other towboats, some with stern-wheels, and diesel-powered with unusual propulsion systems. They included the Duncan Bruce, Geo. T. Price and W. A. Shepard. The Bruce and Shepard were built for the W. C. Kelly

From the Files of The Waterways Journal

The big shoving match—stern-wheel D. T. Lane vs. propeller-driven James Rumsey.

Barge Line and were to be the nucleus of the American Barge Line when it acquired Kelly. American also had the Price.

These boats had been built for W. C. Kelly of Charleston, West Virginia, who had the Kelly Barge Company, one of the biggest manufacturers of axes in the country. The Kelly Barge Company bid for common carrier rights on the Ohio and Mississippi, and in 1927 used all three boats to attempt to move 18 barges up the Ohio to a new river terminal at Glassport, Pennsylvania, on the Monongahela River. However, there was low water on the Ohio, and they didn't make it.

The Bruce and Shepard were chartered by the new Inland Waterways Company that turned into the American Barge Line. W. C. Kelly was its first president, with Patrick Calhoun, Jr., first vice-president; and Andrew P. Calhoun, second vice-president. Garrad Kelly, W. C. Kelly's son, was secretary. So started what is today the big American Commercial Barge Line Company.

Coming back to Carl J. Baer. The pointed barges mentioned were part of the Standard Unit Navigation Company that he built as an attempt to bring barge service to tributary streams. They were to be pushed by towboats powered with chain drives, using a series of paddles like a "caterpillar." There were two boats, the SUNCO A-3 and A-4. They were designed by Carl F. Jeffries, who like Carl Baer was a native of Gallipolis, Ohio. The work was done at the Nashville Bridge Company.

Courtesy of The Waterways Journal

At left: SUNCO A-4's "caterpillar" paddles. This was taken on the port side looking forward showing the double chains and paddles. Note that the paddles are staggered. Right: A head-on view of the SUNCO A-4, taken at Nashville, Tennessee, when she was new.

Left: double width roller chain operating paddle wheel 15 feet in diameter
and 8 feet wide on on a river tug.
Right top: single width roller chain operating paddle wheel on a river boat.
Bottom: Towboat which employs the tractor principle for towing freight-laden barges over shallow river waters. This drive consists of a triple width roller chain with paddle blades attached in a manner resembling the method of attaching flights on a chain conveyor.

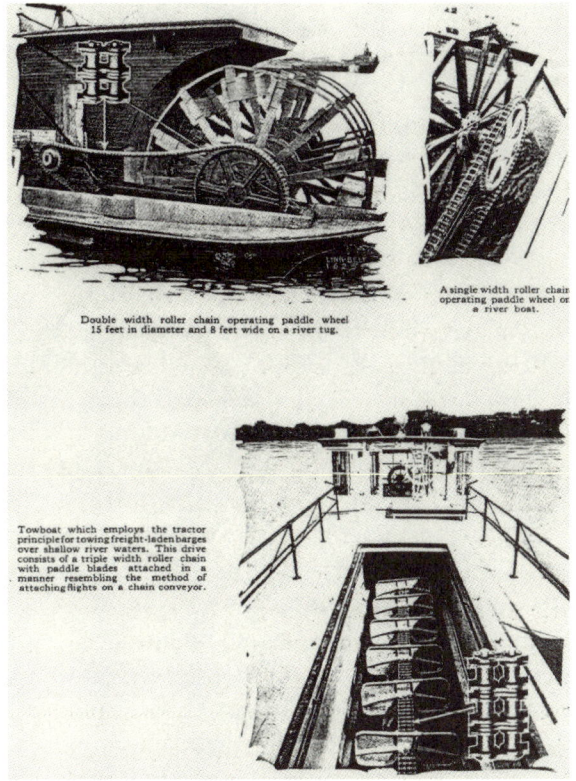

Double width roller chain operating paddle wheel 15 feet in diameter and 8 feet wide on a river tug.

A single width roller chain operating paddle wheel on a river boat.

Towboat which employs the tractor principle for towing freight-laden barges over shallow river waters. This drive consists of a triple width roller chain with paddle blades attached in a manner resembling the method of attaching flights on a chain conveyor.

This innovation of propulsion, which had two chains, one on each side like a side-wheel boat, did not work out. Baer interested the Childress family of St. Louis in the idea of a barge and the pointed barges. Jeffries came along as chief engineer.

Going back to the Mississippi Valley Barge Line, L. Wade Childress is credited with founding it in 1929. He was a St. Louis business man who was also president of the Columbia Terminal Company. He was president, then chairman of the board, until his death on January 31, 1950.

Frank C. Rand was also involved in forming MVBL, and a boat was named for him, as was one for Mr. Childress. (Actually, more than one; the early ones were replaced by more powerful vessels.)

On the rivers, the firm was more commonly called the "Valley Line," and eventually the corporate name was changed to Valley Line. In June 1992 the Valley Line was absorbed by American Commercial Barge Line.

W. J. Barta was later president. The people I knew best at Valley were Capt. L. J. Sullivan, Dewitt "Buzz" Beaver, Capt. Audry D. Haynes, Jr., Nate Haynes, Robert Haynes, and Mrs. Norvell Smith, in the office.

Gasoline

The first internal combustion engines on the rivers were fueled by gasoline. Gasoline engines were quite the thing in the early 1900s and late 1890s. So they came to the rivers, too, on short-trade and low-water packets; and on the tributaries, as well, on small towboats. Many pictures of river landings have gas boats in view as well as steamboats.

There were many manufacturers of gasoline engines. There is a book about them published by Crestline Publishing Company of Sarasota, Florida. One of the firms that made many marine engines was the Red Wing Motor Company of Red Wing, Minnesota. They had two- four- and six-cylinder models, all using four-cycle designs.

The steam towboat directory of the late Capt. Frederick Way, Jr., contains an interesting paragraph on gasoline boats. He made the observation that the gasoline engines "would run happily on almost any fuel that would flow through a funnel...." He also described what these "pop-can boats" sounded like when they started. It is priceless, I think, and would be great if it could be imitated.

Diesel Power

In 1889, Adolphus Busch of St. Louis, best known for his beer, acquired American building rights to the German-originated Diesel engine. Until 1912 Busch controlled Diesel engine manufacturing rights in the United States. Then, through an agreement with a Swiss firm, Sulzer Bros., the Busch-Sulzer Diesel became the American version of the original. The Busch-Sulzer line ranged from 300 to 5,000 hp., many of them being stationary engines.

The Nordberg Manufacturing Company of Milwaukee, Wisconsin, got the manufacturing rights of Busch-Sulzer in 1946.

There is a manual and other information on Busch-Sulzer in the Federal Barge Line papers at the St. Louis Mercantile Library's Herman T. Pott National Inland Waterways Library.

Courtesy of The Waterways Journal

The gas boat era. Several of them are shown on the Little Kanawha River above slackwater, Big Root Shoals, eight miles below Grantsville, West Virginia.

143

This different type of power (Diesel) began to be applied to river vessels, and a number of mechanically minded men, who had been working with gasoline engines, turned to the diesel. (It should be noted that Diesel was once capitalized but now it is not.) The river fleet was on its way to what it is today.

Among those who turned to the diesel was Eddie Erlbacher at Cape Girardeau, Missouri, who had the Mokita, Mishawaka, Papoose and Shawnee. From these efforts came the Missouri Barge Line and Missouri Dry Dock and Repair Company, with Robert Erlbacher and his family, and the late Capt. C. W. "Woody" Rushing and his son Michael.

There were a number of people at Paducah, Kentucky, involved in the evolution of river transportation. Fred W. Olcott, with a boat bearing his name; Hardy L. Roberts, who had the Hardy Towing Company and boats named the Hardy L. Roberts; Louis Igert, whose Igert Towing Company had a number of boats; and Walter G. Hougland, who had the towing company carrying his name.

In Memphis, Tennessee, there was F. M. Graham, of Industrial Marine Service; Capt. Russell Warner, Warner and Tamble; and Ray Waxler, who had Waxler Towing.

Greenville, Mississippi, had many who helped develop the towboat business, and we will devote a chapter to this southern city.

It is always dangerous to detail names like this, because the author will undoubtedly miss some, as I am sure I have here. A whole book could be written about this phase of the river business, and the reader who has additional candidates for it will have their names gladly accepted.

Oil on Water

The oil companies recognized early the advantages of river transportation. Those listed in the 1949 Inland River Record included Ashland Oil and Refining Company, Clark's Super Gas Company, Creole Petroleum Company, Esso Standard Oil Company, Gulf Oil Corporation, Humble Oil and Refining Company, Illinois Farm Supply Company, Independent Oil Company, Lake Tankers Corporation, Magnolia Petroleum Company, Oil Transport Company, Parland Oil Company, Producers Pipe Line Company, Pure Oil Company, Simpson Towing Company, Socony-Vacuum Oil Company, Sohio

Steamer Sprague with Oil Tow.

Petroleum Company, Standard Oil Company of Indiana, Standard Oil Company of Ohio, Streett Towing Company, and the Texas Company.

Of course, many of the barge lines were also towing petroleum products.

The pioneer in this business was Esso, which, as the Standard Oil Company of Louisiana, had moved petroleum products for many years with stern-wheel steamboats such as the Jack Rathbone, Amos K. Gordon, C. J. Reynolds (chartered in 1912-3 as the first sternwheeler in their fleet), C. M. Pate (the first they actually owned), D. R. Weller and, of course, the Sprague.

She was the most famous, being a giant of a boat, 276 by 61 by 7.4 feet. Everything about her was huge. At first, the sternwheel was, as Capt. Frederick Way,, Jr., described it, "40 feet square," meaning that the diameter was the same as the bucket length. It was later cut down.

The Sprague was built at Dubuque, Iowa, by the Iowa Iron Works, a name later changed to the Dubuque Boat and Boiler Company. Originally the Sprague was a Pittsburgh coal towboat. She was chartered by Standard Oil of Louisiana in December 1922 and sold to the Standard Oil Company of New Jersey (Louisiana Division) in May 1935.

She set some records as a tower of petroleum products, just as she had with coal tows earlier in her life. In March 1926 she brought down to Baton Rouge, Louisiana,19 loaded oil barges that made a tow 1,123 feet long and 266 feet wide. In the barges were 11 million gallons of petroleum products.

The Sprague was decommissioned at Memphis on March 5, 1948. Later that year citizens of Vicksburg, Mississippi, led by Dr. Walter E. Johnston, secured the towboat (affec-

Courtesy of The Waterways Journal

The steamer Sprague "Big Mama," with oil tow, and carrying 1927 flood refugees.

tionately known to many as "Big Mama") as a museum and theater. She was towed back to Pittsburgh in 1959 for that city's bicentennial. She burned at Vicksburg May 15, 1974, and was a complete loss. Efforts to preserve parts of her never got anywhere.

Facilities were needed to load and unload the petroleum from the barges, so a series of terminals were built along the river to handle it. Later pipelines were built from the oil fields north, and they cut into the amount of oil moved by river.

An interesting story was told by Andy Franz of the *Journal*. On a trip to Charleston, Missouri, he met H. G. "Chilli" Simpson of the Simpson Oil Company. Charleston is not on the river, but Andy asked him why the firm didn't ship by river. Till then they just hadn't thought about it; so they did, and later Simpson Oil had five boats in the trade (1949).

To show how the river developed, and for nostalgia's sake, I thought it would be interesting to list most of the river operators that were in the 1949 Inland River Record that had been used before. The names will undoubtedly bring back memories.

American Barge Line Co.*
Armco Steel Corp.
Arrow Transportation Co.
B & M. Towing Co.
Barge Transport Co.
The Barrett Line, Inc.
Baton Rouge Coal and Towing Co.
John L. Beatty
Capt. W. A. Bisso
Blaske Lines, Inc.
Edwin Bull
W. T. Burton
 Butcher-Arthur, Inc.
Canal Barge Line*
Cargill, Inc.*
Carnegie-Illinois Steel Corp.
Cenac Towing Co.
Central Barge Co.
Choctaw Transportation Co.*
Choton & Pharr, Inc.
Clifton Towing Co.
Coal City Towing Co.
Colle Towing Co.*
Commercial Barge Lines, Inc.
Costanzo Transportation Co.
Coyle Lines, Inc.
Crain Brothers*
Crucible Steel Co. of America
Cumberland River Sand Co.
J. K. Davison & Bro.
Delta Towing Co.
Deneen River Co.
C. L. Dick Towing Co.
 Dixie Carriers, Inc.
Donahue Bros. Towing Co.
Edmundson Towing Co.
Edwards Transportation Co.

Fabick Tugboat Rental Co.
Falcon Marine Service
Federal Barge Lines
Findlay Towing Co.
Fleet Towing Co.
Franklin Towing Co.
Freeport Sulphur Co.*
G. B. Transporters, Parker Bro.
E. C. Gaines
Chas. Gentel and Sons
J. S. Gissel & Co.
Capt. George B. Gordon
Greenville Towing Co.
Clarence A. Grimm
E. P. Grimm and O. C. Ball
Gulf Atlantic Transportation
Co.
Gulf-Canal Lines
W. D. Haden Co.
W. T. Hardison & Co.
Harms Marine Service
Augustus B. Harris & Son
Harris Boat Co.
Hatfield-Campbell Creek Coal Co.
John I. Hay Co.
Higman Towing Co.*
Hillman Transportation Co.
James R. Hines Corp.
Horton & Horton
Walter C. Hougland, Inc.
Hulett Transportation Co.
Hyer Towing Co.
John M. Hysmith
Igert, Inc.
Indian River Lines
Industrial Marine Service
Ingram Products Co.

Island Creek Fuel & Transportation Co.
Jackson Hope Towing Co.
Jahncke Service, Inc.
Capt. C. A. Johnson
J. M. Jones Lumber Co.
Jones & Laughlin Steel Corp.
E. S. Keeney
T. G. Keeney Sons
Kelley's Creek Barge Line
Kosmos Towing Co.
Cornelius Kroll & Co.
Lake Charles Towing Co. Inc.
Lea River Lines
Lee Wilson Co.
Lipscomb Towing Co.
Curtis Logsdon*
Lone Star Cement Co.
Lucas Towing Co.
McBride Towing Co.*
McCrady-Rodgers Co.
McKay Bros.
McKee Button Co.
Fred R. McKenzie
Russell Maher
Marine Transit Co.
Marine Transportation Co.*
Marquette Cement Mfg. Co.
Material Service Corp.*
Mead Corp.
A. L. Mechling Barge Line, Inc.
Mid-Continent Barge Line Co.
Midwest Towing Co.
Mississippi Valley Barge Line
Missouri Barge Line*
New Orleans Coal and Bisso Towboat Co.*
Norman Bros. Inc.
Ohio & Kanawha Transp. Co.
Ohio Barge Line, Inc.
The Ohio River Co.*
Oil Transport, Inc.
Kline O'Neill
Parker Bros. & Co.

Parker Towing Company*
Parsons Coal Co.
Patton-Tully Transportation Co.*
Pelican Towing Co.
D. M. Picton & Co.
Pittsburgh Coal Co.
Port Arthur Towing Co.*
Portsmouth Steel Corp.
D. J. Potts
Howard Powell*
Powhatan Mining Co.
John M. Raike
Ralph Raike
R. & W. Towing Co.*
Red River Barge Line
Roberts Towing Co.
Sabine Towing Co.
Sabine Transportation Co. Inc.*
O. J. Schwabe
Schwing Towing Co. Inc.
H. L. Seabright
Semet-Solvary, Div. of Allied Chemical & Dye Corp.
O. F. Shearer & Sons
Simms Bros. Towing Co.
Alex J. Slepski
E. T. Slider Co.
Capt. Edward Smith
Charles C. Smith & Co.
Southern States Barge Line*
Capt. Charles C. Stone
Texas Towing Co.
Tex-Mex Towing Co.
C. E. Tinsley
Everett C. Tuel
Twin City Barge and Towing Co.
Union Barge Line Corp.
United States Gypsum Co.
Valentine & Godd
Frank C. Valentine
Victory Towing Co.
Voyageur Towing Co.
Wade Towing Co.
F. B. Walker & Sons

Warner & Tamble
Warrior & Gulf Navigation Co.
West Kentucky Coal Co.
Wheeling Steel Corp.
Harry F. White & Co.
George W. Whiteman
Wilkins Barge Line

Wolf River Transportation Co.
Russell Wolf & Co.
Wood Lumber Co.
N. L. Wright
G. B. Zigler
Zubik Towing Co.

Note: Only those firms followed by asterisks are listed in the Inland River Record of 1999, Many have been absorbed by other lines.

Other companies started after 1949 and were prominent, but some now are gone. Included are:

G. W. Gladders Towing Company
Mid-America Transportation Co.
Nilo Barge Line
Rose Barge Line
Upper Mississippi Barge & Towing Co.
Agri-Trans Corp.
Alamo Barge Line and Chemical Transportation Co.
Alter Barge Lines*
American River Transportation Co.*
Apex Towing Co.*
Bacon Towing Co.
Brent Towing Co.
Campbell Barge Line*
Central Soya Co.
Scott Chotin
Conti-Carriers
Crounse Corp.*
Flowers Transportation, Inc.
G&C Towing, Inc.
Greenville Transportation Co.
Houston Barge Line
Huffman Towing Co.*
Indiana Michigan Power Co.*
Inland Oil & Transport Co.
Inland Tugs Co.
LeMay-Wyant

Logan Towing Service
M/G Transport Services, Inc.
Madison Coal and Supply Co.*
Magnolia Marine Transport Co.*
Marquette Transportation Co.
Mid-South Towing Co.*
Mississippi Marine Transport Co.
Missouri River Barge Line
Mon River Towing, Inc.*
National Marine, Inc.
Northern Towing Co.
Ohio Barge Line, Inc.
The Ohio River Company*
Ole Man River Towing Co.
Orgulf Transport Co.
William B. Patton Towing Co.
Peavy Co.
Plaquemine Towing Corporation*
Port City Towing Co.
Republic Marine, Inc.
Reserve Transportation Co.
Riverway Co.*
Rushing Marine Corporation
SCNO Barge Lines, Inc.
Shickling Towing Co.
O. L. Schmidt Barge Line
Security Barge Line
Selps River Towing

Spanier Towing Corp.	Valley Towing Service
Stapp Towing Company, Inc.*	Vickers Towing Co.
Sun Transportation Co.	Walker Towing Corp.
TPT	Warrior & Gulf Navigation Co.*
Jack Tanner Towing Co.*	Waxler Towing Co.*
Three Rivers Towing	Weathers Towing, Inc.
Corporation*	White Bros., Inc.
Tri-W Towing Co.	George W. Whiteman, Inc.
Trotter Towing Corp.	Williamson Towing Co.
Union Mechling Corp.	Wisconsin Barge Line
United Barge Co.	

Note: Those followed by an asterisk are still in business.

The giants in the river industry are now on the Ohio River— American Commercial Barge Line LLC, Midland Enterprises, and the Ingram Barge Line (but headquartered in Nashville). On the Gulf Coast, Kirby Inland Marine has grown large.

The story of these mergers is well-told by Dan Owen in his foreward to the 1999 *Inland River Record*, where he tells the story of American Commercial Barge Line LLC and how it grew.

The reader can find a good source for towboat business history in the forewards to the *Record*, first by Capt. Fred Way, Jr., and now by Dan Owen.

Readers can get an idea of how the river industry increased by comparing the first issue of the *Inland River Record* and the current one. The 1945 issue had 147 pages of boat names. The 1999 issue has 398, and the type is smaller than it was in the1945 issue.

I have written about the barge lines here, but many of the boats running were owned by construction companies, dredgers, and harbor service firms, which all contributed to the inland waterways commerce. And their owners played a part in developing the mechanical part of towboating.

On the following pages appear pictures selected to show the progression of the towing industry. I attempted to include those representing different shipyards, designs and towing companies. I could not pass up the opportunity to republish an advertisement that indicates how Southern Shipbuilding Corporation of Slidell, Louisiana, went after business.

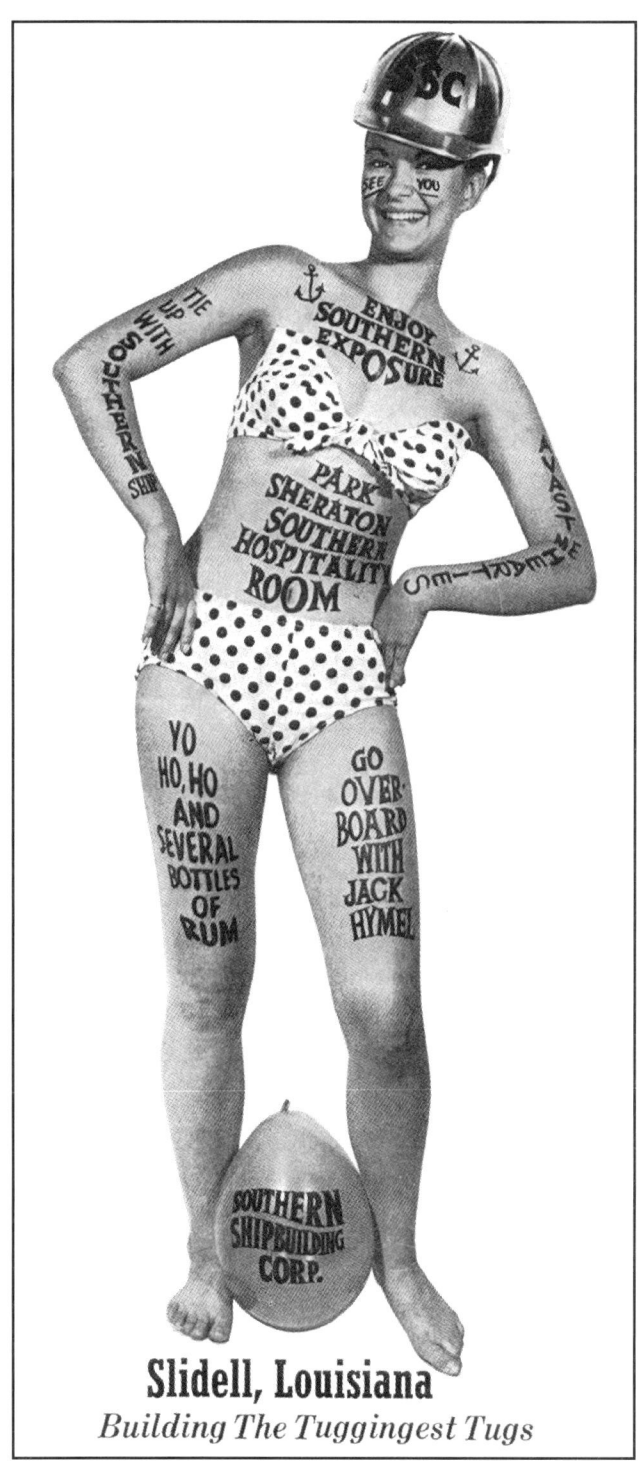

Murphy Library, University of Wisconsin-LaCrosse

John I. Hay Company started business with the steamers Altair and Betsy Ann.

Socony-Vacuum Oil Company Photo

Kansas City Socony, built by Elliott-Fairfax Shipyards, Kansas City, Missouri, in 1937.

Memphis District, U.S. Engineers, labeled this "Mississippi River Commercial Navigation" on August 9, 1939. Boats are Patton-Tully Transportation Company's Diamond A, left, and Kanawha, 180 hp.

152

Courtesy of The Waterways Journal

Memphis District, U.S. Engineers, Mississippi River Commercial Navigation, March 18, 1940. Mokita, owned by Eddie Erlbacher and chartered by the American Barge Line, 1,100 hp.

Courtesy of The Waterways Journal

James H., Walter G. Hougland Sons, built by Nashville Bridge Company, 1940, 800 hp.

Courtesy of The Waterways Journal

Ashland, Ashland Oil & Refining Company, built by Calumet Shipyard and Dry Dock Company, 1941, 2,500 hp.

Courtesy of The Waterways Journal

Havana Zephyr, Streett Towing Company, built by St. Louis Shipbuilding and Steel Company, 1945-46, 2,000 hp.

Courtesy of The Waterways Journal

Commercial Clipper, Commercial Barge Lines, Inc., built by St. Louis Shipbuilding and Steel Company, 1947, with load of automobiles, 1,980 hp.

Courtesy of The Waterways Journal

Jane Smith, Charles E. Smith Company, built by Smith Marine Corporation, 1948, 1,600 hp.

Sam Houston, Butcher-Arthur, Inc., built by St. Louis Shipbuilding and Steel Company, 1948, 1,700 hp.

Henry L. Hillman, Hillman Transportation Company, built by Hillman Barge and Construction Company, 1949, 1,000 hp.

Photos Above Courtesy of The Waterways Journal

A. M. Thompson, Central Barge Company, built by Calumet Shipyard and Dry Dock Company, 1949, 2,800 hp.

Courtesy of The Waterways Journal

J. W. Bedford, built by Maxon Construction Company, 1950, 900 hp.

Courtesy of The Waterways Journal

Kansas City, Sioux City and New Orleans Barge Lines, built by Parker Bros., Houston, 1955, 3,200 hp.

Courtesy of The Waterways Journal

J. W. Hershey, American Commercial Barge Line Company, built by Jeffboat, 1965, 5,000 hp.

Memphis "Press-Scimitar" / The Waterways Journal

Esso Tennessee, Humble Oil and Refining Company, built by Dravo Corporation, 1966, 4,320 hp.

Courtesy of The Waterways Journal

Argonaut, Union Mechling Corporation, built by Dravo Corporation, 1974, 10,500 hp.

Boat Photo Museum

Jessica Brent, Brent Towing Company, with telescoping pilothouse, built by Brent, 1975, 2,000 hp.

Boat Photo Museum

Jim Bernhardt, Wisconsin Barge Line, built by Nashville Bridge Company, 1976, 10,500 hp.

Courtesy of The Waterways Journal

Senator Stennis, left, and Senator Eastland, Brent Towing Corporation. The Senator Eastland was built as the Gladys Flowers, and the Senator Stennis as the Rusty Flowers by Superior Works in 1974, 5,000 hp. They were rechristened on September 2, 1978.

What's Inside a Towboat?
(Pictures of the Mv. Austen S. Cargill)

Boat Photo Museum

Mv. Austen S. Cargill, built by St. Louis Shipyard and Steel Company, 1961, 6,630 hp.

Boat Photo Museum

One of the staterooms.

159

Courtesy of The Waterways Journal

The galley.

Courtesy of The Waterways Journal

Lounge.

Courtesy of The Waterways Journal

Pilothouse.

Courtesy of The Waterways Journal

Engineroom.

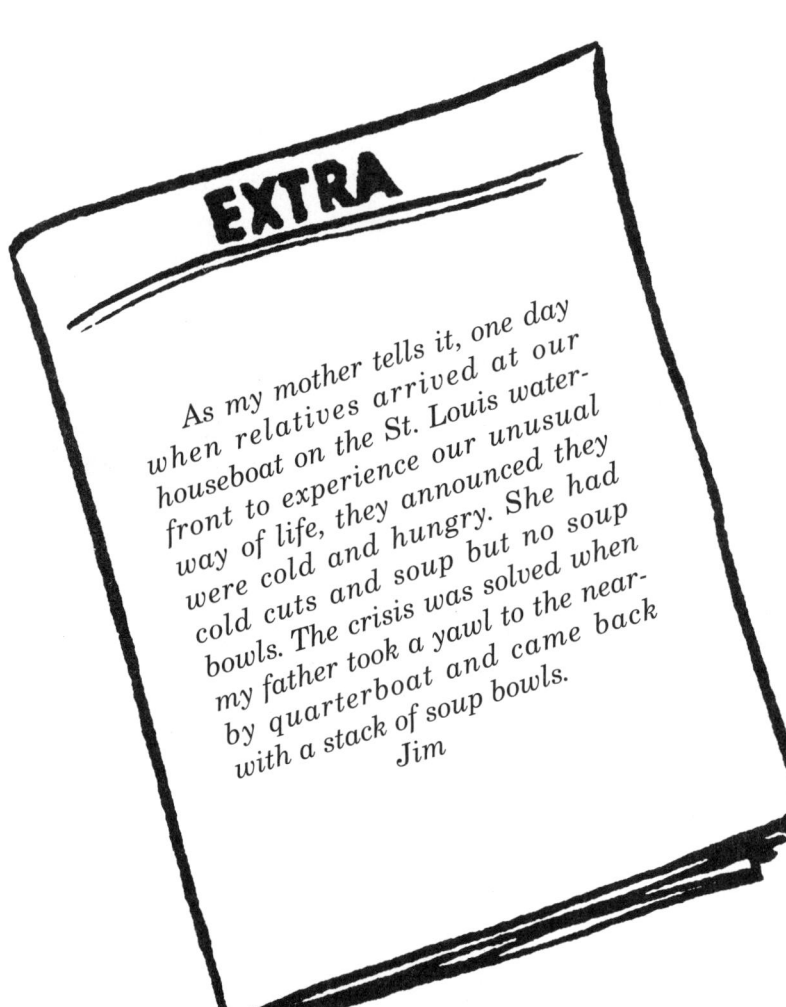

EXTRA

As my mother tells it, one day when relatives arrived at our houseboat on the St. Louis waterfront to experience our unusual way of life, they announced they were cold and hungry. She had cold cuts and soup but no soup bowls. The crisis was solved when my father took a yawl to the nearby quarterboat and came back with a stack of soup bowls.

Jim

Chapter 15 ——

A Boost From Technology

In this day of computers, fax machines and e-mail it is difficult   to realize that in the early days of modern towboating, when the captain wanted to call the office, the crew had to break out the yawl, go ashore and find a land phone.

Regarding communications, Federal Barge Lines, in its efforts to improve the barge line business, put wireless on their boats. Their clerks were also radio operators and used Morse code. One of the men was Herman Radloff, who was on the S. S. Thorpe, now the towboat-museum at Keokuk, Iowa, and renamed Geo. M. Verity.

After World War II voice radio came along. One of the leaders in this field was the Radiomarine Corporation of America, which went out for the river business. (Advertisements we mentioned before; Radiomarine has one of the first exhibits at the MVA convention.)

This revolutionized the communications on rivers. Not only could boat crews call ashore, but they could talk to those on other vessels. The pilots did not have to guess what the boat they were meeting was going to do until there was a whistle signal; they could agree on passing arrangements at a considerable distance.

There was also Channel 4, or the equivalent of the country party line. One could pretty well keep track of what was going on at somebody's home and down on the farm by listening to Channel 4.

On my trips for the *Journal* I had a radio receiver in the car tuned to the marine bands, so I could keep track of the boats. It was especially good on the lower Mississippi River. I could take it out of the car and listen to it in the motel room.

These radio transmissions to and from the boats had to be handled by someone. Federal Barge Lines had a station in Memphis, WPI, to handle its boat traffic; and RCA ran a station in St. Louis for the Mississippi Valley Barge Line. The Missouri Barge Line, in Cape Girardeau, had a 2-mc. station that didn't even reach Memphis.

In Memphis, Capt. Russell V. Warner saw the need for stations with power that could service his boats and others. In 1932 he persuaded his partner, Capt. George Tamble, to set up a radio station with a "Coast" license that could serve all vessels. There was a hearing in Memphis on their application in 1938. It was approved, and in 1939 WJG went on the air. It was first located on the Warner and Tamble operations barge, and in 1944 was moved into the country 10 miles from Memphis.

The radio service was well-received. In 1942 at the request of American Barge Line, Warner and Tamble put in a station at Louisville, WFN. In 1945 RCA put in radiotelephone at WGK in St. Louis. WGK was originally in the Rutger Street terminal of the Valley Line.

Warner and Tamble also put in a station, WCM, at Pittsburgh in 1946. It didn't work, and RCA took it over. RCA sold both WGK and WCM to Ray Gartman on August 1, 1967.

Through the years service on the stations improved with single-side band equipment, VHF, and tape recorders to back up the operators.

As the towing industry increased in size and new communications technology was being developed, the barge lines realized a better system was needed.

In the 1970s, a number of carriers, 10–20 of them, started a movement to organize such a system, but the depression in the towing industry halted it. American Commercial Barge Line came to the rescue, and with its backing started what was to become WATERCOM, or the Waterway Communications System, Inc., based at Jeffersonville, Indiana.

A new series of transmission towers was erected to take out the blind spots that had plagued river radio signals. WATERCOM used the latest in electronics. Their advertisement in *The Waterways Journal* reads: "In one minute you can verify your vessels' locations, call in a pickup or drop off change, report on river conditions, confirm fueling arrangements."

The master can also send facsimiles and other data. WATERCOM also stresses its ability to keep boat crews happier with the use of Datron DBS-4000 systems that deliver laser-disk-quality pictures and CD-quality sound on the television, even when the boat is moving.

During World War II one of the big developments that helped win the war was radar. The Allies perfected it and used it to good effect in tracking enemy submarines, ships and planes. Could it be used in confined areas such as the rivers? That was the question; smaller sets with shorter coverage were necessary. There was no doubt that there was a place for radar on the inland waterways, with their fog, smoke, rain and snow, making visibility at times difficult. Some boats also tied up for the night.

Pioneers in the adoption of radar on the rivers were Ashland Oil and Refining Company and Sperry Gyroscope Company. The mv. Tri-State was the first towboat to get such a system. Capt. Fred Way said it was at Dravo in November 1946.

The Tri-State left Ashland, Kentucky, home of Ashland Oil, on December 5 for Cincinnati, which was reached the following afternoon. Many visitors came to see the new device at Ashland and at Cincinnati. In fact, so many came that M. C. Dupree, Ashland's transportation manager, announced a "moonlight" trip to show off the radar. Robert L. Gray, marine superintendent, was there as a host. Visitors were from the river industry, the Corps of Engineers and Coast Guard. The Coast Guard had set up four radar "targets" to help check on the radar on the Tri-State.

At the end of the operation, Mr. Dupree announced that Ashland had ordered four more Sperry scopes for the towboats Paul Blazer, Jim Martin, Ashland and Tri-State. It was said

Mv. Tri-State, the first Western Rivers towboat to have radar. Note the big antenna atop the pilothouse.

that the Tri-State had saved 20 hours running time on a trip from Cincinnati to Pittsburgh. It was also reported that visitors to the boat were quite impressed with the performance of the radar. The equipment is standard on boats today.

Later, the Tri-State was at Mount Vernon, Indiana, and Andy Franz and I were invited down to see it.

Also on the electronic front, people sometimes wondered what that "stick" is on the lead barge in many tows; it extends down into the water. The "stick" is another help to the pilot—a depth indicator. The depth of the water registers on a graph in the pilothouse so the operator will know where the best channel is. No longer is it necessary to send out the yawl and grope around looking for a suitable way to go.

It's not so hard now to communicate with the mate or deckhand on the lead barge. It is no longer necessary to use a bull horn or megaphone or a loud voice. A walkie-talkie in the hands of the guy on the barge will tell the pilot how close he is to the lock wall and other necessary information.

Also, in those early days of modern towing, when a boat needed food and supplies, it was necessary to go ashore to get them, or land the boat. Most came aboard at the end of the trip, but if the cook ran out of something, like milk, it had to be picked up en route.

The late Jim Walden always said he was the first person to offer midstream service—it was at Memphis. Whether this is right or not, midstream service did develop to the advantage of the towboats. The midstreamers met the tow with anything they desired, from food, spare parts for the engineroom, cigarettes, even comic books. As a service, the boat stores delivered and picked up the mail, and brought out newspapers.

The midstreamers also brought out fuel, so the boat took on a new load of diesel while underway. What a great time-saver all this was!

There are many companies offering these services today; but the leaders in the business, as I recall them from my visits along the rivers, especially at Memphis, were Economy Boat Store, Dee Colborn; Ory Bros., Rene Ory, both at Wood River, Illinois; St. Louis Fuel and Supply Company, Ray Chouner, St. Louis; Waterways Marine, Charlie and Laura Smith; and Frankie and Johnnie's, Memphis.

Some of them, particularly Waterways Marine, had accommodations at its "Boatel" for crews waiting for their boats. At Catlettsburg, Kentucky, Merdie Boggs had what is now The Boat Store; and Bob Kennedy, *The Waterways Journal* correspondent, was there.

Today, Economy is probably the largest midstreamer and boat supplier, having service at six locations—two on the Gulf Intracoastal Waterway in Alabama and Florida. Economy also says it is the originator of midstream fueling.

There was a time when the line boats spotted their barges at the terminals or docks and made up their own tows. At this time, the size of the towboats and their horsepower made it possible.

As the boats got bigger and more powerful, it wasn't so easy and certainly not efficient economically. So, a new business came into being—the fleeting service. Often retired pilots and their sons would get a harbor boat and take barges off passing tows in midstream. When loaded or unloaded, the barge would be taken out to the passing tow. It was an important service that sped things up considerably.

Today, there is a fleeting service at almost every river location with docks and terminals; the barges waiting for space at the dock, or to be picked up by a line boat, grow to quite a sizable fleet. There are hundreds of them at St. Louis south of the main riverfront.

In addition to the fleeting, some harbor services also clean and strip barges, and do topside repairs. They also have pumps available if a barge starts taking on water. Some firms have floating cranes to stack barge covers.

Pilothouse control of the engines was first used on ferries and was adopted by towing vessels. It certainly beat the speaking tube or stomping on the pilothouse floor on smaller vessels. It made for quicker, and often safer, handling of the engines.

The uniform size of barges also helped speed things up in the towing business. At one time barges came in a number of sizes. Federal Barge Lines, for instance, had some barges that were 300 by 48 feet; and there were the pointed ones used by the Mississippi Valley Barge Line. Then, standard sizes began to be used, such as the 175 by 26 feet carriers, and 195 by 35 feet. Some bigger barges were also built—290 by 50 footers for both dry and liquid cargoes.

Integrated and unit tows came along, barges that would fit together to make a smoother riding fleet. Box barges were built to fit in with barges with rakes. The Harry Truman tow of Federal, as described earlier, was a good example of early attempts at integrated tows.

Barges came into being to handle all kinds of items in addition to the traditional loads of coal, grain and dry chemicals in the hoppers. Liquid cargo, such as a number of chemicals, was moved by barge, in addition to petroleum products. Sulfur was moved in addition to other ores. Steel products went in hoppers. Other barges were developed to handle cement. Deck barges moved all types of machinery—often entire industrial plants, and military equipment. One of the most interesting were rockets and missiles; a special barge was constructed to move the Saturn space craft.

For a while there were movements of automobiles out of Evansville, Indiana, on specially designed car carriers and on barges with decks made to carry cars. The car manufacturers then built plants around the Midwest and eliminated the need for this river transportation.

Also, don't forget air-conditioning as part of the crew's comfort. Those were not pleasant days on the lower Mississippi in August with a following wind. And television in the lounge and maybe cabins; radios, and even VCRs. All the comforts of home, which of course it was for 30 days at a time.

The cook has the modern technology of the refrigerator instead of an ice box, TV dinners if necessary, and prepared foods and the like.

In other words, the towboats are up-to-date now, and so is their operation. (See "What's-Inside-a-Towboat pictures in Chapter 14.)

Barges Come in a Variety of Shapes And Sizes

Courtesy of The Waterways Journal

Dump barge.

Photo Courtesy Jeffboat, Inc.

Box hopper barge built by Jeffboat, Inc., in 1991.

Courtesy of The Waterways Journal

Hopper barge built by Dravo in 1983.

Courtesy of The Waterways Journal

Flat deck barge.

Courtesy of The Waterways Journal

Dry-cement barge built by Dravo in 1970.

Courtesy of The Waterways Journal

Automobile carrier Commercial Clipper.

Courtesy of The Waterways Journal

Steel barge designed to haul automobiles.

Courtesy of The Waterways Journal

Barge rake.

Courtesy of The Waterways Journal

Middle box barges of integrated tank tow.

Courtesy of The Waterways Journal

Sun Oil Company integrated tow.

Courtesy of The Waterways Journal

Berthing (hotel) barge.

173

Todd's largest barge.

What kind of barge is this?

Photos Above Courtesy of The Waterways Journal
Refinery column loaded on barge in Holland.

Barge R.B. 2, built for Flour Ocean Services, 1970.

An interesting tow!

Photos Above Courtesy of The Waterways Journal

Smith-Rice crane barge 3 launched by Paceco in 1974.

Photo by St. Louis Distirct, U.S. Engineers

Arkansas National Guard equipment at Alton, Illinois, in 1987.

Courtesy of Dravo

Another interesting tow.

Courtesy of The Waterways Journal

Crounse Corporation vessel tows missile barge.

Courtesy of The Waterways Journal

Another innovation that helped the towing industry was the kort nozzle, developed by L. Kort of Germany. Basically, it is a ring of steel that fits over the propeller. Dravo Corporation obtained the U.S. rights and installed the first one (appropriately) on the towboat Pioneer; she ran a trial trip on May 13, 1937. Use of the kort nozzle, which gives more thrust to the propellers, spread rapidly.

177

While coming back from my trips to the south for The Waterways Journal I would pass through towns along U.S. 61 just before Thanksgiving. They were already preparing for Christmas. Colored lights were strung among the cypress trees in the bayous and lakes, making a pretty picture.

Jim

Chapter 16 ——

Flowing With The River

We have brought the river industry up-to-date, more or less. So now would be the right time to get personal for awhile. (The publisher has reminded me from time-to-time that some of this must be autobiographical.)

I did want a college degree, but time and money were in the way in the late 1930s and early 1940s. I did have a job, which is something a lot of people did not have. There were no junior or community colleges in those days; Washington University and St. Louis University were the major schools in St. Louis at the time.

However, Washington U. did have a night school called University College, and I did enroll there in courses that I liked or that I thought would help me along the way. The credits probably would have worked toward a degree.

After the war I could have taken advantage of the GI Bill, but again, there was the job. Donald Wright was not one to push for higher education either. In fact, he took a dim view of academia as a whole. Also, after the war, even night school was a challenge because the fall semester started about the time my fall trips started for the *Journal*, so I would miss much of the early part of the course.

I had one break though; I took a course in what I recall was economic geography. The teacher let me miss several weeks by reporting on business along the Gulf Coast, the oil drilling, shrimp fisheries and shipbuilding, etc. So, I got credit for that course.

One of my earlier courses had more far reaching effects than the credit. It was on geology, taught by a man named Courtney Werner. He took us on field trips, one of which was to the cliffs above Alton, Illinois, looking for trilobites, those fossil marine anthropods that are found in some numbers in the Alton area. While in one of the caves that we explored I sat next to a girl and exchanged pleasantries. I was surprised to learn she lived only five houses from me on Pershing Avenue. Even more surprising was that she had graduated from Soldan High School the same year I had, but we had never met.

Her name, as she liked to explain, was Brunnhilda Carol Teckula Bock. ("But call me Bea," she would urge people.) As opera people know, Brunnhilda was one of the Valkyries in Wagner's famous Ring series. Her father was under the spell of Wagner, it seems, and he wanted to name his son Siegfried, but Brunnhilda's mother put her foot down on that, and he was named George. Mr. Bock was a professor who taught at various colleges; he was teaching in Columbus, Ohio, when Bea was born.

I found out that Bea was a librarian by trade, and worked for the main St. Louis Public Library downtown at Thirteenth and Olive. She was in the children's room, applied science room, and the reference room, where I found myself on many nights waiting to take her home.

This worked in well with my family. My mother's sister, Sarah R. Bailey, was also a librarian and head of the Crunden Branch Library. Naturally, many of her friends were in the library, so it was a close-knit group. I had leanings toward library work myself, but my aunt didn't think it was a good job for men, and I got little encouragement from her; otherwise I might be a librarian instead of a writer.

Bea earned two degrees in library science from Washington University.

While we were dating, one of our favorite spots was the Coronado Hotel, Spring and Lindell. The dance floor in the Jug had square holes in it, through which colored lights shown. There was also the Chase Hotel roof. In those days before air-conditioning, the hotels had roof gardens to catch the cool breeze—if there was any. The Statler, downtown, had one as I recall.

Another place we went on dates was the Muny Opera in Forest Park. It wasn't too long a walk from our houses, and we sat in the free seats in the back of the open-air theatre; we had no fear of walking out there, nor did we have any while walking to the Coronado. The Muny was still doing the old-time operettas then, such as "The Desert Song," "New Moon," and "The Student Prince," and we would go home singing those Sigmund Romberg love songs.

Marriage came on May 17, 1947, in the chapel of the Second Presbyterian Church, Taylor and Westminster, in St. Louis, now called the Central West End. Our mothers planned the wedding lunch at the Forest Park Hotel. It was a lot of fun.

Then we went downtown to the Lenox Hotel, Ninth and Washington, for the wedding night. I still remember leaning over to sign the register, and rice fell out of my hair, to the amusement of the clerk.

After a little while in our room, Bea getting into more suitable attire, and we were off to the river. There, we were greeted by one friend who remarked, "Nobody except a damn fool like you would come down here on their wedding day."

But, there was a very good reason for me being on the river that day. The steamer Golden Eagle was to leave on her first trip of the 1947 season. The boat had been acquired by Herman Pott, or Pott Industries, and/or St. Louis Ship. She never looked better, for they had really put a lot of money into renovating the steamer. There were many floral arrangements from well-wishers; at the time no one thought anything about it—least of all, a wake.

Many of the Golden Eagle's faithful were aboard, including Marga Sasche (who was to become Mrs. Wilbur Finger) whose camera was to immortalize the voyage.

Bea and I headed up the hill to the Lenox, a fine dinner in the Rathskeller and the wedding night.

The next morning we got on one of the Pennsylvania Railroad's four morning trains to New York. Safe in the hotel in the big city, and relaxing with *The New York Times* what did I see—a picture of the Golden Eagle—sunk! Was anybody lost? It didn't say. All there was was the picture of the wreck. Did anything happen to Irwin Urling, who was in the wedding party and news editor of *The Waterways Journal*? If I hadn't been buoyed up with the excitement of the wedding and honeymoon, it really would have been a dark day.

Our hotel room had views of the Hudson River down a street between tall buildings. One morning we looked out and saw the Queen Mary coming in. We made a most rapid exit, and were now going down to another river—on the run! New Yorkers we passed couldn't figure out what was going on. We made it, and saw the great ship come into the dock. Years later I found out that in the crowd, perhaps standing next to me, was John Zenn, from the Allegheny River.

My Aunt Evelyn Patterson, my mother's older sister, lived in New York and got us tickets to the Broadway shows "Annie Get Your Gun," with Ethel Merman; and "Carousel." They were great treats, but I hate to think what my aunt had to pay for those tickets! Another highlight, I recall, was dinner at the Tavern On the Green, in Central Park.

It was time to head home, and Aunt Evelyn took my hand and said, "Jimmy, I hate to tell you this, but your favorite boat sank." I took her other hand and thanked her for not telling me, then I told her I already knew about it.

We had a busy life. My wife, being a craftsperson, liked to make things like dolls and puppets, and so joined the Greater St. Louis Doll Club and the Puppet Guild of St. Louis. She was also a singer, being in the Second Presbyterian Church Choir and the Washington University Chorus. She worked with Talking Tapes for the Blind, and not forgetting her library days, clipped papers and magazines on hundreds of subjects, labeled under the Dewey Decimal system.

She accepted my love for the river, and as I have mentioned, took trips with me on several boats. We attended river meetings together, especially the Midwest Riverboat Buffs, where she delighted in needling president Bill Talbot.

For that inevitable question, do you have any children. The answer, unfortunately is no. But we tried. We were both 31 when we married and after a reasonable length of time, we visited our family doctor who said to try a bit longer. Now, he was of the old school, and I wondered if he knew something we didn't and wouldn't tell us, or thought if it didn't happen naturally it was not supposed to be. One of our river friends sought such help, got it, and had children.

My wife passed over the big river on October 5, 1999.

EXTRA

One of my favorite Memphis stops was Warner and Tamble Transportation Company's wharfboat, where Capt. Russell V. Warner had his office. There we visited, and he would share interesting river pictures. He told how his partner, Frank Tamble, would get on the wharfboat during icy weather by sitting on a piece of cardboard. He'd slide down over the cobblestones, aiming for the gangway, and then shoot aboard.

Jim

Chapter 17——

The Mark Twain Hotel

A popular meeting place for the river fraternity in St. Louis during the 1940s and '50s was the Mark Twain Hotel at Eighth and Pine. The name and its central location were a drawing card.

At that time the river industry offices and government agencies were all concentrated in downtown St. Louis. The Coast Guard was in the Old Post Office at Eighth and Olive, as was the U.S. Army Corps of Engineers. Federal Barge Lines was in what was then the Boatmen's Bank Building at Broadway (Fifth Street) and Olive; the Mississippi Valley Barge Line was in the Ambassador Building at Eighth and Locust; Lake Tankers was in the Arcade Building at Eighth and Olive; and a number of marine insurance companies and maritime lawyers had offices nearby.

The basement of the Mark Twain had the Steamboat Cabin, a large room with white railings around the walls, and a mural of riverbank scenes painted on the walls. One could eat and imagine they were on a boat cruising on the river. At one time it was open for lunch, and it was used for parties and group meetings.

185

Courtesy of the Missouri Historical Society

The old Mark Twain Hotel in St. Louis.

On the street level there was the Purple Cow, the coffee shop, which was open late, perhaps 24 hours, but certainly past midnight.

But the principal gathering place was the Cypress Room, with its bar. One could find river people there any time of day or night. At that time the boats would lay over while their barges were loaded or unloaded, and the masters often came up to the Mark Twain. A lot of business was done in the Cypress Room.

This brings to mind another phase of the towing industry; a new breed of rivermen was introduced when the Butcher-Arthur boats began coming up from the South. They had French-American (Cajun) crews who had not been in northern waters too much. Some of the captains would become well known, especially Capts. Roy LeBeouf and Eno Dupuis. I want to mention two stories that came out of this period; they may be true:

One concerns a southern boat pilot who was asked by an approaching vessel, "Where are you, Cap'?" The reply was, "I'm on page 29 (of the light list)."

The other was about the threatened mutiny (or maybe it actually happened) of a southern crew unless the cook served them red beans and rice.

Regardless, the Butcher-Arthur boats got the job done.

On the mezzanine floor was the "Propellor" Club Room (that was the way it was spelled) where the St. Louis Propeller Club met for lunch every Monday. (The club also had monthly meetings in the Steamboat Cabin.)

The organization had started on the East Coast, and its home "port" was New York. Many deep-sea ports had Propeller Clubs, and soon the river cities followed. Harry Parsons was the torchbearer, so to speak, and he boosted the formation of the inland ports.

St. Louis was one of the most influential and largest. The biggest meeting was the one held yearly during the MVA convention, when the club sponsored the luncheon. The luncheon drew many dignitaries, and there was also a well-known speaker.

One of the most interesting I recall was the year in the Chase Club when we found out that Richard Bissell, the author of several river books and "7½ Cents" (which became the Broadway hit *Pajama Game)* was to be there. Ed Renshaw, the president of the St. Louis Propeller Club that year, got the girl singer from the Chase Club to sing one of the show's hits, "Something's Always Happening on the River." Bissell was surprised, and the audience gave him a big hand.

The other entertainment, which became a Propeller Club classic story, was the club's stag at the Mark Twain. A stag party was always popular with the members, as it was with many male groups. At this particular one, word got around that we might have a visit from the vice squad. To stall this, an invitation was extended to the mayor of the city of St. Louis. Fred Hume, of *The Waterways Journal*, had been an aide to Mayor Al Kaufman. Well, sure enough, the party had just started, and the first girl was on the floor, when the vice guys arrived at the head of the stairs leading to the Steamboat Cabin. The club's president, Ruel Bridges, who rivermen will remember as a very gentlemanly person, quiet and reserved, met them. He explained that we were expecting the mayor, but they could join the party if they wanted to. The expected arrival of the mayor gave them cause to hesitate, and in the meantime people were trying to get rid of the evidence. The trouble was that she was sitting on the lap of William J. Keith, an elderly gentleman about 80, who was enjoying it very much. He wouldn't let loose of the girl; she was finally pried off Billy's lap and thrown into the ladies room before the authorities got down the stairs. By that time everyone was drinking and talking in a normal manner. But the incident was enough for the proprietors of the Mark Twain; it was the Propeller Club's last stag at the hotel. (Others were held on the river.)

There was always a disagreement as to whether the Propeller Club should be a social organization or that it should be political in backing the waterways. Because of its size the organization could have an important role to play.

The great cause of the National Propeller Club was the American Merchant Marine. The deep-sea part of it, that is. It is hard for blue-water people to understand that brown-water vessels (vessels of the inland waterways) are also part of the merchant marine, indeed the most viable part today. But this fact is one reason for the expansion of the Propeller Club to inland cities.

There were some serious debates about the ocean-shipping part of the merchant marine during the Propeller Club luncheons. I recall one time when something was said that caused Capt. Oscar Lane, of Lake Tankers, to get so angry that he left the room. Capt. Lane had been on the deep seas and was sent to St. Louis when Shell Oil Company began its river operations. There were also others with previous sea duty that came inland.

After World War II, the interest in Mississippi River towing spread. We had several foreign visitors guided by the Coast Guard.

The big event in the Propeller Club's year was the annual convention. Someone from St. Louis was chosen to represent the club. St. Louis got the convention in 1968, the first time it had come to inland waterways headquarters was the Chase-Park Plaza Hotel (October 8-11).

It so happened that the St. Louis Cardinals won the pennant that year, so the convention coincided with the World Series. It is not difficult to imagine the shortage of rooms, and also the great number of requests for World Series tickets for visiting friends and customers of the local towing industry.

On Thursday, October 10, there was a river ride on the Mv. Huck Finn. The Cardinals were also in the deciding game of the series, and many radios were tuned to the game. The Cardinals lost!

St. Louis was after another national convention several years later. Various clubs would submit bids for the privilege of holding the convention, so it was a job trying to persuade the board and members to choose your city. During the year when it was to be decided whether the convention should be in St. Louis, or elsewhere, the national meeting was to be in Honolulu, Hawaii. I was authorized to go and, hopefully, bring back the prize. It was a long way and a great opportunity to travel.

Our opponent for the convention was Washington, D.C. I don't remember what I had in addition to literature to entice people to vote for St. Louis. But Washington had straw hats with bright bands that invited people to visit the Capitol City. There was one problem, though. When the hats were shipped to Honolulu, they were packed in boxes that previously held fishmeal. The hats smelled so bad that they could not be worn! St. Louis got the convention.

In the long run it wasn't to be. To qualify for the convention the home port had to put up a lot of money in advance. By then the bottom had fallen out of the river industry. I did not realize how bad it would be until Tom Gladders, of G. W. Gladders

Towing Company, came to a meeting and said we shouldn't send the money nor have the convention. He saw into the future. We had to forfeit. It was the beginning of the end for the Port of St. Louis, too. The club itself ceased meeting, and the remnants of the St. Louis river industry now have the Muddy Waters Social Club, which holds golf tournaments and (like the name implies) social events from time to time.

One more comment on the St. Louis Propeller Club before closing this chapter. Sorry to say, the organization was strictly for males, as so many groups were in those days in the 1940s and '50s. When Mrs. Louise Merrill, president of Merrill Marine Service—she took over the business when her husband, E. M. "Jack" Merrill, died—applied for membership in the club, she was turned down by the board of directors. She was a fine businesswoman, well respected in the river industry, but even she could not break the gender barrier.

The restriction against women rankled me, and when I was president of the club, I instigated a resolution to make Louise an honorary member. First I called Al Filiatrault, executive secretary at national headquarters in New York to tell him what I planned to do. He said, "Go ahead, the president of the Alaska club is a woman." How times had changed. Mrs. Merrill had moved to Arizona by then, and I always hoped she would come back so she would be able to be recognized correctly. She never did.

Lastly, the Mark Twain Hotel was torn down in early 1975 to make way for a State of Missouri building complex.

Propeller Clubs in 1968

Due to the locations of various Propeller Club ports, it was convenient for some to serve the needs of both blue-water and brown-water mariners. Others served mostly one or the other. There were, of course, Propeller Club ports overseas, and quite a few student ports on college and university campuses.

In the following list of U.S. ports, some will be followed by a "B" for blue water, others by an "I" for inland, and still others by "B/I" for both.

Local Propeller Club Member Ports

Anchorage, Alaska - B
Baltimore, Md. - B
Baton Rouge, La. - I
Bellingham, Wash. - B
Boston, Mass. - B
Brownville-Port Isabel,
  Texas - B/I
Buffalo, N.Y. - B
Camden, Ark. - I
Charleston, S.C. - B
Chicago, Ill. - B/I
Cincinatti, Ohio - I
Cleveland, Ohio - B
The Columbia River, Ore. - I
Corpus Christi, Texas - B/I
Detroit, Mich. - B
Duluth-Superior Minn./Wis.- B
Evansville/Owensboro,
  Ind./Ky. - I
Galveston, Texas - B/I
Georgetown, S.C. - B
The Golden Gate, Calif. - B
Greenville, Miss. - I
Honolulu, Hawaii - B
Houston, Texas B/I
Huntington, W.Va. - I
Jacksonville, Fla. - B
Joliet, Ill. - I
Key West, Fla. - B
Lafourche, La. - I
Little Rock, Ark. - I
Los Angeles/Long Beach,
  Calif. - B
Louisville, Ky. - I
Memphis, Tenn. - I
Miami, Fla. - B
Mobile, Ala. - B/I
Muskogee, Okla. - I
Narragansett Bay, R.I. - B
Nashville, Tenn. - I
New Orleans, La. - B/I
Newport News, Va. - B
New York, N.Y. - B
Norfolk, Va. - B
Paducah, Ky. - I
Pittsburgh, Pa. - I
Port Everglades, Fla. - B

Portland, Me. - B
Portsmouth, N.H. - B
The Quad Cities, Ill./Iowa - I
The Sabine, Texas/La. - B/I
San Diego, Calif. - B
St. Louis, Mo. - I
St. Petersburg, Fla. - B
Savannah, Ga. - B
Seattle, Wash. - B
Tacoma, Wash. - B
Tampa, Fla. - B
Tulsa, Okla. - I
The Twin Cities, Minn. - I
Washington, D.C. - B
Wilmington, Del. - B

Overseas

There were also more than 20
  overseas ports.

U.S. Student Ports

Baruch College of C.U.N.Y.
California Maritime Academy
Florida J.C. of Jacksonville
The Great Lakes Marine
  Academy
Jacksonville University
Marine Maritime Academy
Marshall University
Massachusetts Marine Academy
Pacific Lutheran University
San Francisco State University
So. Maine Voational. Tech Inst.
State University of New York
  Maritime College
Texas Maritime Academy
U.S. Merchant Marine Academy
University of Florida
University of Maryland
University of New Orleans
University of North Florida

EXTRA

In New Orleans I would call on Capt. Joseph Chotin, president of Chotin Transpor-tation, Inc. His offices were on the upper floor of a downtown building, and he could see the river only down one street. He kept a telescope focused on that spot so he could get a good view of what was going by on the Mississippi.

Jim

Chapter 18 —

Greenville

You could say that Greenville, Mississippi, was the ultimate in river cities in the 1960s and '70s. No other place on the inland waterways had such a concentration of towing companies, shipyards, and related industries. The area was given a special four-page section in the Annual Review issue of *The Waterways Journal*.

The 1970 Annual Review had, in the Greenville section, advertisements for the:

> Greenville Port Commission
> Greenville Towing Company
> Port City Barge Line
> Marine Welding & Repair Works
> Greenville Propeller Works
> M and M Towing Company
> Couey Harbor Service
> Warfield Towing Service
> Vickers Towing Company
> The Marina (on Lake Ferguson)
> KGW Towing Company
> S & W Barge Line
> Brent Marine Supply Company

Wasson Towing Service
Specialized Electronics Company
Brent Towing Company
Greenville Shipbuilding
Greenville Manufacturing & Machine Works
Williamson Engine & Supply Company
Logan Charter Service Company
M and M Transportation Company
Moyse & Moyse & Wasson (insurance)
Delta Towing Company
J & H Diesel Service
Weathers Towing Company
Feeder Line Towing Service
Big T Towing Company
Greenville River Services
Security Barge Line

From the Files of The Waterways Journal

Lake Ferguson at Greenville, Mississippi.

Also impressive was the list of Greenville towboats presented in the same section. Listed in 1970 were the following:

Ace	.660 hp.	Karen	.2,880 hp.
Ann Brent	.3,200 hp.	Kathy	.330 hp.
Annilou	.760 hp.	Kyle T	.580 hp.
Barbara Brent	.3,200 hp.	Lee McCourt (Dredge)	.300 hp.
Beaver Island	.760 hp.	Lesta K	.3,200 hp.
Ben McCool	.2,400 hp.	Leta Jane	.1,200 hp.
Betty Brent	.2,400 hp.	Lil Arthur	.300 hp.
Betty K	.495 hp.	Linda	.3,000 hp.
Bob Aycock	.650 hp.	Little Jessie	.165 hp.
		Lucille	.1,400 hp.
C. R. Clements	.1,800 hp.		
Chuck Hobart	.660 hp.	Mac	.330 hp.
City of Greenville	.3,200 hp.	Mama Lere	.3,200 hp.
		Margaret K	.615 hp.
Danny P	.600 hp.	Margie Taylor	.700 hp.
David Vickers	.1,800 hp.	Marlin	.1,170 hp.
Debbie Lee	.2,250 hp.	Mary Ann	.1,700 hp.
Del Rio	.3,200 hp.	Mary Ann (Dredge)	.300 hp.
Delta	.760 hp.	Mary C. Thompson	.1,400 hp.
Denis Brown	.1,800 hp.	Miss Carolyn	.800 hp.
Dorothy Lee	.1,130 hp.	Miss Nancy	.600 hp.
Double D	.3,200 hp.	Miss Susan	.760 hp.
Drake	.755 hp.	Mo-Ark	.1,800 hp.
		Mustang	.330 hp.
Everett McCourt	.1,000 hp.		
		Nita Vickers	.3,200 hp.
Forsythia	.800 hp.		
		Ohio	.4,300 hp.
George Weathers	.2,400 hp.	Ole Miss	.3,200 hp.
Greenville	.3,200 hp.		
		Patrick D. Condon	.1,140 hp.
Henry McCourt (Dredge)	240 hp.	Polliwog	.1,800 hp.
Hilman Logan	.5,000 hp.		
		Ricky	.500 hp.
Issaquena	.5,000 hp.	Ruth Brent	.3,000 hp.
Jackie Lewis (Dredge)	.240 hp.	Sally B	.1,800 hp.
J. E. Vickers	.3,000 hp.	Superior	.3,200 hp.
JAG	.2,400 hp.	Susan Vickers	.3,200 hp.
James Faris	.1,600 hp.		
James L. Williams	.3,200 hp.	Templeton	.495 hp.
Jesse Brent	.4,300 hp.	Tennessee	.2,500 hp.
Joe Taylor	.1,050 hp.	Tri-W	.4,800 hp.
John K	.760 hp.	Tunica	.1,800 hp.
Johnny Dan	.1,950 hp.		
Julie Ann	.3,200 hp.	Walter Williamson	.2,400 hp.
		Washington	.5,000 hp.
		Weatherwood	.800 hp.
		Wm. H. Craig	.3,200 hp.

Also listed in the Greenville section were names of the city officials, mayor, fire and police chiefs, etc., as well as members of the Port Commission. Bringing these names up-to-date was one of the final chores of getting the Christmas Issue (Annual Review) ready. Concentrating the Greenville ads into one section had been my idea. So, of course, getting the names was my responsibility. Col. Milton P. Barschdorf, Greenville port director, was my helper on this, for which I was always most grateful.

Lake Ferguson, on which all of these river companies were located, was once part of the Mississippi River that had been separated by one of the Corps of Engineers' cut-offs whose purpose it was to straighten the river to help with flood control. In its slack-water state, it was ideal for docking, shipbuilding, etc. Warfield Point was the entrance to the Greenville enterprises.

When I first went to Greenville, I had people to meet who were not in the river business. My mother knew Kathleen Harty, so my first duty was to call on her. She was a genuine southern lady who did not quite understand the booming river business, nor did she recognize many of the families running the towing companies.

Her brother, Emmett Harty, was a prominent judge in town, and when I mentioned his name as a means of reference, it sometimes brought a wry smile; they had been before the judge for some infraction of the law, like a traffic infraction. Judge Harty knew many of Greenville's older generation, of course, including Will Percy, who wrote the classic, *Lanterns On The Levee*. A city park is named for Judge Harty.

Because Greenville was such a place of importance, The American Waterways Operators held their southern region's quarterly meeting there. After the MVA and OVIA, it got to be the most popular gathering of the river fraternity.

The first event of these AWO meetings was the Friday night fish fry, sponsored by Capt. Jesse Brent. His neighbors, or at least citizens of Greenville, would come with big iron kettles in which they cooked the catfish and hushpuppies. Fresh and hot, it was really good eating.

The fish fry was held at the Brent house. I recall two memorable experiences there. The first year there was a monkey in a tree that offered a bit of amusement. Another year the driver of the car I was in looked at the sky and said we

From the Files of The Waterways Journal
The Marina, Port of Greenville, Mississippi.

ought to get back to the motel. We got there just before the heavens opened up. It really did rain, and it soaked the grass parking lot at the Brents. Greenville's tow trucks had a field day getting all those cars out of the mud!

The next day things got down to business at the motel, with Coast Guard and U.S. Engineer reports and river business.

Going back to the catfish, catfish "farming" had become a big business around Greenville. When flying into town, one could see all those rectangular ponds where they were raising the fish. The catfish farmers were having meetings at the motel.

The river industry was blessed by having in it men willing to spend a lot of time in Washington, D.C., on industry's behalf. Jesse Brent was one of these, and he did a most effective job.

The Port of Greenville was an active one under its director, Col. Barschdorf. It was there that he conceived the idea for one of the waterways' important organizations—Inland Rivers Ports and Terminals. He also tells about the development of Greenville in his book, *A History of an Inland River Port.*

Before leaving Greenville, mention must be made of its famous restaurant—Doe's. It is well-known all over the South, and in a nation-wide poll of eating places published in the St. Louis *Post-Dispatch*, Doe's came out No. 1 for steaks. It was an unusually plain place where patrons enter through the kitchen.

EXTRA

The Mississippi between the Mouth of the Missouri and the mouth of the Ohio River at Cairo, Illinois, is known as the "Steamboat Graveyard." It is estimated 268 wrecks lie in that reach, excluding St. Louis. There are big concentrations at Goose Island, Mile 161–172; Devil's Island, 55; Hat Island, 203–209; Liberty Island, 101–101.6; Turkey Island, 126.3–126; and Carroll's Island, 168. Boats were lost also at major landings such as Cape Girardeau, Ste. Genevieve and Commerce in Missouri, and Chester and Grand Tower in Illinois.   Jim

Chapter 19 ──

The Competition

*D*onald Wright was very allergic to competition. It made him angry and worried him. The river is not that large of a field for advertising, and he could see some of the money for the *Journal* going to someone else.

However, the other publications were monthlies, so it could be truthfully said that *The Waterways Journal* was the "only weekly river paper."

The major competitors were *Waterways* out of Pittsburgh; *Maritime Reporter* still publishing out of New York City; and later *WorkBoat*, then published in the New Orleans area. The Pittsburgh publication began as *National Waterways* and later became just *Waterways*. It was done, Donald said, to confuse people and make them think they were subscribing *to The Waterways Journal*.

John W. Black was publisher of *Waterways*, and he did a good job; it was well-printed and contained good pictures and articles. The problem was that Black had a tendency to enjoy his refreshments too much. There is one story that may or may not be true; as the story goes, at one MVA convention Andy Franz put him on a train back to Pittsburgh and had his magazine burned in the hotel's furnace.

There may have been some deep-seated animosity between Black and Wright that I don't know about, but at the time Donald took over the *Journal*, he got a letter containing best wishes from Black. But this changed. Another *Journal* story is that at a meeting in Pittsburgh Donald had Fred Way sit behind as a sort of body guard, because he was afraid Black was going to attack him.

Black did get after Donald later—in print. He accused him of getting his captain's license illegally, through connivance with high officials. Black did not mince words, among which were "a weasel." The reader can imagine the affect this tirade had at *The Waterways Journal*, at least in the publisher's office. What to do? The *Journal's* lawyer said, "Forget it. It will die." And it certainly did. I don't recall anyone ever bringing it up; those who did read it probably thought, and they were undoubtedly right, that Black was getting desperate to keep his paper going and hoped slander would hurt *The Waterways Journal*. The last issue I can remember of *Waterways* was January 1956.

Harry Peace started *WorkBoat* in the Greater New Orleans area to cover the Gulf Coast but, of course, a lot of people down there also had business up the rivers, so here was another competitor. This also made a problem for *Journal* writers, because there is a tendency to call towboats "workboats," but this would help call attention to the competing publication. The real test came when Harry Peace started to put together his WorkBoat Show. It was intended, I suppose, to rival the MVA expositions or be a Southern version of them.

Donald ignored the whole thing for a long time, but finally talk about it and questions from other river people as to if we were going to attend, etc., made him realize he had to do something. We had to know what was going on. We reserved a table, and I got the assignment to be there. I felt a little like a spy in enemy territory. The only thing I really remember about it was that at the pre-convention reception for exhibitors (held the night before the show opened) I was included because of the *Journal's* table. When I joined the food line I ended up right back of Harry Peace. Of course, some joker had to call out, "Hey Harry, do you know Jim Swift from *The Waterways Journal?*" Harry nodded with a steely smile.

There were other publications such as *Southern Marine Review*, *Motor Ship* (that became *Rivers and Harbors*), and *River Pilot*.

EXTRA

This is the 200th anniversary of the founding of the Library of Congress, which was put up under the direction of Gen. T. L. Casey of the Corps of Army Engineers. Somewhere in Washington, D.C., there is a gargoyle fashioned after a Corps officer who built the building it's in. (Maybe its the Library of Congress.) There was a towboat named for Gen. Casey; it ran in the St. Louis District.

Jim

Chapter 20 ——

Preserving History

A block up Locust Street from the *Journal* office was the St. Louis Mercantile Library. A private institution, it had been founded in 1846 to be the oldest library west of the Mississippi. It has a great collection on western history.

At lunch time it was a great place to go and do research. They had many publications from historical societies one could check monthly to see if there were any river-related articles in them.

The reference librarian, Elizabeth Tindle, kept a card catalogue of interesting items she saw in newspapers and other magazines. It was a source of leads for stories and projects.

In the *Journal* office there were many file cabinets full of valuable river material but not readily available to researchers and historians. Could it be made part of the Mercantile Library? Elizabeth Kirchner, Mercantile's chief librarian, thought so and so did the Board of Directors, at Mercantile. Ray Spencer agreed to the transfer and River Library was born.

I spent many early mornings sorting the material out before it was moved. The Herman T. Pott Foundation, established by the longtime president of St. Louis Ship generously donated money to develop the collection, and so the name is now the Herman T. Pott National Inland Waterways Library. (A long name but there is another library on the rivers at Cincinnati and it was thought best to use a title different from it.)

Peter Fanchi, Jr., former president of the Federal Barge Lines, has been chairman of the Pott Library Board of Directors.

Shortly after the River Library got started, the John W. Barriger III Railroad Library was founded, so Mercantile has become a real source of transportation history.

The River Library was augmented by the collection of Ruth Ferris who had collected a tremendous amount of river material as we have mentioned before.

My aim when promoting the library in the first place was to preserve modern river history, for the towboat era, so Ruth's collection has widened the scope.

Other collections have followed, including Federal Barge Line items; the Anton Drabik library on marine surveying, diving, ship repair, etc.; the collection of author Dorothy Heckmann Shrader of the famous Missouri River Heckmann family; the John A. Creedy papers; the Ray Covington photo collection; American Waterways Operators papers; the Capt. Thomas Kenny photo collection; and Chief of Engineer reports from 1874. *The Waterways Journal* has given the Library additional material from its "morgue" this being the newspaper clippings and documents used by the news editors in writing the stories carried by the paper. The Library has also become somewhat of a museum in itself, with the pilot wheel from the tug Susie Hazzard, the roof bell from the DPC steamer Buna, and a cannonball from the Civil War that damaged the gunboat Essex at Fort Donelson.

There is an outstanding collection of modern river watercolors by artist James Godwin Scott whose works are also on the covers of several Mercantile Library publications.

Mercantile has had two major projects underway, microfilming and indexing *The Waterways Journal*. When completed it will be a great asset to historians and genealogists and libraries everywhere.

For those interested in river ancestors, the *Journal* files are invaluable with hundreds of biographies on individuals, obituaries (for years the annual review issues listed deaths by dates) and registration lists from conventions giving the correct spelling of names and who they were affiliated with.

Because of financial and other problems the Mercantile Library has moved from its long time location in downtown St. Louis to the campus of the University of Missouri-St. Louis on Natural Bridge Road. There are advantages, of course, but to many it will never be the same library.

Among the advantages of the move is that the library's space has doubled, and it is available to the thousands of students at UMSL, as the University is nicknamed.

There was criticism that the new library location at 8001 Natural Bridge Road in St. Louis County (zip 63121-4499) was too inconvenient, but it is only a few blocks from Highway I-170. It is also close to Lambert International Airport; those facing lengthy plane delays, or those having lengthy layovers in St. Louis, could get to Mercantile Library easily.

In this age of fast communications,there are several ways to communicate with the library. Bette Gorden, curator of the Pott Library, has her own line—314-516-7244. The library's fax number is 314-516-7241, and her e-mail address is bgorden@umsl.edu. The library is also going on the Internet *with The Waterways Journal* collection guide and other materials.

At the university the Mercantile Library is in the Thomas Jefferson Library building. A new garage and entrance to Mercantile has been constructed.

The library has published *a Guide To The Research Collection of The Waterways Journal*, done by Ann Morris in 1989, and *The Waterways Journal Index, 1891-1900*. An index to later issues is underway.

Mercantile has a long history of inviting notable and interesting people to address the membership. A series of luncheon lectures was held downtown and continues at UMSL.

Mercantile Library published a very interesting book on its history in 1998, *Cultural Cornerstone: 1846-1998*, which has very good pictures pertaining to the past of the library and St. Louis. In addition to lists of officers and directors of Mercantile, the book contains a list of people who gave programs there. Notable writers and celebrities included Susan

B. Anthony, 1867 and 1875; H. W. Beecher, 1873, 1877, 1881, 1882 and 1884; Thomas H. Benton, 1850; Ralph Waldo Emerson, 1862 and 1867; Horace Greeley, 1870; Bret Harte, 1873; Harriet B. Stowe, 1873; Mark Twain, 1867 and 1885; Artemus Ward, 1864, 1865; Oscar Wilde, 1982; James Godwin Scott, 1986; and Tom Thumb, 1864, 1869, 1874 and 1882.

River personalities visiting Mercantile included Commodore Rollingpin (John Henton Carter), 1873, 1874 and 1879; Ben Lucian Burman, writer, 1984; Capt. William Carroll, 1983, 1984 and 1986; Peter Fanchi, Jr., 1991; Ruth Ferris, 1974; Tom Rollins, 1992; and Capt. Frederick Way, Jr., 1991.

There were some more exotic programs at the Mercantile, such as Aunt Polly's Basset's Singing Skewl, Berkley's Serenaders and Ethiopian Burlesque Opera Troupe, Christy Minstrels, Drieberthyesr's Swiss Bell Ringers, Koral Komic Kosume Koncert, Prussian Military Band, and Scottish Clans of St. Louis (concert). There were a number of minstrel shows.

John Neal Hoover, director of the St. Louis Mercantile Library, did this impressive collection guide.

Chapter 21 ——

On The River Road

*I*t was Donald Wright's philosophy that *Waterways Journal* advertisers should get a personal visit by a *Journal* staff member at least once a year. If you look back in the *Journal*, you will find reports from almost all of the male staff members who made such visits.

The best time for these calls were in the fall, as we were gearing up for the Annual Review Issue (better known as the Christmas Issue).

Donald, of course, and appropriately so, had the big places set out for himself—Pittsburgh, Cincinnati, Louisville and New Orleans. He wrote full accounts of his visits; by reading them you can get a good idea of river history. The same is true if you follow the stories of others, including those written by me and J. Mack Gamble.

Discovering Texas

I am not sure how Texas came into the *Journal*'s field, because it certainly wasn't on the rivers. It could have been because of the increasing number of southern boats coming north, or maybe visits to the Gulf Intracoastal Canal

Association conventions, but Donald began to realize this was a place we should go.

Through the years I had been slowly expanding my business trips to Alton, Illinois, Cape Girardeau, Missouri, and Paducah, Kentucky, but it was a bit hard even to visit those places close to St. Louis, as I had all the paper work to do at the office as well.

But then I got the chance to go down to Houston and the Gulf Coast. I went by train, of course, because as I mentioned previously, Donald was a railroad lover (at least for passenger trains) so it was the only way to go.

The Missouri Pacific ran the Texas Eagle south and, I must say, it was great lying in the berth watching the country roll by, and eating in the diner. The Texas Eagle was a long train that split at Palestine, Texas, some of the cars going to Fort Worth-Dallas and the rest to Houston; one even was switched off for Port Arthur, Texas.

The Rice Hotel was my headquarters in Houston; it was the big hotel then. I divided the territory up for time and convenience, doing downtown Houston one day, then going to Harrisburg and Greens Bayou.

Texas is a big place; the Houston area is really spread out, too. If you know Houston, you know how high the humidity is and also how hot it is; walk two blocks and you are soaked. I did as much as I could by walking and public transportation, because rental cars were not high on the *Journal*'s priority list.

After Houston there was the "Golden Triangle" of Orange, Beaumont and Port Arthur. There was much industry, shipbuilding and towing companies there, and they also were spread out.

One pleasant stop on the way from Houston to Port Arthur was always the White Heron Fish Fry at Liberty, Texas, on the Trinity River. They were enthusiastically backing the canalization of the Trinity to Dallas-Forth Worth, and this was an enjoyable visit.

The Fish Fry would also have a part in my most exciting Texas experience, really the most notable in all my travels. In 1961 in Port Arthur we began hearing advance reports of a hurricane. No one knew exactly where it was going to hit, but it was going to be around Houston and maybe east of there. People were getting ready, just in case. I stood on the levee along the ship channel and watched a procession of boats of all sizes and types heading inland to safety. It was quite a sight.

Heading back to Houston the next morning, I stopped off for the fish fry, and it was announced over the public address system that Port Arthur was to be evacuated. Fortunately there was another bus for Houston; I went back to the Rice and stayed for several days.

The oil companies had called in their people from the coast and had put them up at the Rice—along with their pets. There were all kinds of dogs running around, and the downstairs cafeteria was really full.

Carla came ashore at Pass Cavallo about 3 p.m. on September 11, with Matagorda Bay near Port O'Connor receiving the brunt of the storm; but the effect of the hurricane was felt from the Rio Grande to Grand Isle, Louisiana. The eye of the storm could be seen on television, and for awhile it looked like it was headed for Galveston.

You could hear the glass breaking in the store fronts along Main Street outside the Rice.

When it was over, I was on the scene to check on damage to the marine industry.

I must admit, now, that the first trip to Texas was not a financial success. I had not paid my way; it was my fault, because the trip was in April and my heart was not into selling ads for an issue in December; not understanding the importance of those sales was stupid.

Anyway, things were a bit frosty in the *Journal* office as Donald Wright examined my expense account, but then a miraculous thing happened. We had a visit from H. M. Robertson of Maxon Construction Company at Tell City, Indiana, who had been in Texas after me and praised my coverage of the area; he had used it as a guide. Now, I have mentioned how Donald could be very difficult and then do something very nice. And that is what happened. The coldness disappeared, and on the next trip he suggested I take Brunnhilda along at the *Journal's* expense. She could look for steamboat pictures at libraries while I called on the trade!

Along The Bayous

This trip would take us to another area I visited on occasion for the *Journal*, through the bayous of Louisiana, approaching

209

Texas from the east. I made those trips, to at least part of it, many times.

There was plenty of marine activity there, including towing, oil operations, fishing and shrimping. It came in cycles; one year the oil industry would be up and everyone was busy, but the next year oil production was done and people were singing the blues.

Houma and Morgan City were the most important places to visit; there was a particularly good mixture of industry there.

I still recall several things from that trip. We got into Baton Rouge and, naturally, headed for the river. A car came up behind us, and the gentleman in it asked if I was James Swift. It came as a great surprise to be addressed by name so far from home. It turned out to be Capt. Frank Leahy, who was doing the *Journal*'s work around New Orleans. He was a long-time friend of Donald's and a notable person in marine circles. I don't recall now if Donald had warned him that I was coming or not, or if he had read it in the *Journal*, but he knew where to look for me—down by the river! Mrs. Leahy was with him, and we had a most enjoyable evening.

Another thing I remember was spending the night in a large, white, wooden building that was used as sleeping quarters by men on oil-production sites; there weren't a lot of motels down there. Anyway, the bathroom was down the hall. About 5 a.m. the guys started to get up, clumping down the wooden floors in their boots.

A funny thing I recall was rolling up to the Rice with socks hanging out the window. I was trying to pull them in. I was running out of socks and had washed them. They weren't drying in the humid air, so I hung them over a coat hanger and out the car window, hoping the moving air would do the job.

Green as Grass

That was what I was on my first long business trip for the *Journal*—green as grass. I hadn't been on the road before, nor on any extended voyage.

It was decided that I was to tackle the lower Mississippi but not including, New Orleans. The first and worst mistake I made was not making advance reservations. That became evident quickly when I went into a motel at Hayti, Missouri, near Caruthersville. The desk clerk, in a soft southern voice, said,

"Oh, Sir, we have no rooms. This is the cotton picking season." This was pretty obvious, of course, for those giant cotton pickers were in the fields everywhere with those big round headlights blazing, but the lady continued, "There is a Holiday Inn Jr. down the road a few miles."

This place did have a room, and it is the only one like it that I ever have seen. The bathrooms probably came from a railroad car roomette, where things fold up. But it was a place for the night, and a lesson to me.

On the the subject of Holiday Inns, where I usually stayed, I never heard it said, but I am sure the idea came from the World War II movie with Bing Crosby (I saw it about ten times while I was in the service). Of those days a couple of things linger in my mind: the girl at the desk was always talking on the phone with a girl or boyfriend, while customers waited for service, and in the restaurant, even if it were empty, customers were always seated facing somebody at the next table.

Another memory of that trip: I called on a Mr. Hebert, who was a leader in the Mississippi Valley Association in Plaquemine, Louisiana. We had a pleasant conversation, during which I addressed him as Mr. Hebert. As I was leaving he said to me, "Son, you pronounce it Aybair."

A final lesson of this trip also came in Plaquemine. I stopped in for a cup of coffee at a cafe and got a little cup, a demitasse. Thinking what a cheap bunch the operators were, I drank it down quickly. As the rich mixture coursed through my stomach, I realized I had been introduced to chicory or cajun coffee and that it was supposed to be sipped.

Another leg of my travels included Cape Girardeau and Caruthersville in Missouri, Memphis in Tennessee; Greenville, Vicksburg and Natchez in Mississippi; and Baton Rouge and Plaquemine in Louisiana.

In Mack's Footsteps

One of the earliest correspondents for *The Waterways Journal* was J. Mack Gamble from Clarington, Ohio, on the upper Ohio River. His father had been a steamboat man who operated many boats. His son, being in education, did not go on the river, but he loved the river and kept the *Journal* up-to-date on news from that part of the Ohio.

Mack also made a yearly trip downstream to get news and ads for the Annual Review issue. His yearly visit became a part of life on the upper Ohio. But Donald's sharp eye on expenses led to a memorable event. Donald wouldn't pay Mack for getting his car washed at the end of his trip one year. Mack as much said, "Shove it!"

So here was another crisis—the Ohio River had to be covered. Guess who got the assignment. I left home on Labor Day to call on people from East Liverpool to Portsmouth, Ohio. During the first year I also called on some big advertisers like The Cooper-Bessemer Corporation, National Supply Company, Cummins Diesel Engine Company, and Maxon Construction Company, where offices were off the river in Dayton, Ohio.

The first stop on this eastern swing was the annual meeting of the Allegheny Valley Improvement Association, usually held on the Allegheny River at Oil City, Pennsylvania. I represented Donald, who was an officer and leader in the organization until his death. Then I was elected a vice-president, which was really strange when you come to think of it.

When I got to Marietta, Ohio, there was the annual meeting of the Sons & Daughters of Pioneer Rivermen, which was a bit bitter-sweet; everybody else was having a good time, and I was still working.

Those Ohio River trips were marred by mishaps, probably because it was the start of my travels for the year and I wasn't in the mood yet. One year my car blew a cylinder and I had to limp up those Pennsylvania hills to Oil City. Another year I had a tooth pulled before leaving home, and I had to go to a dentist on the first night out. Yet another year I pulled the handle off my suitcase at Marietta and, if that were not enough, my plumbing (as my wife would describe it) went bad and I had to visit the hospital emergency room at Marietta. I had been visiting the restroom at almost every firm I visited.

A highlight of the trip was seeing Mack in his big, white frame house on the hill at Clarington. His great collection of river pictures and artifacts could have kept me there for days. After his death I always blew a long whistle when I drove by his house.

With this kind of an itinerary I was gone from home from Labor Day to Thanksgiving except for a couple days.

One Ohio River trip feature I always looked forward to was a "steamboat" session at the Holiday Inn at Huntington, West Virginia. One year I came up with the idea of getting some kindred souls together. I contacted Jim Wallen, who did the *Ashland Oil Log* for Ashland Oil for many years; Bob Kennedy, Wallen's friend who wrote for *The Waterways Journal* out of Catlettsburg, Kentucky; Ben Gilbert, a genuine steamboat man originally from Paducah, Kentucky; and Capt. Harold Wright, a friend of Jim Wallen. We would have dinner and then adjourn to my motel room for a very interesting session on river matters. This annual get-together continued for several years.

The year 1965 was a pivotal one for *The Waterways Journal,* and two of my trips that year are noteworthy. H. N. Spencer, Jr., or "Ray" as he was always called, was in the process of buying the paper. To acquaint him with the river business, Donald asked me to take him with me on the Ohio River trip.

A high point was when, at Marietta, Durward Hoag of the Hotel Lafayette gave us the penthouse overlooking the Ohio River; the low points were the hotels we stayed in at Donald's suggestion. I don't think Donald had ever stayed in a motel; he remembered those hotels from his days of travel when they were the only place in town. As we were in the hotel in East Liverpool, with its torn shades, Ray said, "I'll never do this again!"

During the trip I would type my notes for the day, while Ray went for a walk. For a long time I didn't realize I was driving him out with my cigar, for I did smoke then, including cigarettes and a pipe. I got the cigar habit in the Army, because I would trade my cigarette rations for cigars, which most of the guys didn't care for. Amazingly enough, I was able to stop all of this smoking "cold turkey" when my wife developed respiratory problems.

The second trip of 1965 came about because, for the first time, Donald decided not to go to New Orleans. Perhaps he wasn't feeling well then. Anyway, the New Orleans trip was added to my schedule.

Donald also told me he would reserve his favorite room for me at the Roosevelt Hotel, a room the proprietors saved for him each year. When I saw it I know it wasn't for me, and

One way to promote the barge industry.

regardless of the expense account, I asked to be moved. His room, by the elevators, had a big round table in the center and a couch that opened out into a bed!

Donald had also arranged for me to take a trip back in the bayous with his good friend Capt. Barrett Woods, a marine surveyor for the notable New Orleans marine insurance firm Geo. S. Kausler Company. It was to be quite an experience. Barrett Woods had made friends with boat operators on the bayous when the Cajuns were getting into the towing business and knew nothing about insurance matters. Barrett had always helped them and worked well with them, and they liked him. With him was his associate, James Bond, whose license plate was, appropriately, 00–7.

I remember vividly one place we stopped. Barrett went into the captain's office, but when I started in the door was slammed in my face. I didn't know what to do for a minute; the office manager said, "Don't worry, the captain is having some marital problems that he wants to talk to Mr. Woods about."

The next stop was at the captain's house, where his wife called him the worst names I have ever heard. When, on the following year, I asked how the matter had turned out, the answer was, "Oh, they're doing fine. They're back in the house again."

For lunch we adjourned to a big white building on a hill...in Houma, I believe. The drinking went on and on, and I could see my schedule going to pieces with each round. But we had great seafood, and for me the trip was certainly one to remember.

214

Heading north, my longest run was from Baton Rouge to Memphis at night. Things were going all right until I got just outside of Greenville, where a tire went flat. The worst thing was that I found out I did not have a tool to take off the lug nuts. I tried to flag somebody down but without success. Then I saw the lights of a vehicle coming down a side road a short distance away. I ran toward it and flagged down what turned out to be a pickup pulling a trailer containing two white mules. The truck passengers were two hunters, who accompanied me back to my car. They not only furnished the lug-nut tool but also changed the tire! I hope they saw the letter of thanks which I later placed in the Greenville newspaper.

I continued my trip, but I wasn't feeling very well, and I got sicker as I drove. I bought a bottle of cough medicine and took a swallow of it from time to time. I was able to finish up in Memphis, though, and headed home. The doctor diagnosed it as walking pneumonia.

Then the telephone rang. It was Ray Spencer. Donald had died!

EXTRA

To find anything in the National Archives in Wash-ing-ton, one must know what to look for—which record group. Record groups are found in a three-volume "Guide to Federal Records in the National Archives of the United States." Vol. 3 is the index. There are 2,428 pages in the three books. Corps stuff is in Record Group 77; Coast Guard in RG 26, and Marine Inspection Service in 41.   Jim

Chapter 22 ──

The Christmas Issue

As I have explained before, the Annual Review and Directory Issue of *The Waterways Journal* was more often referred to as the Christmas Issue. It came out in the middle of December, and many advertisements in it had Christmas themes. Donald Wright also referred to it as the Mardi Gras issue; the boats often went to New Orleans during Mardi Gras, for what was hoped would be the biggest and most profitable trip of the year. The Christmas Issue was certainly the biggest of the year for the *Journal*.

All of those trips I have been describing were focused on this issue as far as advertising was concerned. My responsibility during this effort was to put together an ad dummy with all the ads in place. Because the issue was so large it required a series of multi-page forms, each of which had to be coordinated with the printers for press time. Because of the number of pages, the printing process went on during a two-week period prior to the publication date; two regular issues of the *Journal* were printed during that period as well. Working with the forms required getting ads with color in proper sequence for the presses. When the ad dummies were done, the news editor could tell how much space he had to fill. He had been preparing for the Christmas Issue for weeks.

Von Hoffmann Press at Ninth and Walnut streets in St. Louis did our printing and had done so for many years. The *Journal* was published letterpress in those days, which meant that everything in the book had to be converted to metal form—the news story type and the plates for the ads. One nightmare I had was when ad plates arrived late and I had to go to the Railway Express office to get them, praying that they would be there.

I may have already mentioned that during my first year with the Christmas Issue the book was all ready for publication except for a two-inch hole where an ad "cut" should have been. We went back to the office and tore it apart, trying unsuccessfully to find that cut. Providentially, somebody began checking pockets and found it in Capt. Sam Smith's overcoat. I certainly did feel sorry for Sam!

I don't know how it came about, but we were the only publication whose staff were allowed on the floor at Von Hoffmann's. In most printshops it is taboo for anyone to get anywhere near the type, other than those printshop employees who belong there. Being permitted there was a great convenience to us. For the regular *Journal* issues we would arrive in the morning about seven, read the new type that had been set overnight and the older type that had been corrected. We took necessary changes back to the linotype machines; each line had to be set in metal. The man in charge of these machines was none other than Don Summers. I am sure that it was his work on *The Waterways Journal* that led him to a life on the river, including a period as pilot on the Admiral and the New Orleans ferries.

At that time, the *Journal* was printed on Friday and mailed on Saturday. The final forms of the Christmas Issue were crucial ones, because the closer we got to deadline, the less time there was to allow for complications and corrections. Von Hoffman press time was allocated carefully to avoid idle presses. Any delay in our forms was going to cost us. Donald would come down for the finale and was given the royal treatment. He brought with him his little notebooks in which he had recorded changes in ads, such as new telephone numbers and addresses. He would check the press proofs to be sure all of these changes had been made. While he was doing that, the presses were being held idle, and we could see the price going up minute by minute. Once he had finished, the forms were rushed downstairs and the printing began.

Donald would then retire to the Mark Twain Hotel, leaving instructions that he wanted to see the forms when they were printed. About 2 a.m., I would hike over to the hotel and Donald would come to the door in his nightshirt. "All right," he said, smiling. I don't think he ever looked at the paper.

The Christmas Issue ran 196 pages in 1965 and was approximately in that range throughout the 1960s and 1970s.

With the big issue put to bed, and after a little relaxation, we would have the only staff meeting of the year. Donald would go through the issue page by page, and we hoped he wouldn't find something wrong and bring it to everyone's attention. But there was a good thing at the end—envelopes with Christmas bonuses in them!

Things were to change in the future, and we faced a crisis. Von Hoffmann announced that the firm would go into book production and stop doing work for customers like us. Fortunately, the other publication they had been doing, *The American Paint Journal*, agreed to print the WJ as well.

The other big change was that this was an offset operation. We didn't have to worry about hot metal anymore; the images would go directly to paper, making it unnecessary to transfer them first to copper or zinc plates. It freed up a lot of old boat pictures and also made obsolete some plates with old boat pictures we had already made.

My duties varied through the *Journal* years, as one can imagine with the small staff that we had. I even did the editorial for awhile. I was also the book-review editor, and I had the reviews in the paper often with my own byline. Into this column went all sorts of material, including pamphlets and literature from manufacturers and shipyards. I was able to introduce to the river industry a number of publications that today are deemed river classics.

Regarding the old boats, Donald liked to do them himself. In fact, many early issues were primarily old boat issues, with large pictures of steamboats illustrating the stories. In those days there really wasn't much else to write about.

When Roy L. Barkhau joined the staff he brought with him a love of river history and a lot of knowledge about steamboats, for he had worked with the Greene Line and knew a lot of Ohio River people. He did many of the old boat stories. (Roy also wrote a story about the Eagle Packet Company in booklet form and another on the race between the Robt. E. Lee and the Natchez.

It was when Roy left the *Journal* that I really got into the old boat stories. But, I did not have a byline until February 18, 1978, when I got one thanks to Jack Simpson. This means that, officially, I will have done 1,117 old boat columns by the end of July 2000.

When I retired I continued writing the old boat column, which got switched to the aft end of the book; but it is gratifying to hear that many readers go to the back of the paper first when they get their *Journal*.

I have tried to tie the old boat columns into current events like meetings, conventions and anniversaries. There is more than the old boat in the column, too—items such as meetings and notices of people looking for ancestors and boat information.

The Annual Review and Directory Issue is just what its name implies. A summary of the year's events. It also carries a lengthy article aptly titled The Annual Review. The principal review articles were first written by J. Mack Gamble, then Bob Kennedy after Mack's death, and later by Susan Eastman of Alton, Illinois. The men tended to be more interested in the construction end of the river business, and Mack was especially interested in the things that happened to the passenger-carrying fleet. Susan, to a greater extent, covers legislation and its impact on industry. The history of the rivers is there in The Annual Review issues.

These special issues also carry tables listing new boats, boat name changes, boats lost, and vessel pictures carried during that particular calendar year. (Dan Owen keeps up on the boat tables.) For many years the issue listed the names of river-related individuals who had died during the year. As space allows, each Annual Review Issue highlights important or interesting pictures that were published during the year and messages from Christmas cards sent by *Journal* readers.

Another column that highlights important activities of the year and lists them by date is "Do You Remember."

Branching Out

I heard through the famous "grapevine" that Capt. Frederick Way, Jr., in Sewickley, Pennsylvania, was thinking of retiring from publishing his *Inland River Record*, a book he had been publishing since 1945. It listed towing vessels and gave their history, horsepower, size, and other pertinent data.

It was a valuable asset to any inland marine operator and others doing business on the waterways. The *Record* (or IRR as it was often referred to) had grown in popularity each year since the first issue, which was not a great success. In fact, Capt. Way was so discouraged that he buried hundreds of unsold copies in his back yard.

It seemed to me that there was something *The Waterways Journal* could do to make sure the *Record* continued to be published.

Ray Spencer, our owner and publisher, agreed, and he contacted Fred Way. An agreement was reached, and since 1968 the *Inland River Record* has been a *Waterways Journal* publication.

Dan Owen, of East Liverpool, Ohio, had been working with Capt. Way on the *Record*, and he agreed to come to St. Louis to continue the work. He also brought with him a great collection of towboat pictures, which he had been taking since a teenager at Babbs Island in the Ohio River. These pictures of the "new" river augmented the large file of steamboat pictures that Capt. Wright and others had accumulated through the years.

Capt. Way was not totally happy about giving up his authorship of the *Record*, and he wrote some rather harsh comments about the new ownership.

Among the items that came across our desks over the years were publications for Great Lakes and Pacific Northwest consumption. The books listed various businesses such as shipyards, docks, ports, fueling services, etc.

Could such a list be useful on the inland waterways? The concensus was that it could. Shortly thereafter, the *Inland River Guide* came into being, and Dan Owen was given the additional task of compiling it.

The inland river terminals and dredging companies, which had been included in the *Record* for some years, were moved to the *Guide* (soon to be referred to as the IRG), which today also lists such things as fueling services, divers, surveyors, shipyards and marine repair facilities, insurance firms, etc. It is a loose-leaf book, while the *Record* is hardbound. The *Guide* has some 700 pages. An example of how the inland marine industry has grown is illustrated by the *Record*, which has about 500 pages; the 1945 edition had 147.

Many Loyal Friends

Throughout the years, *The Waterways Journal* was lucky to have many loyal friends, who sent in material from their respective areas so as to keep the newspaper up-to-date on what was going on. Capt. William H. "Steamboat Bill" Heckman, from Hermann, Missouri, submitted many stories in addition to news items. A young Fred Way contributed many stories. Columns were published almost every week by Frank L. Sibley, Gallipolis, Ohio, and George A. Zerr, Pittsburgh. Those with by-lines included:

Alfred C. Andersson, Memphis; Mabel Bartenhagen, Muscatine, Iowa; Virginia Bennett, Covington, Kentucky; Marion Bragg, Lower Mississippi; Claude Brown; Capt. H. T. Crouse, Hickman, Kentucky; Forrest Crutchfield, Paducah, Kentucky; Joe Curtis, Memphis; Parnin DeGaris, Cumberland;

Capt. Bert Edwards, Davenport, Iowa; Capt. Elmer Fancher, Cincinnati; Capt. Joseph Goold; Harold Henning, Cumberland; Charles S. Henry, St. Louis; Don Heuchan, Florida; Robert Kennedy, Upper Ohio; James H. Lavely, Illinois River; Ed McLeod, Memphis; Charles B. "Shep" Shepard, Greenville, Mississippi;

Frank L. Sibley, "Gallipolis Gossip"; George D. Stuart, Allegheny River; Capt. J. R. Tompkins, Tennessee River; Mr. and Mrs. Ralph E. Vennum, Paducah; Capt. Harris D. Underwood, Tennessee River; James Wallen, Huntington, West Virginia; C. A. Wetzel, Upper Mississippi; Roy A. Wykoff, Jr., Upper Mississippi; John Zenn, Allegheny River; and George A. Zerr, Pittsburgh.

Chapter 23 ——

Greater Than God?

*T*he word of God, as given to us in the Holy Bible, includes these words from the beginning, in *Genesis*, Verse 27:

> *"Then God said, "Let us make man in our image, after our likeness; and let them have domination over the fish of the sea, and over the birds of the air and over the cattle, and over all the earth, and over every creeping thing that creeps upon the earth."*

We find today that mankind is dominated by the welfare of such things as snail darters, spotted owls, pearly shelled mussels, clawed frogs, Alabama sturgeon, and furbish louseworts.

An innocent book, *Silent Spring*, written by Rachel Carson, was published in 1962. It was to revolutionize everything, including government and business during the years following, for it was the first step in building up the religion of the "environment."

I should explain that I love nature and don't like waste and pollution and wanton destruction of the land, but I think it has been taken too far. Organizations have been formed that have this cause; the officers of these groups are making a living out of the environment, and they are never going to let it go, even when they have been proved wrong. When budget time comes they are bound to start another campaign declaring a river is the worst polluted in the country, another animal is close to extinction, and so on. They need money to keep the organizations going.

I saw a threat to the waterways as the environmental movement grew and, indeed, I spent a lot of time writing letters to Congress and the press to combat this movement, which seemed to be against progress. It seems to me that they (the environmentalists) just don't like people. I didn't have the complete backing in this campaign from Ray Spencer, who thought my time would be better spent on other things. But it was I who had the duty to tell him that the environmentalists had stopped the rebuilding of a new lock and dam on the upper Mississippi River at Alton, Illinois. The case of Locks and Dam 26 remains one of the biggest actions yet taken against the waterways industry.

The pet enemy of the Sierra Club and its friends remains the U.S. Army Corps of Engineers, because of their dam building, and since the biggest customer of the Corps is the barge and towing industry, we, too, became the enemy.

The first objective of these people was to stop the spread of navigation to waterways not yet developed. And, they were successful in stopping the Trinity project to Fort Worth and Dallas, a link of the Gulf Intracoastal Canal along the west coast of Florida, and worst of all, the Cross-Florida Barge Canal, which was already partially done. It is hard to estimate how much taxpayers' money was lost in the killing of those projects through surveys, public meetings, and reports, not to say how much benefit continues to be lost because shippers are denied the benefits of water transportation on these routes.

Locks and Dam 26 had become a great bottleneck, because its 600-foot main lock and 360-foot auxiliary chambers could not handle the traffic that came down the upper Mississippi

Courtesy of The Waterways Journal

Looking downstream from Locks and Dam 26 in April 16, 1976.

and Illinois rivers. The same was true for upbound tows. There were waits of many hours, with towing companies losing money every minute.

The St. Louis District of the Corps of Engineers was set to accept bids on the Locks and Dam 26 replacement project, when 21 western railroads, the Sierra Club and the Izaac Walton League filed a lawsuit in Federal District Court, asking for an injunction to stop the project. The bid-opening was, in fact, halted. Those planning to attend the opening in August, arrived at the established bid-opening site, only to discover a sign stating that it was postponed to September 4, 1974. The case was assigned to Federal Judge Charles R. Richey. Separate suits had been filed originally, but the court ordered them combined. This resulted, appropriately, in the plaintiffs being labeled as "strange bedfellows."

There was heated debate on the Locks and Dam 26 project in Congress, in the press, and in numerous hearings held by the Corps and private organizations. The case even went to the U.S. Supreme Court. It was not until November 13, 1978, that the U.S. House of Representatives passed H.R. 8537 to appropriate money for the project. But the river industry paid a price. User fees were included in the legislation.

The price for the long delay, the lawyers fees, hearings, meetings, travel, and delayed tows is estimated to be $1.1 billion.

Reports on the hearings, environmental impact statements and press reports on the Locks and Dam 26 case, plus the briefs filed by the railroads and environmental organizations are in the Herman T. Pott National Inland Waterways Library at the St. Louis Mercantile Library.

The building of a bigger lock would mean increased traffic on the upper river, environmentalists contended, and would hurt the fish and wildlife on it. They could not understand, or didn't want to, that there would not be any more traffic, that tows moving north would not have to waste money waiting for lockage.

Courtesy of the St. Louis Engineer District

The Corps used this crack in the wall of one cell to help promote a replacement for Locks and Dam 26.

The upper Mississippi is a beautiful river, which has been called "The Rival of the Rhine" because of its scenery, wide expanse of water in places, and many islands. But despite this, the upper Mississippi has been the subject of the greatest number of environmental studies of any river in the country.

The Upper Mississippi River Basin Association has been studying this river for years, and is continually coming up with some new angle that members say needs study and analysis. It appears to me that it is a group of people who are enjoying travel and meetings at the public's expense for things that don't really need to be done. They are in the U.S. Engineers' way all the time in what appears to be perpetual search for perfection.

There is a proliferation of environmental groups, nonprofit, that are syphoning money away from organizations that are working to help mankind live a better and more healthful life.

You must be very careful to study and understand what these environmentalists propose. I recall the time when I went to one of the early meetings of the upper Mississippi group, at which a Coast Guard officer was the representative of the towing industry, since he was from the Department of Transportation. He came out practically in tears he was so mad; while he was out of the room they tried to change rules on dredging that would have hindered river maintenance.

While I do not recall specifically which group meeting I attended, it might have been one of the newly established Great River Environmental Action Teams, of which there were three. According to some industry spokesmen, team membership was monopolized by environmentalists. One person told us that when a team member could not attend a meeting, his alternate could, but he could not vote. Fair play apparently was not the order of the day.

The other upper Mississippi River locks above Alton also have 600-foot chambers and no auxiliary chambers. The congestion has moved up the river, and the locks are getting old—50 to 60 years old. The river industry would like to see those locks enlarged to accommodate today's traffic, and a comprehensive study is underway of both the Upper Mississippi and Illinois rivers.

The feeling among many is that if the recommendation is for building new and larger locks, there will be another lawsuit by the environmentalists to stop the projects, undoubtedly joined by the railroads, as was the case with the Locks and Dam 26 lawsuit.

Having stopped the spread of navigable waterways, there appears to be a move to get commercial transportation off rivers completely. The Missouri River is the present target; many published articles have attacked improvements on this river. The use of water from the upstream reservoirs is being questioned, because it interferes with recreational use of the lakes in the northern states in the Missouri Basin.

The release of water for barge traffic is also in question, because higher flows interfere with the nesting of birds such as plovers. The Corps is working on a new manual to govern the use of the Missouri River.

This reference to the plovers leads into the endangered species part of this chapter. It would appear that the creation of the Endangered Species Act was engineered as a convenient way to stop projects. If you don't want something built, find a fish, bird, flower or animal that is rare and you can stop it. One encyclopedia says there are 1,075 endangered species on the list (probably more now) and you can bet many are there because the environmentalists opposed the building of something. New listings are being proposed frequently.

These can be frivolous like the snail darters that almost killed the Tellico Dam project in Eastern Tennessee in the late 1970s. After delays and litigation and lots of publicity about the little fish, someone found in November of that year that there were snail darters in other rivers in the area, including the Hiwassee. This did not occur, however, until after much legal rangling. The U.S. Supreme Court agreed late in 1977 to review the snail darter and dam issues. The U.S. Court of Appeals for the Sixth Circuit had ruled against the dam in late January. The controversy was ultimately brought to an end when word spread that the tiny fish was no longer endangered. But the $116 million project, virtually completed at the time of the discovery of the snail darter in 1973, was held up for the better part of a decade at considerable expense.

As frustrating as the environmental intervention must have been for supporters of the Tellico Dam, some incidents occurred that added a touch of humor to the issue. Snail darters were displayed in tiny vials by individuals appearing before various groups to support the dam. Cartoonist Johnny Hart featured the snail darter in an installment of his B.C. comic strip. It was not humorous, however, when an employee of the Fish and Wildlife Service attempted to transfer 98 snail darters from the Little Tennessee River; he used a contaminated pail, and all of the fish died. That, too, drew headlines.

The snail darter issue was similar to many in the past where a specie thought to be endangered was used by environmentalists as a weapon to shut down multi-million-dollar projects with which they disagreed. One example cited by the *Journal* on numerous occasions was that involving a proposed industrial park at Houston, Texas. Over the years, the habitat of the Houston toad had virtually disappeared. No one had spotted one in more than a decade. Yet the EPA used the Houston toad to stop the industrial park in its tracks. The valuable development was abandoned—at least at that site.

What rose out of many frustrations of the past, capped by the snail darter incident, was the establishment of a special seven-person committee to review the Tellico Dam project and one in Wyoming. This was accomplished by amending the Endangered Species Act in a manner that would exempt both projects if the committee did not vote otherwise. When committee appointments were not finalized within the prescribed 30 days, the exemptions became final. We never heard about the committee again.

With the wide range of climate and types of land and water cover in the nation, these endangered species could be transplanted from the area they are in and be saved. That is the idea of zoo and wild animal parks. Many species can be preserved in habitats where they would be safer than they would be in the wild.

There is a particular move underway now to "save" mussels from propeller wash and sediment. And I ask you: What is so important about something you can't see, you can't eat, and you cannot find a use for? Of course, there are varieties that can be used for buttons and producing pearls, but these are not the endangered variety.

One of the few humorous things that have occurred since the beginning of the environment movement came with the Cro-Con Canal incident. *The Waterways Journal* editorial on the subject reflects the attitudes of that time about what was taking place.

Don't Believe Everything

We have pointed out before that everything the environmentalists have been saying about our planet, pollution, and the U.S. Engineers, doesn't have to be swallowed, hook, line and sinker. You can still doubt some of their statements and not be judged anti-motherhood, anti-American and Communistic. We have even gone so far as to say the readers of "Editor and Publisher" screen environmental statements.

Now we have proof that some newspapermen, and news gathering organizations, can be gullible. We're speaking now of the Sierra Club's infamous Cro-Con Canal.

Jonathan Ela, midwestern representative for the Sierra Club, came up with a study in the "Sierra News" recently entitled "From Sea to Shining Sea." Or "Through the Rockies at 31 Knots." "Conservationists are expressing concern," Mr. Ela wrote, (with tongue in cheek?) "over a proposal just announced to construct a Cross-Continental Barge Canal linking Boston with San Diego. The joint project of the U.S. Engineers and the Atomic Energy Commission would be the largest public works ever constructed in the U.S...." The story goes on to say that the proposal of the canal is to float aircraft carriers across the country (they are now too big to go through the Panama Canal), enhance the capacity to transport coal, and make deep-water ports of such cities as Cincinnati, Louisville, Tulsa and Aspen, Colo.

The effect of this proposal (said to be contained in an Engineer "Preliminary Framework Analysis" of 610 pages) upon the environment can easily be predicted. (A Xerox copy of a map of the project—also shown in the article—was said to have been procured by a disgruntled associate of Jack Anderson). In answer to the critics of the canal, Mr. Ela quotes Lt. Gen. R. R. "Brute" Thwackem, the Corps of Engineers public relations as saying, in part, "...no posy-plucker is going t tell us how to run our shop."

It makes amusing reading but unfortunately some newspaper people didn't see it as a farce and the Cron-Con has now been blasted as if it was a real thing. Lt. Gen. Frederick J. Clarke, Chief of Engineers, in a speech in Alaska August 4, took notice of the story and told the audience that "General Thwackem is doing a fine job for the Corps in mapping the route of the canal, carrying only a compass and a slide rule. Actually the author may be guilty of a breach of security because the Navy has a TOP SECRET classification on the plans to send aircraft carriers through the Rockies at 31 knots."

We'd say at least two things should be learned from this story. One, some environmentalists do have a sense of humor, and second, newspapermen should take some ecology statements with a grain of salt.

I want to assure readers that I am a nature lover, in spite of the harsh things I have written in this chapter about environmentalists. I like green areas and birds, etc., but there is a limit to this. Unfortunately, it is the people on the fringe that have brought the very name "environmentalist" into disfavor with many people. In protecting the environment, reason must be used so people can live, work and travel with impunity.

One major complaint by the scientists who take issue with some environmental findings is that environmental scientists frequently use what is called "pseudoscience," that is, their unsupported conclusions are presented as fact but are not shared with other scientists for evaluation beforehand.

It must disturb many environmentalists to see all those kids in the McDonalds, Burger Kings and other fast-food places. They are all going to need places to live when they grow up and take over more land. There is a move to get people out of the flood plains and turn them over to nature, but if these people move out, they will have to go to higher ground and cut down trees to build homes. That won't be good either.

There is a need to talk, not fight, about these things. There must be compromise.

EXTRA

Steamboat travel could be deadly. Records show there were some 111 accidents in the 1800's in which 10 or more people were killed. The explosion of the Sultana (April 25, 1865. above Memphis) was one of the worst. It had been carrying Union troops home from Confederate prison camps when the boiler(s) blew. Some 4,975 other people died in major mishaps on the Mississippi River System (45 boats burned, 19 were snagged, 18 were lost in collisions, two sank and one was stranded.)

Jim

Chapter 24 ——

The Bubble Bursts

*T*he river industry had smooth sailing through the years until the 1970s, when it ran into snags—the environmental movements first, and then the user taxes (fuel tax) that came with the Locks and Dam 26 fight.

But the worst was yet to come. In 1979 the Russians invaded Afghanistan, and President Jimmy Carter imposed an embargo on grain going to Russia from the United States. It may have hurt Russia, but it certainly did hurt the American farmer; other countries stepped in to sell the grain, and America lost grain markets it never got back.

To the river industry it was devastating. Millions of tons of cargo was lost overnight. Bob Kennedy, in his "Annual Review" for 1979, had this to say:

> John W. Lambert, chairman of the board and chief executive officer of Twin City Barge & Towing Company, spoke to the Minnesota Farm Bureau Federation on December 7, 1979, at its 61st annual meeting held at Bloomington, Minn.
>
> In making a comparison, Mr. Lambert said, "One hundred and two years ago Gen. George Armstrong

Custer led his Seventh Cavalry into an ambush at the Little Big Horn. As his 220 some troopers were surrounded by some 4,000 Sioux and Cheyenne, one of his junior officers pleaded, 'My God General, what are we going to do?'

"Custer, outnumbered 20 to 1, snapped back the command 'Take no prisoners!'"

He continued by saying, "This illustrates the fact that it is often hard to gain a proper perspective in the midst of chaos.

"Chaos is what we have today in agricultural transportation and government seems incapable of putting the problems into perspective. And based on the outlook for 1980, things aren't going to get any better for transportation than they did for General Custer."

At the time this happened, the industry had geared up for a rosy future as predicted by government forecasters. It was so rosy in fact, that it seemed the shipyards would be unable to supply the equipment needed to handle the increased tonnage. At the *Journal* we were happy to use this prediction with potential advertisers and shippers.

The Kearney Consultants report projected that the total transportation market was to increase by 121 percent by the year 2000, and on the inland waterways to 868,821,100 tons. Fleet requirements by 2000 would be 4,000 to 5,000 towboats, 20,000 to 25,000 dry cargo barges, and 3,500 to 4,000 tank barges.

The marine brokers had also used these predictions and had sold barges as a good investment to people outside the industry (such as doctors and lawyers), financed the construction of barges as a long-term investment and waited for the money to come in.

But now, the freight had evaporated and the barges were sitting idle.

This all was devastating for the river shipyards, too. The operators looked into the future, and they could see no business coming in for the immediate future. There was nothing to do but shut down. It was hard to believe, but Dravo, St. Louis Ship and its affiliate Paducah Marine Ways all closed. Jeffboat cut back but kept operating.

Now, all these were big advertisers in *The Waterways Journal*, so one can well imagine the effect on the paper's revenue and size.

There was also trouble on the upper Ohio River. The steel mills were closing all along not only the Ohio but also along the Monongahela, and with these closing went the towage of coal, and steel going south for export. This was, of course, offset to some extent by the steel coming in from abroad, which was the cause of the domestic steel production dropping off.

The smaller yards, such as those in the Louisiana area, did not feel the blow from the lack of business as much as the bigger yards. They continued to build smaller craft such as excursion boats, and to fill the needs of increasing commerce on casino boats.

All through the troublesome period consolidation was rampant within the industry. The number of firms in industry today stands at about one-third what it once was.

In 1999, the building of barges and some towing vessels is coming back; Jeffboat, which held on during the lean times, is turning out many, as is Trinity Marine Products, headquartered in Dallas, Texas.

EXTRA

To and from St. Louis my parents rode the packets, including the Belle of Calhoun. As my mother recalled, her decks were often underwater from the weight of the barrels of Calhoun County apples she was bringing into St. Louis. Another packet was the Cape Girardeau. My mother recalled that Capt. William "Buck" Leyhe warned her to be careful as she left the boat. When the Cape sank at Fort Gage, Illinois, (October 21, 1916), some of the chairs were rescued from the river for our houseboat.   Jim

Chapter 25 ——

The Agencies

*T*he two government agencies most affecting the water-way industry are the U.S. Army Corps of Engineers and the U.S. Coast Guard

We met the Engineers earlier in their role of clearing the rivers of snags and building the locks and dams. Their mission today, as shown on the next page, was taken from the *Inland River Guide*.

THE CORPS OF ENGINEERS
U. S. ARMY

STATEMENT OF MISSION

- Investigates, plans, designs, constructs, operates and maintains improvements of rivers, harbors, and other waterways for navigation, flood control, recreation, and other water uses and related purposes.

- Administers the laws for the protection and preservation of the navigable waters of the United States including water pollution control.

- Directs emergency flood control operations in connection with potential or actual flood conditions, and collects information of flood states and flood damage.

- Collects and forwards to appropriate authorities information on waterborne commerce.

The Corps is now involved in two big projects on the water-ways, one on the Missouri River, where a plan is being developed to organize a new Missouri River Operating Manual, and on the upper Mississippi River, to plan a new maintenance and operating plan, the latter with a hope of alleviating delays at the old and small locks (see Chapter 23).

The Engineers on the Missouri have a problem not only with the environmentalists, who would like to see navigation off the Missouri, but also with the Indian tribes who are asking for water rights, and the politicians of the upper Missouri States, who want to see the big reservoir always full for recreational purposes no matter what happens down-river.

The Illinois-Upper Mississippi study seems to be going around in circles, with neither the industry nor the environmental side about to accept all the Corps' proposals.

The Corps and industry worked together for a long time, in a lawful way, but unfortunately things have changed. The older people in the Engineers have retired and it seems that many of the newer staff members do not have the enthusiasm for commercial navigation that their predecessors did. Some now see the Corps as an enemy—not a helper.

There are, constantly, proposals to consolidate Corps districts and make changes in territory, etc., but at this time the structure on the inland waterways is:

Great Lakes and Ohio River Division (Cincinnati, Ohio)

> Chicago Engineer District
> Huntington Engineer District
> Louisville Engineer District
> Nashville Engineer District
> Pittsburgh Engineer District

Mississippi Valley Engineer Division (Vicksburg, Mississippi)

Memphis Engineer District
New Orleans Engineer District
Rock Island Engineer District
St. Louis Engineer District
St. Paul Engineer District
Vicksburg Engineer District

Southwestern Engineer Division (Dallas, Texas)

Fort Worth Engineer District
Galveston Engineer District
Little Rock Engineer District
Tulsa Engineer District

Northwestern Engineer Division (Portland, Oregon)

Missouri River Regional Headquarters (Omaha, Nebraska)
Kansas City Engineer District
Omaha Engineer District
Portland Engineer District

South Atlantic Engineer Division (Atlanta, George)

Mobile Engineer District

The Coast Guard came on the rivers with President Franklin D. Roosevelt's influence, taking under its wing the various agencies that operated with civilian crews. To many, the trouble with this military role is that there is a constant change in personnel, while the civilians stayed put and got to know the territory. A standing joke is that by the time a Coast Guard officer has

The Coast Guard

learned the ropes, he is transferred out to far distant places. Most of the people coming in don't know anything about river craft and river conditions.

The Coast Guard took over the steamboat inspection service and the U.S. Lighthouse Service, the latter in July 1939, just after the Lighthouse Service's 100th anniversary on the rivers. It had started 50 years before that on the coasts. Known as the 15th District, it's superintendent was Walter G. Will, and it was headquartered in St. Louis.

The Coast Guard organized its operations according to the system of Naval Districts already in place. The Second Coast Guard District, with headquarters in St. Louis, was the largest in the lower 48 states, encompassing 22 states. All matters relating to the Mississippi River system above Baton Rouge were supervised by this office. In 1996, bowing to budgetary pressure, the Coast Guard decommissioned the Second District office and attached its territory to the Eighth District headquartered in New Orleans. Many in the inland industry felt that the Coast Guard was abandoning the river system. As a compromise, the Coast Guard agreed to place a senior officer in St. Louis who would supervise river operations and work with the river industry. This officer, called the Director of Western Rivers Operations, reported to the District Commander in New Orleans. The compromise proved only temporary, however; for while there are marine safety offices, groups and detachments throughout the region, the agency moved all operational supervision to New Orleans in mid-1999. A senior staff officer there now has collateral responsibility for liaison with river interests.

Backing Hard Into River History

The Coast Guard Mission, again as it appears in the *Inland River Guide*, is as follows:

> Protects the environment through a comprehensive
> Program of preventive regulation, inspection
> Response, and enforcement.

> •

> Responds to emergencies caused by man-made or
> Natural disasters with active duty and reserve
> Personnel trained in waterborne rescue operations.

> •

> Promotes the safety of recreational boating by
> Establishing mandatory construction and equipment
> Standards and directing a comprehensive program
> Of boating safety education by Coast Guard and
> Coast Guard Auxiliary personnel.

> *

> Supervises the safe design, construction, and
> Operation of tank and hazardous cargo barges and
> The licensing of towboat operators and tankermen.

The Engineers, aware that the agency needed the expertise of its "customers," began holding navigation conferences during the annual Mississippi Valley Association meetings in St. Louis. (It was always a question as to the first year this was done. Jim Peterson, head of the operations section for the St. Louis Engineer District, kept asking me the question and, unfortunately, I had to admit I didn't know, having forgotten to look it up.)

Anyway, heads of different sections would discuss at these conferences current projects and future work in dredging, lock and dam operations, dike and shore construction and the like.

Representatives were present from the other districts and divisions to describe what was going on in their areas. Members of the river industry gave their opinions on what the Corps was doing or planning. A report especially awaited was that from the Missouri River Division, because it dealt with how much water there was in the reservoirs; this affected not only the Missouri

River navigation but also navigation on the Mississippi between the mouth of the Missouri and Cairo, Illinois.

There was some emotion shown at the Engineers' session, but nothing like that at the "Industry Days" begun by the Coast Guard. The Coast Guard had so many rules and regulations on vessel inspections, pollution control, vessel construction, marine sanitation, and rules of the road that it is easy to see where there would be conflicts. They got pretty heated at times; the Coast Guard hated to see people like Capt. Charles Lehman, Capt. Edgar Allen "Wamp" Poe, Frank Stegbauer and Jack Lambert stand up, for it almost always spelled trouble.

Bridges across rivers often spelled trouble for the towing industry, especially railroad bridges that had to be opened to let tows pass. The Coast Guard also inherited the headache of overseeing bridges. The Bridge Branch was then headed by Stan Thoroughman, who had a fantastic memory; he would rattle off the bridges on all the rivers, giving their current status as far as construction, problems with guard structures, complaints with openings, etc. Then would come the comments from the audience; they would go on and on, to the annoyance of the marine inspection people whose program it really was. Because of these complaints, the operations of a lot of the bridges did improve and some were reconstructed.

Roger Weibusch took over the Bridge Branch when Stan retired.

These meetings took two days, and the two agencies cooperated on them; the Coast Guard would go first one year, and the Corps first the next. At first the Coast Guard was not prepared for such conferences and had to borrow the Corps' sound systems and operators. Following the demise of the Water Resource Council (which had taken over the MVA), the conferences were held independently in St. Louis, but now they are moved around, often to Louisville.

Looking back at those early Industry Days, often there was disagreement within the river industry as to the policies and practices between the Second District (covering the brown-water vessels) and the Eighth District, which had more to do with the blue-water operations. What will happen now that the Eighth District is in charge?

The Maritime Administration

The U.S. Maritime Administration, under the Department of Transportation, calls itself the "good agency," because the river industry doesn't have to worry about it imposing rules and regulations.

MarAd, as it is usually called, is best known for its administration of the Title XI program, which guarantees the financing of merchant vessels, including those on the inland waterways. MarAd has been doing this for 44 years (without any direct cost to the taxpayer) using funds obtained through the issuance of private corporate bonds.

The agency issues an annual report in which it reports on shipbuilding, with major contracts awarded, vessels on order, delivered, Title XI guarantees, capital construction and construction reserve funds, shipyard improvements and crane and school ships; ship operations, with a U.S. fleet profile, operating-differential subsidies, passenger/cruise service, foreign transfers, and environmental protection such as incinerator and asbestos control; domestic operations on the inland waterways and Great Lakes; market development; port and intermodal development; research and development in shipbuilding, ship machinery, fleet management technology, ship performance and safety, cargo systems, advanced ship systems, marine science, Arctic shipping and university research; marine labor and training; and national security, marine insurance, emergency operations, reserve fleet, ship sales and exchanges for scrap, and war risk insurance. MarAd also has maritime relations with China, discussions with the Philipines, Brazil, Iceland and Malaysia, and has consultants with Japan.

So MarAd, busy with maritime matters, publishes a number of reports, including financial data on ports and terminals, and has legal, legislative and litigation services.

Robert G. Goodwin, Jr., is MarAd's midwestern representative in St. Louis.

Chapter 26 ⸺

Saving The Past

*T*o a river historian, saving papers and relics dealing with past steamboat days, and now towboat days, is an important challenge. To many a river wife the river was her greatest challenge, for it took her husband away from her for long periods at a time, and he thought about that a lot whenever he was home. At the death of their husbands not a few widows had revenge—their husand's river stuff went in the furnace or trash can—a real nightmare for those who want to keep the river record straight!

Fortunately many wives don't feel that way and are as much a part of the river heritage as their husbands (some even worked on the boats as cooks or maids). There are organizations and museums that are pleased to receive and preserve this heritage.

The granddaddy of them all is the Sons and Daughters of Pioneer Rivermen. How did it get started? Let us go to Frederick Way, Jr.'s account in the first issue of the *S&D Reflector*, 2 March, 1964:

> The idea of S&D originated with a school teacher in Clarington, O., Miss Elizabeth Litton. Her inspira-

tion brought together a small group, not over a dozen, at the Hotel Lafayette, Gallipolis, O., on June 3, 1939. Capt. And Mrs. Phil C. Elsey were there and it is noteworthy that Capt. Phil picked up the check for the dinner party—the first and last time an individual played host. Miss Litton's objective was an annual river get-together, something like a family reunion. J. Mack Gamble suggested the name, Sons and Daughters of Pioneer Rivermen. Officers selected there at Gallipolis were: J. Mack Gamble, president; Capt. Phil C. Elsey, vice president; Elizabeth Litton, secretary; Ben D. Richardson, treasurer; Capt. Mary B. Greene, honorary president. An executive committee was appointed with three members: B. L. Barton, Bert Noll and J. W. Zenn.

The first annual meeting was held later that same fall, on September 10, 1939, in the Riverview Room at the Hotel Lafayette, Marietta, O. About 30 or 40 persons attended. There were informal talks and a few songs were sung. I well remember suggesting that a permanent River Museum would serve to bond the organization, an idea hatched the year prior at Pittsburgh. Mrs. Edith S. Reiter was in the audience and promptly invited S&D to consider placing such a Museum at Campus Martius where she was the curator. J. Mack Gamble was asked to prepare a constitution and also, at this first formal meeting, the S&D insignia, a pilotwheel enclosing a headlight, was adopted.

The incentive to build a River Museum really dates to September, 1938. Pittsburgh at that time was celebrating the sesquicentennial of Allegheny County. Capt. William B. Rodgers (Jr.) was chairman of the River Committee and he decided to display river relics in the old Music Hall near the Point. The building was in bad repair, a dismal place at best; the lighting was inadequate, the hall was clammy and cold. John W. Zenn, J. W. Rutter and I were involved in the actual work. We formed display tables of rough-cut lumber held up on sawhorses. Nevertheless, during the three weeks the show was on some 20,000 persons viewed the steamboat models built by Robert Thomas and others, the section of a coalboat built by "Sandbar" Zenn, the enormous pilotwheel from the towboat Boaz, and an attractive array of pictures and photographs.

These exhibits of course were on loan. Soon as the show was over everything was returned to the good persons who owned the material, most of whom said they were willing to donate these things if a permanent museum could be arranged for.

Capt. Tom Greene expressed hope that the museum would be in Cincinnati, and B. L. Barton and others were for an historic house in Bellaire, Ohio. Mrs. Reiter showed the group a room in the basement of the Campus Martius Museum in Marietta, and it was there that the museum was placed. (The second S&D meeting was held in New Martinsville, W.Va., in the fall of 1940. Ben D. Richardson, Malta, Ohio, was elected president.)

A Museum Committee, headed by William Knox Richardson, Marietta, had unanimously recommended the Campus Martius site, and some of those who wanted the museum at Bellaire withdrew from S&D.

The museum opened on March 16, 1941. At 2:30 p.m., master of ceremonies Mack Gamble formally introduced the celebrities; some had to stand because chairs had not been provided. Robert G. Thomas had made the stands and railings and gave the museum some of his models.

A dinner followed at the Lafayette Hotel and the March 1991 issue of the *Reflector* carried pictures of the people present, an interesting view of some prominent members of S&D at an early age.

Campus Martius was run by the Ohio State Archaeological and Historical Society (now the Ohio Historical Society) and it soon became apparent that there were more river relics than would fit in the original museum. The result was the construction of the present Ohio River Museum, one of the most interesting on the rivers, with hundreds of models, paintings, and artifacts from both the steam packet and towboat eras.

Moored on the Muskingum River below the museum is the genuine steam towboat W. P. Snyder Jr., donated by Crucible Steel Company. It is open to the public so viewers can see what a towboat looks like.

Fred Way became president of S&D in 1941 and was the catalyst for bringing people to the annual S&D meetings. There was usually a surprise at the sessions, and even Fred wasn't sure what was going to occur. The meetings were at Marietta in September, now the third Saturday, with the Hotel Lafayette as headquarters.

There were the Saturday morning business meetings that were pretty lively, especially if there was a raise in dues or something like that on the agenda. Then there would be considerable comment from people like Mack Gamble or John Zenn that would make things very interesting.

The luncheons were held out-of-doors at the Marietta Yacht Club, with food served picnic style. The banquet was served in the Lafayette in what is now the bar room. With this little space there would be a throng of people trying to get a table; many didn't and had to eat elsewhere. Now, with the expanded banquet room, there is no problem accommodating them.

In those early days there was no reception on Friday nights before the meeting, and if you were not in a group, you were pretty much left out. The Lafayette's dining room was booked up and you had to find a place elsewhere to eat, which wasn't easy in Marietta. (The Becky Thatcher hadn't arrived yet.)

For me, there were some memorable S&D meetings. Donald Wright was miffed that he hadn't been asked to speak at S&D, and when he finally was, he sent me—out of spite or because of some legitimate reason. I was to read his speech. I was, of course, nervous to start with, and then the waitress dumped a dish of succotash on me. When I pulled out my pocket handkerchief, corn and beans sprayed everywhere. I got through the presentation all right, especially where Donald had written in the sound of a whistle—which sort of brought down the house!

Another famous memorable speech at S&D was given by Mack Gamble—he called it "Progress." Presented in that slow Gamble drawl, he explained why some things weren't really progress at all.

When Mack died he willed money to S&D. It became the J. Mack Gamble Fund, to be used for helping river history projects. I understand that part or all of it was railroad money; Mack sold some of his riverfront land to the Pennsylvania Railroad, which needed it to build a spur line to an industrial

Photo by Larry Geisler

Fred Way (seated) and Mack Gamble on the Lady Grace at the Valley Boat Docks in 1966.

plant nearby. That some or all of it was railroad money has always pleased me.

Another S&D highlight is the night that Lexie Palmore, wearing kilts, ushered Fred Way into the dining room with a bagpipe. It was his birthday, if I recall. Lexie lived at Tyler, Texas, at the time. Today, Capt. Lexie and her husband, Capt. Jim McMillen, operate the Caddo Lake Steamboat Company at Uncertain, Texas, where they operate the Graceful Ghost, a small steamboat Capt. Lexie had built.

Another incident I thought was amusing has to be explained. Fred Way was the perennial president of S&D; and the year the incident occurred, women's lib was in full swing. Bill Talbot, who was chairman of the nominating committee, nominated Delly Robertson as president. Before the shocked crowd could react, Delly got up and announced she was refusing the nomination.

Then there was a man from Baltimore who had a crush on (or liked very much) two ladies from Memphis. He would sit by the only elevator in the hotel, waiting for them. They, in the

Photo by S. Durward Hoag

The author, left, and *Waterways Journal* publisher H. N. "Ray" Spencer at the S&D conference at Marietta, Ohio, in 1967.

meantime, were trying to figure a way to get around him.

The S&D magazine was and still is called the *S&D Reflector*. The first issue was dated March 1964, and it has come out quarterly ever since. Fred Way was the editor until his death on October 3, 1992, at which time J. W. "Woody" Rutter took over. The magazine has a world of information and some fine pictures. Following the meetings it also carries a list of those who attend, so it is a good source for the spelling of names.

At one point it became apparent that an index was needed for the *Reflector*. Alan L. Bates stepped in and did the first index for the years 1974 to 1978, and then went on to do the rest. What a great contribution he has made for river historians! Fred Way had some interesting things to say about the quarterly and the indexes in the 1974-78 index:

> When Vol. 1. No. 1 of the S&D REFLECTOR was issued in March 1964 the chances for its survival were slim. The urgency which prompted the attempt was little other than a means of providing S&D members with a quarterly bulletin.
>
> To pad the columns the fledgling editor used a sprinkling of old-time photographs, repros of old packet advertisements and historical articles. What he could not forsee [sic] and which happened right away, were contributions in the mail, comments, photographs and articles. These have increased over the years, always interesting, often fascinating and sometimes block-buster [sic] revelations both of historical and current value. Sometimes it seems that the 'impossible' picture or story is right here on the editorial desk, and we can hardly wait to set up such

nuggets for the next issue. It sure is fun being editor of the S&D REFLECTOR.

The urgency for an Index was first impressed upon your editor by Dr. Agnes Starrett, then in charge of publications for the University of Pittsburgh. 'Do it now,' she stated twelve years ago in her soft kindly voice. But we didn't do it and in some bewilderment to us Jerry Sutphin, Tom Kenny and others plunged into the task independently and with no prospect of reward other than accomplishing a service. Andy Anderson of the Inland Rivers Library, Cincinnati, impressed upon us not only the magnitude of the task but that making a workable Index is a specialized maze of references, cross-references, names, titles, subjects, ad infinitum. It has to be tackled by somebody with training and complete dedication.

That's where Alan Bates arrived on the scene. Alan, despite his self-depreciation which you may have noticed in the last paragraph of his Foreword on another page, is a plunger. He goes in where angels fear to tread, gets mad when he's thwarted, hangs on like a bull dog, has a stunning record of successes tempered with a few interesting blunders and all of a sudden he wanted to index the S&D REFELECTOR and would not take 'no' for an answer.

Alan saw right away that he was going to have to bite into the project in chunks. So he chose the five years 1974 through 1978 for openers. As this is written Alan is well along on the preceding five years 1969-1973. This will be published next. Then he proposes to do 1964-1968, the first five years when the magazine wasn't so hefty.

That all of this commotion could have been caused by a typewriter and a glue pot continues to delight your editor.

Frederick Way, Jr.

July 15, 1980

The foreword to this index is also interesting. Alan Bates, compiler, writes:

The S&D REFLECTOR, the house organ of the Sons and Daughters of Pioneer Rivermen, is unique. The casual reader assumes that it is about steamboats. Not so, although steamboats are the catalyst for its actual subjects. These are people...real people. The persons in the magazine are nice, ornery, mad, obtuse, honest, crooked, alive and dead.

Capt. Frederick Way, Jr., the editor and writer of the REFLECTOR, is fascinated by relationships and no single thing or person stands alone in these volumes. This is the delight and the despair of the indexer. The mercurial flights of Fred's typewriter can transport a reader from the muddy shores of Vevay, Indiana, to an examination of a yacht called FAID GEHAAD on the Nile with the smallest flicker of an eye and, improbably, these things are not incongruous. The effect on the indexer is to make it impossible to assign a 'subject' to an article. For this reason we have listed single articles under as many as fifty headings, occasionally more.

We have attempted to list every person's name each time it appears. Same for each boat name. Titles are listed and subjects itemized. Owners are indicated and the professions of a number of persons, especially river persons, are given. This was done by a listing of each mention of these things. Where an item is more than a 'mention' the page number is underlined but we adjure the reader to not scorn the pages not accented in this way.

This index is conceived as a means to find a page...nothing more. The researcher is well-advised who remembers this simple fact for we have not traced the relationships of the items herein excepting where two or more persons or boats happen to have the same name. Even in those instances we do not claim absolute accuracy. For example, there is a poem on page nine, March 1975. We defy anyone to state, with certainty, whether the VERNE SWAIN there mentioned is (lst) (2nd) or (3rd)! Blame the poet, not the indexer.

There are approximately fifteen thousand page numbers presented here. Mistakes do occur in projects of this magnitude and complexity and these mistakes are the sole responsibility of the indexer. He has done his best but he wishes to make it known that his best is none to good. The reader is begged to give absolution for these inadvertant errors."*

* *The index is now being done by Frederick Way III.*

The slogan of S&D, by the way, is "You don't have to be a son or daughter to belong to the Sons and Daughters." This is due to the fact that some people thought they couldn't belong because of having no river roots. The mailing address is J. W. Rutter, 126 Seneca Drive, Marietta, Ohio 45750.

Inland Rivers Library

The artifacts owned by the S&D have a resting place in the Ohio River Museum, but the pictures and papers are cared for by the Inland Rivers Library, part of the Rare Books and Special Collections of the Public Library of Cincinnati and Hamiliton County. The library has accumulated many river items since it was established and is now in new and larger quarters, doing special exhibits and lectures as well as working with the paper items and images. Mrs. Dorothy Powers was the first librarian, followed by Yeatman "Andy" Anderson III. Now Sylvia Metzinger is in charge, with M'Lissa Kesterman as first assistant manager. The library is at 800 Vine Street, Liberty Square, Cincinnati, Ohio 45202-2071, phone 513-369-6957.

S&D branched out after a few years. Those interested in the Kanawha River got together and formed the O-K Chapter, that is the Ohio and Kanawha Chapter, with headquarters at Point Pleasant, West Virginia. They meet regularly with Capt. Bert Shearer as president, and Capt. Charles Henry Stone, who as spokesman gives the chapter's report at the S&D business meetings. Capt. Stone's address is 2105 Mount Vernon Avenue, Point Pleasant, WV 25550.

There was a feeling that too much attention was being given to the Upper Ohio River, so the Middle Ohio River Chapter came into being on a cold night, October 19, 1975, when nine river rats gathered to keep warm in the captain's cabin of the Belle of Louisville. The Middle Ohio Chapter has a busy schedule, with a number of trips to various river locations. Rick Kesterman is president and M'Lissa Kesterman, secretary.

The Middle Ohio Chapter puts out a newsletter, *Riverview*, three times a year, with Fred Rutter as editor. The address is Post Office Box 193, Lithopolis, OH 43136-0193. The Kesterman's address is 3118 Pershing Court, Cincinnati, OH 45211-6915.

The Mississippi River Chapter is the latest spin-off of the parent organization. J. Thomas "Tom" Dunn of Gateway Riverboat Cruises in St. Louis conceived the idea and is president. The board of directors has members from St. Paul to New Orleans. The group has a variety of programs. Tom Dunn's address is 50 South Leonor K. Sullivan Boulevard, St. Louis, MO 63102.

Midwest Riverboat Buffs

William L. Talbot, a postmaster of Keokuk, Iowa, came to the S&D meetings each year with Doris Foley, librarian at the Keokuk Public Library, and Mr. And Mrs. Leroy Pratt from Des Moines, Iowa. Bill was a real river historian, who was responsible for Keokuk getting the towboat Geo. M. Verity, now a towboat-museum.

Bill and I would "steamboat" into the night at S&D in the lobby of the Lafayette Hotel, and I recall the clean-up man working around our feet with his vacuum cleaner. Anyway, our common theme often was that there were steamboats on the upper Mississippi as well as on the Ohio River. I do believe the seeds of the Midwest Riverboat Buffs were really planted in the lobby of the Lafayette Hotel.

A notice went out calling a "River Rat Rally" at the Keokuk Public Library on May 20, 1972. One of the questions was: "Should Upper Mississippi steamboat fans (have) some type of annual meeting?" The notice was signed by Bill Talbot and A. Willard Heimbeck. On October 13 there was a Midwest Riverboat Buffs meeting called at the Hannibal, Mo., Presbyterian Church, although there are minutes of a meeting dated October 21, 1972, from the Public Library at Keokuk. Nevertheless, this was the start of an organization that celebrated its 25th anniversary in 1996.

The annual meeting is held each year at Keokuk, the place of its founding, with spring meetings held on a lot of rivers, including the Mississippi, Missouri, Illinois, Des Moines, St. Croix and Rock. The Buffs ' semiannual newsletter is called *River Ripples*; it has been edited by A. Willard Heimbeck, Bill Talbot, Robert L. Miller, John Miller, John Dommerman, Pat Welsh and, now, Dean Gabbert.

Bill Talbot died January 26, 1984, at his home in Keokuk.

Sonie Liebler, 9720 Lakeland Terrace, Oklahoma City, OK 73162, indexed the *River Ripples* in time for the 25th anniversary. Robert Soule is president of the Buffs, and Charles Anschutz, treasurer, at 14 Rainbow Drive, Keokuk, IA 52632-2253.

Missouri River Rats

For Missouri River people there is the Missouri River Rats organization that meets once a year at Brownville, Nebraska.; it is based on the big side-wheel dredge Capt. Meriwether Lewis, which is a museum now at Brownville. The Rats have their own Missouri River Hall of Fame. They induct three notables from the Missouri each year and have been meeting on the excursion boats Belle of Brownville or Spirit of Brownville.

The organization's address is Route 1, Box 38, Brownville, NE 68321, and the phone number is 402-825-3341. Ken Murdock has been president, and Clay Kennedy, secretary.

Mon River Buffs

On the Monongahela River there are the Monongahela River Buffs Association. The group has a paper, *Voice of the Mon*, and is interested in the Monongahela River Museum in Monongahela, Pa. Dr. J. K. Folmar, who taught at California (Pa.) State University, edits the newsletter and is president of the Buffs. His address is 847 Wood Street, California, PA 15419. The Buffs address is Monongahela, PA 15063; the museum is at 175 Second Street.

Steamship Historical Society of America

You might say The Steamship Historical Society of America is to the deep-sea and coastal waters what the S&D is to the inland waterways. It collects material and photographs of ocean liners, freighters, eastern and western coast vessels. SSHSA has chapters, too, in many coastal cities. *Steamboat Bill* is its journal, published quarterly since 1940. There is an "Inland Rivers" section done by David F. Massie, 952 Annapolis Ave., Akron, OH 43310, and a "S.E. and Gulf Ports" column. Massie also does a column on casinos.

The Steamship Historical Society has a library at the University of Maryland, and it agreed recently to participate in the development of the Heritage Harbor History Museum at Providence, RI. The Society has its headquarters in Providence at 300 Ray Drive, Suite 4 (the zip code is 02906).

Association of Retired Marine Personnel

This energetic organization is, we believe, the brainchild of Capt. H. Paul Striegel, Calvert City, Kentucky. He certainly has a lot to do with it. Centered in Paducah, Kentucky, the group holds its meetings monthly in Kincaid's Crossing Steak House Pub in the Executive Inn. Their menu states, "There has always been a river in Paducah's history," and there is a little history related to this on the menu. The walls of the pub are lined with river pictures and memorabilia.

The Association publishes a monthly newsletter, *The Wheelwash*, edited by Capt. Jack W. Clark.

Paul Striegel's address is 48 18th Avenue, Calvert City, KY 42029.

Chapter 27 ——

Still Fighting

*I*n past chapters I introduced organizations that worked hard to get the inland waterways cleared of snags, dredged, and then dammed and locked for slack water navigation.

When these challenges were accomplished, those who used the waterways had other problems with the government agencies, with regulations, and during World War II, with priorities such as Selective Service, and the great demands for transportation of war materials and the basic items to produce needed weapons and other fighting equipment.

The first effort was the formation of the Western Rivers Panel in 1943, to better coordinate the towing industry with the needs of the Coast Guard. The first panel met on April 14 of that year in St. Louis. Donald Wright had a lot to do with putting the panel together. The Coast Guard officers most directly involved were Vice Adm. Russell R. Waesche of Washington, D.C., and Capt. Stephen S. Yeandle. In years following, the chairman of the Western Rivers Panel was the president of The American Waterways Operators (AWO).

During the following year, the need for an organization that would represent all carriers, as well as shore facilities and shippers, became apparent. So AWO was incorporated under the laws of Delaware on May 22, 1944, and its first meeting was held May 26, 1944, in St. Louis. During that meeting a constitution and by-laws were approved and a temporary organization set up. The board of directors then met in Pittsburgh on June 9, 1944. Henry F. DeBardeleben, Coyle Lines, New Orleans, was named chairman; and Chester C. Thompson, former chairman and president of the Inland Waterways Corporation (Federal Barge Lines) was named president.

Executive offices were placed in Washington, D.C., with field or regional offices in New Orleans and New York.

In addition to its work with legislation and government rules and regulations, the organization also worked in public relations. It published a 108-page book on the towing industry called *Big Load Afloat*, which turned out to be a basic text for the public on inland waterways and the towing industry. AWO also published a series of papers on "Waterways Economics," which gave a continuing list of plants being built on the inland waterways; and a weekly newsletter. The organization also produced and distributed two films: *The Wonder of Water* and *Forever Free*.

In the 1950s, due to a rift over the so called "mixing rule," regulated carriers left AWO and set up the Inland Waterways Common Carrier Association. Later it became the Water Transport Association, led for 25 years by John A. Creedy, who played an important role in barging history on the Washington scene, dealing with Congress and the Administration. The regulated carriers rejoined AWO in the 1970s.

AWO celebrated its 25th anniversary on May 21-22, 1969, at the Chase-Park Plaza Hotel in St. Louis during a navigation conference with the U.S. Engineers. The Coast Guard participated, with Rear Adm. Russell R. Waesche, Jr., commander of the Second Coast Guard District, and staff in attendance. *The Waterways Journal* gave the anniversary a four-plus page review. On March 28, 1994, it published a special 50th Anniversary addition.

AWO now has its corporate office in Washington, D.C., at 1600 Wilson Blvd., Suite 1000, Arlington, Va. 22209. The phone number is 703-841-9300, and the fax number is 703-841-0389. It has other offices in New York City, and Seattle, Wash.; and in New Orleans at 601 Poydras Street, Suite 1621, phone 504-

524-3366. Ken Wells is the vice-president for the Southern Region. The Midcontinent Region has Paul J. Werner as vice-president. His office is at 319 North Fourth St., St. Louis, Mo. 63102. The phone number is 314-434-2534. At the time of this writing, Thomas A. Allegretti is president of AWO.

National Waterways Conference

In 1955, the Second Hoover Commission on the Organization of the Executive Branch of the U.S. Government recommended that user charges be placed on inland waterways traffic. This sent a shock wave through the industry and alerted the leaders that something had to be done to fight the proposal.

The Inland Shipping Conference, organized by The American Waterways Operators, met in St. Louis on September 7 to set up a steering committee for the purpose of establishing a National Waterways Conference. Chester C. Thompson, AWO president, was chairman, with Braxton B. Carr, Warrior-Tombigbee Development Association; E. K. Davison, J. K. Davison and Brother, representing the National Sand and Gravel Association; Francis T. Green, American Marine Institute; William J. Hull, Ashland Oil and Refining Company, representing The Ohio Valley Improvement Association; Robert E. Mayer, Pacific American Steamship Association; Dale Miller, Intracoastal Canal Association; G. C. Taylor, Mississippi Valley Barge Line, representing Regulated Water Carriers; Herbert G. West, Inland Empire Waterways Association; Everett T. Winter, Mississippi Valley Association; and David A. Wright, Lake Tankers Corporation, representing Exempt Water Carriers.

The steering committee held an organizational meeting at the Hotel Knickerbocker in Chicago on October 12, 1960. NWC was off and running.

The organization fought hard against tolls, with a series of imaginative pamphlets, a Toll-Meter for figuring what tolls would cost, and buttons that read "Look to the Waterways," and "Waterways Make the Difference." All of this work is detailed in a book, *History and Accomplishments of the National Waterways Conference-1960-1985*. It was published as a 25th anniversary testimonial.

The annual meetings of NWC are considered to be among the best, and it was so described by Randy Tardy of the *Arkansas Democrat* of Little Rock on October 16, 1983:

Attending the conference is one of the highlights of my work year because of its usually well-planned and executed programs, top-notch speakers and panelists and their timely topics.

From a personal standpoint, arrangers of the conference usually do a lot of little things to make it easier for the working press—such as reserving a place for us near the head table; arranging for a press room equipped with phones and typewriters, helping us find key people and providing other assistance.

Harry Cook came to the NWC as managing director from the Tennessee-Tombigbee Waterway Development Authority, became executive vice-president in 1965 and president in 1978, a position he still holds. At the time Cook left the Tenn-Tom Authority, Col. Gilbert M. Dorland (USA-Ret.), president of Nashville Bridge Company, was a member of the Tenn-Tom Authority and also president of NWC. He is to this day an individual member.

NWC's good fight was compromised by the Locks and Dam 26 controversy, which resulted in the fuel tax. The money collected goes into the Inland Waterways Trust Fund that for the first quarter of fiscal year 1999 had revenue of $29.5 million ($25.6 million from fuel taxes and the rest from interest) with outlays of $21.1 million, leaving a balance for the fiscal year of $8.4 million and an overall balance of $345.5 million. In the last fiscal year, the fund had revenues of $114.7 million ($96.4 million from fuel taxes and $18.3 million in interest). Expenditures were $76.8 million for shaft-draft construction and major rehabilitation, leaving a year-end balance of $37.8 million and an overall balance of $342.3 million.

NWC publishes an informative newsletter, *Washington Watch*, which Harry Cook edits. It also has published many valuable reports pertaining to waterways issues over the years. National Waterways Conference offices are at 1130 17th Street, N.W., Washington, D.C. 20036. The phone and fax numbers are 202-296-4415 and 202-835-3861 respectively. The e-mail address is hcook@waterways.org.

Ports and Terminals

Down in Greenville, Mississippi, in 1973, the Greenville Port Commission was involved with mini-ships and LASH (lighter aboard ship) barges. The Commission became involved, as its port director Col. Milton P. Barschdorf put it, "in this new world of direct export/import (the first inland port to have done so) and having gone through the agonies of seeking relief from the railroads and Federal Trade Commission without success, could best fight this inequality with an all-out effort to organize a coalition of the nation's shallow-draft river ports as a united voice."*

Col. Barschdorf wrote a letter to selected port directors, expressing this idea; due to the unanimous response, he followed up with an invitation to a meeting to set up the organization. More than 400 responded favorably, and the original meeting was held at Stouffer's Riverfront Inn at St. Louis on May 29, 1974. So, Inland Rivers Ports and Terminals, Inc., was formed. It was chartered in the State of Missouri, with headquarters in St. Louis.

IRPT is today a going and busy concern, with directors divided between the basins of the Upper Mississippi, Lower Mississippi, Ohio River, Illinois River, Missouri River, Arkansas-White-Red-Ouachita Rivers, Southeast Rivers (Tennessee, Tennessee-Tombigbee, Black Warrior-Tombigbee, Coosa, and Alabama), and the Pacific Coast (Columbia, Snake and Sacramento).

IRPT has started a new educational program, with Dr. Linda Beckham as educational consultant. She was traveling in the summer of 1999, doing teacher-in-service training and making plans for a web site during school.

IRPT keeps abreast of legislation and problems that do or might effect the ports and terminals on the waterways. The annual meetings have been held in conjunction with those of the National Waterways Conference. The headquarters of IRPT is now in Jackson, Mississippi. The P.O. Box is 4363, and the zip code is 39296-4363. The telephone number is 601-352-IRPT (4778), the fax 601-355-1506, the e-mail address is admin@irpt.com, and the home page is www.irpt.com.

MARC 2000

As efforts to modernize the locks on the Upper Mississippi began to draw opposition, it was evident that an organized effort would be needed to get the work done. The Midwest Area River Coalition 2000 was formed for the purpose of informing the public and legislators about the issues.

MARC 2000, as the group is best known, is (according to an organization brochure) a "group of agribusinesses, agricultural shippers, producers, carriers and other interests concerned about the future of the Upper Mississippi River and the Illinois Waterway as a cost-effective form of transportation and as a natural resource important for wildlife habitat, recreation and other public use."

They are doing a good job in "spreading the word" through a monthly newsletter, *The River Alert*, edited by Lynn M. Muenchm, vice president. Spokesmen for MARC 2000 have been visiting Upper Mississippi River areas, and using radio advertisements and public workshops to disseminate their message.

The organization is also sponsoring barge/boat tours so people can see the lock and dam system and river transportation.

MARC 2000 has offices at 908 Olive St., Ste. 1010, St. Louis, MO 63101. The telephone and fax numbers are 314-436-7303 and 314-421-3374 respectively, and the e-mail address is marc2k@aol.com.

Christopher J. Brescia is president of MARC 2000.

DINAMO

The Association for the Development of Inland Navigation In America's Ohio Valley (DINAMO) was launched in 1981 to expedite the modernization of the lock and dam infrastructure on the Allegheny, Monongahela, and Ohio rivers. In 1983, it merged with the Ohio Valley Improvement Association (OVIA) and took on the responsibility for capital improvements on the entire Ohio River Navigation System. Its focus today is singular. Gradually, after the OVIA had achieved so many of its navigation modernization successes, particularly those initiated in the mid 1950s, many people wanted OVIA to promote the needs of flood control in the Ohio Valley. OVIA, while predominantly representing a navigation constituency, took on that added advocacy at the prodding of congressmen and U.S. senators. DINAMO tightened its focus when they merged.

Since 1981, fifteen locks and dams on the Ohio system are under construction or complete. When all of these projects are complete, they will represent an investment of nearly $5 billion. Another eight lock and dam modernization projects have been targeted for construction authorization in this decade.

The association's address 425 Sixth Ave., Pittsburgh, PA 15219. The phone number is 412-392-4550, fax 412-392-4520, and e-mail: linda@pittsburghchamber.com. The web address is www.dinamo-waterways.org.

R. Barry Palmer is executive director of DINAMO.

Chapter 28 ——

Precious Images

W hat would the river historian of today do without those images of the boats and men and women of the past? It would be pretty bleak. By images I mean photographs, drawings and paintings.

As I probably mentioned before, during the time just preceding Donald T. Wright's death he thought all steamboat pictures had been collected. How wrong he was! Thanks to Ralph R. DuPae, of LaCrosse, Wisconsin, thousands more have been saved for posterity, and this super sleuth for steamboat pictures is still bringing them in for the Murphy Library at the University of Wisconsin-LaCrosse.

His collecting started in an interesting way. Ralph was an engineer for Northern Engraving in LaCrosse and was assigned the job of tearing down an old building. In it were two vaults, and in one there were some glass negatives. He asked the president of the company what to do with them, and Charles D. Gelatt suggested taking them to the University (where he, Galett, was on the board). Six of the negatives were of steamboats, and the rest were of LaCrosse street scenes and buildings. It was suggested that pictures of LaCrosse fires be collected. Gelatt also ask Ralph about boats, since he (Ralph) was already interested in river history.

Ralph talked with Capt. Walter Karnath, Dr. Lewis Younger of the Winona (Minnesota) Historical Society and Capt. Alan F. Fiedler of the U.S. Engineers to see what they thought about the idea, and they said, "Go ahead"; they also let Ralph copy their collections.

Then he visited with Capt. Fred Way, Jr., who estimated that there might be 8,000 steamboat photos still around. When Gelatt asked Ralph how long he thought it would take to bring them all in, Ralph estimated two years; that was in late 1969; and in 2000 he is still finding them. The latest estimate is that the Murphy Library has 45,000 steamboat pictures and 52,000 all told, including those of river work, river towns and scenes.

Edwin L. "Ed" Hill was curator of the Murphy Library and worked closely with Ralph on the river collection. He has now retired, and Paul Beck is the new curator.

Fires, storms and especially floods have taken a toll on collections of river pictures and albums with boat photos in them. Those who have boat pictures should not risk losing them; let Ralph DuPae copy them or give them to a museum or library that will take care of them. When we consider the number of boats that have been built versus the number of river pictures that exist (especially on the smaller rivers), it is easy to see that we have not accounted for many of them.

An early collector of steamboat photographs was Capt. Sam G. Smith, business manager of *The Waterways Journal*, who operated the Marine Photo Company. Many of the best known lower Mississippi River boat pictures were in Capt. Smith's collection. They eventually came into the possession of Donald Wright.

Other collections in steamboat days were those of J. Mack Moore of Vicksburg, and Henry C. Norman and his son Earl of Natchez. Moore's photos are in the Old Courthouse Museum at Vicksburg, and Norman's have been preserved by Dr. Thomas H. Gandy at Natchez. Gandy found them falling into ruin on a porch. Many of them are in a book Dr. Gandy and his wife Joan W. Gandy compiled, *The Mississippi Steamboat Era In Historic*

Photographs: Natchez to New Orleans 1870-1920, published by Dover Publications, New York, in 1987.

Some photographers had studios on boats. One of the best known was operated by Thorton Barrette, J. P. Doremus and Hazael C. Williams.

These pictures are from the steamboat period. A collector of the diesel age is Dan Owen, who won't fool with steamboats. Dan started collecting when he was a boy at East Liverpool, Ohio. He utilized an observation point on Babbs Island, in the Ohio River, to photograph the boats as they passed. Dan started then what was known as the Babbs Island Photo Company. He worked for Union Barge Line for awhile and helped Fred Way with *the Inland River Record*. When *The Waterways Journal* acquired the *Record*, Dan moved to St. Louis, where he took over the *Record* and also became editor of the *Inland River Guide*. Because his work was so closely related to the WJ, he also held a third title: he was associate editor. He is still in the photography business, so anyone in need of diesel-boat pictures can contact the Boat Photo Museum, 430 Joseph Dr., Maryville, IL 62062. He has more than 36,000 pictures.

In Keokuk, Iowa, where Lock 19 offers a great observation point for taking photographs, John R. Miller has compiled a good collection of towboat pictures. His address is 729 Hazelhurst, Keokuk, IA 52632. His phone number is 319-524-6491.

A noted photographer of today is Allen Hess, who has presented several shows of his fine pictures, many with river themes. He lives in Pittsford, New York. In 1981 he published a calendar with steamboat pictures; his own photograph of the steamer Julia Belle Swain in the fog was on the front cover.

I mentioned earlier the collections of river pictures at the St. Louis Mercantile Library and the Public Library of Cincinnati and Hamilton County. Contact the latter at phone 513-369-6900; rare books and special collections, 513-369-6957; fax 513-369-3122; and E-mail: rarebooksasst@pich.lib.oh.us.

Others include the Lilly Library at the University of Indiana, Seventh St., Bloomington, IN 47405, phone 812-855-2452. It contains many of the Howard Shipyard pictures and artifacts, including 10,000 blueprints from 1834 to 1942. The

fax number is 812, 855-3143, and E-mail address is liblilly@indiana.edu. The web address is:
www.indiana.edu/~liblilly.

The Howard-Tilton Library at Tulane University, 7001 Freret St., New Orleans 70118-5549. The library has Donald T. Wright's photo collection, which they bought from his widow. It is part of the Joseph Merrick Jones Special Collections. The phone number is 504, 865-5685. The fax is 504-865-5761, and the E-mail address: leinbach@nmailhost.tos.tulane.edu. The web site address for Special Collections is:
www.tulane.edu/~lmiller/SpecCollHomePage.html.

University of Louisville, South Third Avenue, Louisville, KY 40292, has the Standard Oil of Louisiana (ESSO, EXXON) photo collection, which includes the river photos taken by Edwin and Louise Rosskam for the book *Towboat River.* The library phone number is 502-852-6745. The fax is 502-852-7394. The photo archives are on the Belknap Campus; the direct phone to the archives is 502-852-6752, and the fax is 502-852-8734.

Louisiana State University, 1 University Place, Shreveport, LA 71115-2399. The university has the papers of Red River historian Dewey A. Somdal. The phone is 318-797-5000.

Memphis-Shelby County Library, 1850 Peabody Ave., Memphis, TN 38104-4025, has papers of Rees V. Downs, Pine Bluff, Ark, the Tennessee Valley Authority, and other river-related items. The phone number is 901-725-8895. The fax is 901-725-8883. E-mail is drescherj@memphis.lib.tn.us.

The Murphy Library is located at 1631 Pine St., LaCrosse, WI 54601-3792. The phone number is 608-785-8505, and the fax is 608-785-8639. Ralph DuPae's address is 2222 Onalaska Ave., LaCrosse, WI 54603. His phone number is 608-781-3333.

The photo collection of Capt. Thomas Kenny is located in St. Louis Mercantile Library's Herman T. Pott National Inland Waterways Library.

Chapter 29—

The River on Canvas

*T*here are images of the river, man-made, by brush and pen.

During those days out West in Albuquerque I kept in touch with the river through a book of poems and illustrations of paintings. It was *The Great River* by Frederick Oakes Sylvester. He was the great portrayer of the river as it passed the palisades it had created (with the wind) between Alton and Grafton, Illinois. Sylvester was painter in residence at Principia College on the bluffs above Elsah, Illinois. The paintings in the book are of scenes from that area, but before going up there, Sylvester had done a number of paintings of the St. Louis riverfront and Eads Bridge. (Some of these are in the Missouri Athletic Club.)

There is a poem in *The Great River* that has inspired me all of my life and, indeed, helped to lead me into writing about the Mississippi:

> *O River, river, never yet*
> *Was half your glory sung;*
> *And never skill of painter's brush*
> *Nor praise of poet's tongue*
> *Shall half reveal the majesty,*
> *The charm, the primal grace*
> *That clothe thee and attend thy ways*
> *And shine from out your face.*

The painter that I feel captured the towboat era best is James Godwin Scott through his sketches of towboat life and watercolors of St. Louis harbor scenes and fleeting and towing scenes. Many are in the St. Louis Mercantile Library and have been used on the covers of the library's publications. Jim, of course, has done, and is doing, other subjects in his studio, now located in Cottonwood, Arizona, and during workshops he presents worldwide.

The steamboat era, of course, draws many artists; probably the first to gain fame from them was John Stobart. Though living in the East, he has come out to the rivers to study them (and boat pictures) to make sure his work is accurate.

Artists who live on the rivers have also done some fine paintings. Michael Blaser lives in Davenport, Iowa. A favorite at many of his shows is that of the steamer Golden Eagle going under Eads Bridge, with Streckfus boats in the background.

Gary Lucy lives on the Missouri River in Washington, Missouri, and has done a number of studies of Missouri River boats and many others. Before he paints boats, he has models made of them.

Also on the Missouri River, far up in Fort Benton, Montana, is James E. "Jim" Trott, who likes the mountain boats that ran on the upper Missouri. His *Sinking of the Bertrand* has been widely used. In 1993, Trott did a calendar containing his paintings for the Montana "River Edition" of the History Calendar. A bit of Montana history was given for every day of the year.

Many painters do such work for their own pleasure; the meetings of the Sons and Daughters of Pioneer Rivermen are made more interesting by works from Forrest F. Steinlage and Dr. Martin C. "Pete" Striegel from Jeffersonville, Ind.

In steamboat days there were artists who specialized in painting steamboat cabins.

Today Capt. Lexie Palmore-McMillen has done some fine murals, a number of them on casino boats. She also does book illustrations.

During the Great Depression, the U.S. Government helped artists through the Works Progress Administration (WPA) and the Civil Works Administration. Among its programs was one involving the painting of murals on the walls of post offices and other government buildings. Naturally, in river towns, some of these depicted river-related scenes. The National Archives and Records Administration issued a book about this, entitled *A New Deal For The Arts* (1997). (I wrote to see if they could furnish a list of murals with river themes. They did send a list, although I am sure there are more. The list contained only one by William Bunn, but I have seen others.) In any case, here are the ones of which I am certain:

William Bunn, Dubuque Post Office—head-on view of sidewheeler; and boats in Hickman, Kentucky Post Office.

John Folinsbee, Paducah Post Office (It looks more like a courtroom.)—steamboat at wharf-boat.

Purser Stuart, Gretna, Louisiana—five boats loading cotton.
Fay Davis, Chester, Illinois—southern landing with boat.

Richard Zoellner, Portsmouth, Ohio—nice stern-wheeler with wharfboat and a coal tow.

Paul Kelpe, Franklin D. Roosevelt Library, Hyde Park, New York—history of Southern Illinois with boats.

> Philip S. Brinkman, Englewood, Florida. Has
> done some 179 murals, including some for the
> Holiday Inns in Memphis, Tennessee (perhaps
> the steamboat mural at West Memphis,
> Arkansas).

An interesting item in the book is the reproduction of a poster used to promote the documentary *The River*, made by Paul Lorentez in 1938. It has flood scenes and a steamboat.

Today, murals are being painted on floodwalls. At Cape Girardeau, there is a good likeness of the steamer Cape Girardeau and also a towboat and barges. Paducah has a view of the riverfront there in Civil War days and steamboat ties, with another panel coming of the towboat period. After all, floodwalls don't have to be gray.

Murals turn up in some unexpected places. There is one in the lobby of the Holiday Inn in West Memphis, Arkansas, and one of the race between the Natchez and Robt. E. Lee in the Canton, Missouri, Public Library. There was a southern scene with a side-wheel boat in the Park and Eat Restaurant at Monmouth, Illinois.

Another Robt. E. Lee-Natchez race mural (by Mary Brehm) is in the Nellie Peck Room of the Ramada Inn, Portsmouth, Ohio.

Back in the 1940s, there was an artist in the Quad-Cities area who did some fine boat paintings that are very valuable today. Ralph Law only did them, it is said, when he needed money; but they were worth waiting for. (It was also rumored that he put a nude woman in each of his works, but I've never been able to find one.)

Going way back in history there are the famous river artists such as George Caleb Bingham, who did the float boat studies, and Karl Bodmer, who painted on the Missouri River.

Another form of river art involves letterheads with boats on them and logos with towboats and tugs. Many are clever and enjoyable to look at.

I am aware that I have, unintentional though it was, omitted from this list the names of some river artists who deserve to be here. I apologize. It is all but impossible to compile a complete list that is accurate.

If you are interested in contacting the most prolific painters described, here are some addresses:

> Michael Blaser, 1019 Mound St. #101, Davenport, IA 52803-3923.

> Gary R. Lucy, P.O. Box 233, Main and Elm Streets, Washington, MO 63090.

> James Godwin Scott, 565 Mill Dr., Cottonwood, AZ 86326 or Kodner Gallery, 7561 Forsyth, St. Louis, MO 63105.

> John Stobart, 23 Town House, Union Wharf, Boston, MA 02018.

> J. E. "Jim" Trott, 1904 Franklin St., Fort Benton, MT 59442.

EXTRA

Two of the low days of my life occurred during my service career. The first was on the day I took the oath. At the time, the Allies were on the retreat everywhere in the Pacific, North Africa and Europe. It came over me that I was in for the duration, and things looked gloomy. Would I ever get out? The second was in Aachan, Belgium, where we got our first shower in weeks. We would wet down, step out in the cold air to soap up, then get under the water again to wash off the soap. I really felt low that day.   Jim

Chapter 30——

Wood, Plastic And Metal

*I*mage might not be the correct word for another form that reminds us of what vessels of the past looked like. But models certainly do that in the best way. They come in all sizes, from the giant replica of a packet in the Ohio River Museum to the precise but small towboat models (made by Jack Sintich of Woodridge, Illinois) in the Golden Eagle River Museum. Right now I have to say I am skating on thin ice; there are so many model-makers that should be recognized whom I don't know.

I have mentioned the big model named Pioneer, which can be steered by a man sitting at the head of the boat. Another large model is that of the gunboat Carondelet in custody of the Carondelet Historical Society in St. Louis; it can be taken apart to show the engineroom. The model was built by Ron Bolte.

The largest collection of models would appear to be in the Gray and Blue Naval Museum at Vicksburg, Mississippi, where they have 53 built by Bill Atteridge of Arcadia, Louisiana; 31 by Harold Morris of Crystal Springs, Mississippi; plus models from the collection of Lamar Roberts, director of the museum.

A model-maker of some renown in the St. Louis area is Glenn Hensley of Kirkwood, Missouri. He has made a series of

273

models for the Mystic Seaport Museum and is known locally for his radio-controlled model of the excursion steamer Admiral and the Columbia River's Bailey Gatzert. The Golden Eagle River Museum is fortunate to have models made by its members: George Mitchell, who built the Far West and Bixby; and William Paule, who built a smaller version of the gunboat Carondelet and a flatboat. In looking back through *The Waterways Journal* we noted an article about six Monongahela River boat models made by Walter Otto of Charleori, Pennsylvania.

We should remember, too, the big working model of the steamer Delta Queen that was shown at many S&D meetings by Guy Williams. (It will be in Paducah River Heritage Museum.) Paducah also has the working model of the the towboat Russell Lord.

There is a large model of the Sprague in The Mattress Factory at 500 Sampsonia Way in Pittsburgh, Pennsylvania. William F. Wiseman of Memphis has done some beautiful models, including one of the Far West. Robert G. Thomas built many of the models for the early S&D museum.

From where do the ideas and, indeed, plans for many of these models come? John L. Fryant, now of Mainville, Ohio (formerly of Alexandria, Virginia,) has many plans and many models to his credit. He always has some new ones at each year's S&D meeting. His new calling card has on it a picture of his model of a steamer.

Also supplying plans is Alan L. Bates of Louisville, Kentucky, who is well-founded for this, having compiled *The Western Rivers Steamboat Cyclopoedium* and *The Western Rivers Engineroom Cyclopoedium.*

These models are of steamboats, packets and steam towboats. There is a new era today. It involves diesel towboats, tugs and even barges as well as radio-controlled vessels. Around St. Louis much of this interest is centered with William "Ole River Bill" Zumwalt, who lives in New Florence, Missouri. He is a member of the St. Louis Admiral Radio/Controlled Boat Club. Zumwalt and Joe E. "Towboat" Brown, Flatwoods, Kentucky, have put out a very informative booklet on the towing industry, with facts about life on the boats, and with sketches of types of working boats and equipment on them. Both men have plans for towboats and videos of towboating.

A good place to see radio-controlled models is at the annual regatta held by the St. Louis Admiral Radio/Controlled Boat Club. It usually takes place in September on the lake at St. Louis Union Station.

Some other makers of radio-controlled models from years back—they may or may not still be involved in the pursuit— include Bob Eastwood, who had one of the Patrick Calhoun and a tug; and D. G. Pickett of Paducah, who had a large one named for himself (D. G. Pickett) and one of the Miss Hattie Mac, a vessel upon which he worked. (*The Waterways Journal* carried a story about him and the models.)

Model-makers on the Ohio River at Point Pleasant, West Virginia, go by the name of George and Maxine's Airplane Factory and Boat Yard (George and Maxine McClintock). According to their card, they specialize in desk-top display aircraft and boat models, custom built in full detail.

Sam DeSastis built a large flatboat model for the Gabler Maritime Library of the Monongahela River Buffs, Monongahela, Pennsylvania. (Pictures of its construction appeared in the December 1997 issue of the *Voice of the Mon*, the Buffs' newsletter.)

One of the early dispensers of models, both towboats and barges, was Randy Mayse, Kincaid, Illinois, who organized Cherokee Barge and Boat. He has sets of boats and barges, complete with buoys to steer on. Cherokee also has a drydock and a Corps of Engineers mat tow. Buyers can pick the colors they want on the boat's stacks and pick the names of the boats.

I got the urge way back to make a model of the Robt. E. Lee. The urge didn't last long though. The pieces of that ill-fated boat are still in the closet, I think.

The model I became acquainted with very early on was that of the steamer Mary Morton, which sat on top of Donald Wright's roll-top desk. (It can be seen in the early picture of the *Journal* office on page 62.) It was Donald's pride and joy; rumors were that he bought the paper to get the model.

Tragedy struck it, though, as told by this story from the August 5, 1939, issue of the *Journal:*

Even models of packet boats find the going rough in the current era of planes, trucks, and of course railroads. This was demonstrated in the office of The Waterways Journal about 4:10 p.m. last Saturday just after the U.S. steamer Wakerobin had arrived in St. Louis from St. Paul and Capt. Homer Melton, first officer and pilot, had gone post haste to The Waterways Journal office to gaze once more upon what he calls "the finest model of a packet boat in existence"; also to show the model to his friend Bill R. Griffin, a member of the Wakerobin's crew.

Donald T. Wright, Editor of The Waterways Journal, was sitting at his desk on top of which rested the Mary Morton's model in a large glass case. Capt. Melton and Mr. Griffin had just stepped back from a close examination. Without warning a section of plaster an inch thick and fully three feet across at the center let go. The Editor jumped in the nick of time but his coat, draped over the back of the chair, was slashed to pieces. The glass top of the model case broke at the center; and the half over the forward end of the Mary Morton held, in a slanting position. This saved the Mary Morton as far aft as amidships but dumped huge chunks of plaster down upon the pilot house, after end of the texas, and after end of the cabin skylight and boiler deck roof. Davits supporting four lifeboats went down, both hog chains, and wheel chains were broken, gingerbread work on the pilot house and texas roofs was damaged, and the roof of the cabin was caved in just aft of the end of the skylight.

The management of the Chemical Building was not available so late on Saturday afternoon but on Monday had the Mary Morton removed to a separate office and offered to pay for its restoration. What shipyard would be competent to undertake the job has been worrying The Waterways Journal all this week and no arrangements have as yet been made or bids invited. It was not learned whether or not the local steamboat inspectors would require a hearing with eyewitnesses of the accident present to testify.

For some of the model-makers named in this chapter, information is presented on the following page:

Alan L. Bates, 2040 Sherwood Ave., Louisville, KY 40205-1112. He provides a list of plans and his books for $1 if a return envelope and 55 cents postage is included; otherwise it costs $3.

Joe E. Brown, 1010 Turley Ave., Flatwood, KY 41139. Phone 606-836-1431; E-mail jbrown@dragg.net; web site www.dragg.net/jbrown.

Cherokee Barge and Boat, Randy Mayse, P.O. Box 105, Kincaid, IL 62450, phone 217-237-2400.

John L. Fryant, 7672 Crystal Cove, Maineville, OH 45039; E-mail jonboat@aol.com.

Harbor Models, 17457 Appalachian St., Fountain Valley, CA 92708, phone 714-435-0716. (Handles model work boat kits and accessories.)

Gary Harmon Design Group, 5251 Pattison Ave., St. Louis, MO 63110; fax 314-773-7762. (White metal castings, scale steamboat fittings.)

Hartman Fiberglass RC/Kits, Box 86, Melrose Street, Argentina, IL 62301. (Fiberglass hull kits, including one for John Fryant's generic towboat.)

Tower Hobbies, P.O. Box 9078, Champaign, IL 61826-9078 (Handles complete kits for boats and planes.)

George & Maxine's Airplane Factory and Boat Yard, 107 Vansickle Court, Point Pleasant, WV 675-2383. Can be reached April-October at 740-992-3677.

William Zumwalt, Sink'um & Float'us Salvage Co., 448 Tree Farm Road, New Florence, MO 63363; phone 573-835-3158. E-mail is wzumwalt@ktis.net. The web site is www. Ktis.net/~wzumwalt.

Musically, the song for the towboat era is "Proud Mary—Rollin' on the River." Somehow it just seems to fit in with the Memphis and Greenville boats and their crews.

Jim

Chapter 31——

See The Past in River History

*M*any dedicated people have collected and preserved river history for museums, and actual vessels; many more have volunteered their time to show current generations this past. We should thank them for their efforts by visiting and supporting these places.

I have listed many here, and I know that I have missed some with which I am not familiar. The hours listed may have changed, too, so a call for confirmation may be a prudent move.

Missouri River

Steamer Bertrand Museum—DeSoto National Wildlife Refuge, U.S. 30 from I-75 at Missouri Valley, Nebraska. One mile south of refuge entrance on U.S. 30, in visitor center.

This was the first Missouri River boat to be excavated. A vast amount of tools, clothing, household goods and food is preserved in the Cargo Gallery and Artifact Storage room. Open daily 9 a.m. to 4:30 p.m. except New Year's Day, Thanksgiving and Christmas. Phone: 712-642-4121. Address: DeSoto National Wildlife Refuge, 1434 316th Lane, Missouri Valley, IA 51555. E-mail: r3bertrand@fws.gov. Internet:

Backing Hard Into River History

http://refuges.gov/NWRSFiles/CulturalResources/Bertrand/Bertrand. html.

Sergeant Floyd Museum—Welcome Center, Sioux City, Iowa. Blair Chicoine, manager. Phone 712-279-4840. Open 9 a.m. to 5 p.m. The Sergeant Floyd was a Corps of Engineers survey and inspection boat for the Missouri River, out of the Omaha District. When retired, the boat took a trip along the inland waterways with U.S. Engineers exhibits. She was then at St. Louis as a museum several years. The museum has river archives, including Capt. Joseph Giesler and Paul Giesler collections. Near Floyd Monument. National Historic Landmark.

Capt. Meriwether Lewis—Museum of Missouri River History, Brownville, Nebraska. Big side-wheel, former U.S. Engineers Missouri River dredge. Artifacts from the Nebraska Historical Society show development of Missouri River and its history. A National Historic Site. Open daily 10 a.m. to 5:30 p.m. Memorial Day to Labor Day; Saturdays and Sundays from 10 a.m. to 5:30 p.m. May, September, October. Brownville, NE 68321. Phone 402-825-3341.

Treasures of the Steamboat Arabia—Kansas City, Missouri. Another Missouri River boat that was excavated, uncovering 220 tons of buried "treasure." In addition to thousands of items on display, the museum has a working steamboat engine and other Missouri River artifacts. This very excellent display is open Monday-Saturday 10 a.m. to 6 p.m. Sunday, noon to 5 p.m. Closed New Year's Day, Easter, Thanksgiving and Christmas. Phone for general information, 816-471-4030; group reservations, 816-471-1856. Address: 400 Grand Ave. (downtown), Kansas City, MO 64106.

Historic Hermann Museum-Old German School—Hermann, Missouri, Steamboat legacy exhibit has models, steamer Pin Oak pilothouse, and many pictures. Capt. Delmer Ruediger and Kermit Baecker were curators here for many years. Open April-October, 10 a.m. to 4 p.m. Sunday. Closed Thursday. Address: 312 Schiller St., Hermann, MO 65041. Phone: 573-486-2017. Fax: 573-486-2017. Hermann is the home of the Heckmann family of river fame. There is a memorial pilothouse to Capt. Ed Heckmann at the end of the Missouri River bridge. Dorothy Heckmann Shrader of Hermann has written two books on the Heckmann family and in late 1999 was completing a third.

Goldenrod Showboat—St. Charles, Missouri. One of the largest showboats, and one of two still in existence. The showboat is operated by the City of St. Charles, and plays and concerts are presented. Address: 1000 Riverside Dr. Phone: 314-946-2020. National Historic Landmark.

Illinois River

Illinois & Michigan Canal History Center—Lockport, Illinois. (Will County Historical Society) At east end of the Illinois & Michigan National Historic Corridor that runs from Chicago to the Illinois River. Artifacts, tools and pictures from the building and use of the 100-mile waterway. In a ten-room museum. Mail to: 803 South State St., Lockport, IL 60441. Phone: 815-838-5080. Open 1 to 4 p.m. daily. Closed mid-December-early January.

I & M Canal Visitor Center—200 West Eighth St., Lockport. In Gaylord Building, former canal warehouse. (Near History Center) Phone: 815-838-4830. Open 10 a.m. to 5 p.m., Wednesday-Sunday.

Illinois Waterway Visitors Center—Rt. 1, Dee Bennett Road, Ottawa, Illinois. The center is at Starved Rock Lock and Dam, with indoor and outdoor observation areas and the pilothouse of the towboat John M. Warner.

Washington Park—Ottawa, across from Washington Park at 100 West Lafayette. Dislays on waterway, canal and towboats. Phone: 815-434-2737. Open Monday-Friday, 9 a.m. to 5 p.m.; Sunday, 10 a.m. to 4 p.m.

Beardstown River Museum— Beardstown, Illinois. Most material deals with towboating. Models of Material Service Corporation towboats, pictures, artifacts. Mail to 121 South State St., Beardstown, IL 62618. Phone 217-323-3271. Open Monday-Friday, 9 a.m. to noon and 1 to 5 p.m.

Calhoun County Historical Society—second floor, Farm Bureau building, North County Road, Hardin, Illinois. River pictures and artifacts. Mail to P.O. Box 2496, Hardin, IL 62049. Phone 618-576-2359. Open Wednesday 8 a.m. to 4:45 p.m.; Friday, 9 a.m. to 11:30 a.m.

Grafton Museum and General Store—Grafton, Illinois. Pictures, maps, artifacts. Address 203 East Main, Grafton, IL 62037. Phone 618-786-3220; Fax 618-786-3220; Pager, 618-338-3449 (Jerry) or 618-646-6203 (Jarney); E-mail: mr-fix-it@primary.net or mamalew45@primary.net. Open Thursday-Sunday, 10 a.m. to 5 p.m.

Mississippi River

Julius K. Wilkie—steamboat replica, Winona, Minnesota. Used for meetings, etc.

Riverside Museum—410 East Veterans Memorial Dr. (on riverfront), LaCrosse, Wisconsin. River items include relics from steamer War Eagle that burned at LaCrosse. Mailing address: P.O. Box 1272, LaCrosse, WI 54602. Phone: 608-782-1980. Open daily Memorial Day to Labor Day, 10 a.m. to 5 p.m.

City of Clinton Showboat—On riverfront, Clinton, Iowa. Formerly towboat Omar, then the Rhododendron.

Fred W. Woodward Riverboat Museum-National Rivers Hall of Fame—Second Street Harbor, Dubuque, Iowa. This is a top river museum because of its displays and variety of exhibits, including the side-wheel dredge William M. Black, the towboat Logsdon, and smaller vessels. Plans are underway to expand the museum into a Mississippi River Discovery Center with a riverwalk, aquariums, wetlands and docks. The present museum is near the site of the Dubuque Boat and Boiler Works that built such famous vessels as the Sprague. It is on the Dubuque Ice Harbor. Jerry Enzler, the director, has done a wonderful job in developing the museum complex. The mailing address is P.O. Box 266, Dubuque, IA 52004-0266. Open 10 a.m. to 6:30 p.m., May to October; and 10 a.m. to 4 p.m. Tuesday-Sunday, November and December. Closed on national holidays.

The National Rivers Hall of Fame is located in the Welcome Center and Diamond Jo Casino Building near the museum. It honors men and women who are notables in river history. Those deceased are in the Hall of Fame, and those still living are given Achievement Awards.

INDUCTEES:

PATHFINDERS
Zadock Cramer
Louis Jolliet & Jacques Marquette
Rene-Robert Cavelier La Salle
Meriwether Lewis & William Clark
Stephen Long
Alexander Mackenzie
John Wesley Powell
Sacajawea
Henry Rowe Schoolcraft

RIVER PEOPLE
Betty Blake
John W. Cannon
Mary B. Greene
Daniel Smith Harris
Black Hawk
Thomas Leathers
Grant Marsh

Mary Miller
Diamond Jo Reynolds
Nicholas Roosevelt
Isaiah Sellers
John Streckfus

BUILDERS AND INVENTERS
DeWitt Clinton
James Buchanan Eads
John Fitch
Robert Fulton
William Hopkins
James Howard
James Rees
John and Washington Roebling
James Rumsey
Henry Miller Shreve

ARTISTS, MUSICIANS & WRITERS
Louis Armstrong
John James Audubon
Geroge Caleb Bingham
Richard Bissell
Karl Bodmer
Henry P. Bosse
J. P. Doremus
Steven Foster
E. W. Gould
Constance Skinner
Mark Twain
Captain Fred Way, Jr.

ACHIEVEMENT AWARD WINNERS
Col. Milton Barschdorf
Vernon Behrhorst
Donald Bollinger
Capt. William Bowell
Jesse Brent
Betty Bryant
Capt. Scott Chotin
Capt. Ralph Clark
John E. Connolly
Harry N. Cook
U.S. Senator John C. Culver
Albert J. Dawson

Bailey T. DeBardeleben
Neil Diehl
Majory Stoneman Douglas
Wilbur Dow
Ralph DuPae
Peter Fanchi, Jr.
Ruth Ferris
King Fisher
Bernard Goldstein
Robert Gray
Capt. Noble Gordon
Jesse Gunstream
Robert Guthans
John Hartford
Capt. Clarke C. Hawley
J. W. Hershey
Capt. William James Hudson
Capt. Jesse P. Hughes
William J. Hull
Joseph Merrick Jones, Jr.
Capts. Robert & Ruth Kehl
Catherine Reynolds King
Capt. Wm. "Buck" Leyhe
Capt. Charles Lehman
F. A. "Bud" Mechling
General Jack Morris
Dr. William J. Petersen
Capt. Edgar Allen "Wamp" Poe
Herman Theodore Pott
Capt. John Streckfus & Family
James Swift
H. K. Thatcher
Capt. Fred Way, Jr.
James Walden
General Walter K. Wilson
David Wright
Capt. Donald T. Wright & *The Waterways Journal*

Buffalo Bill Museum—LeClaire, Iowa (just north of the Quad Cities off I-80 and U.S. 61). Don't let the name fool you. They do have a lot of material on Buffalo Bill (William Cody) who grew up nearby, but the main focus is river history, particularly on rafting and Upper Mississippi rivermen. Alongside the museum is the Lone Star, a stern-wheel towboat that went out of service in 1966 and was pulled out on the bank in 1968. Address: Foot of Jones Street, LeClaire, IA

52573. Phone: 319-289-5580. Open 7:30 a.m. to 4:30 p.m., in summer; Saturdays and Sundays, 7:30 a.m. to 4:30 p.m. in winter. The mv. Twilight is tied up just below the museum.

Putnam Museum of History and Natural Science— Davenport, Iowa. There is a river display, and they have the famous Flying Eagle wood sculpture from raft boat days. Address: 1717 W. 12th St., Davenport, IA 52804. Phone: 319-324-1054. Open Tuesday-Friday, 9 a.m. to 5 p.m.; Saturday, 10 a.m. to 5 p.m.; Sunday, noon to 5 p.m. Closed on major holidays.

President Casino—Davenport. Now a gambling boat, but for a long time it was the St. Louis excursion boat and also tramped on the Upper Mississippi and was in New Orleans.

Geo. M. Verity Towboat Museum—Johnson Street at Victory Park, Keokuk, Iowa. Originally the S. S. Thorpe of Federal Barge Lines, the Verity went to the Ohio River and in 1962 was decommissioned by the Armco Steel Corporation and came to Keokuk. She was put on land and is now a fine museum, showing how life was on the river in steam towboat days. Phone 319-524-7465. Open 9 a.m. to 5 p.m., Monday-Sunday, 4th weekend in April to October 31.

Mark Twain Museum—Hannibal, Missouri. A new museum building near the Mark Twain home. Features a replica of a steamboat pilothouse. A pilot wheel is in it, with a view of the Mississippi. There is also a steam whistle to blow. Various exhibits are on display, including items from the Treasures of the Steamboat Arabia museum from time to time. Henry Sweets is director of the museum and Mark Twain-related buildings. Address: 208 Hill St., Hannibal, MO 63401. Phone: 573-221-9010, fax: 573-221-7975. Open June, July, August, 8 a.m. to 6 p.m.; May, 8 a.m. to 5 p.m.; November-February, 10 a.m. to 4 p.m. and Sunday 12 a.m. to 4 p.m.; March 9 a.m. to 4 p.m. and Sunday noon to 4 p.m.; April, September and October 9 a.m. to 5 p.m. Closed Thanksgiving, Christmas and New Year's Day. Internet address: www.hanmo.com/twainweb/

Alton Museum of History and Art—At Loomis Hall, Alton, Missouri. Formerly in the *Alton Telegraph* building. The museum is on the second floor of the building formerly part of Shurleff College. It has a pilot wheel, models, photographs and artifacts. Open Monday-Friday, 10 a.m. to 4 p.m.; Saturday and Sunday, 1 to 4 p.m. Address: 2809 College Ave., Alton, IL 62002. Phone: 618-462-2763.

Great Rivers National Museum and Visitors Center Melvin Price Locks and Dam—south of Alton, Illinois, off Illinois 3. In 1999 the museum was under development to be the only regional visitors center on the Mississippi River for the Army Corps of Engineers.

Admiral Casino—St. Louis riverfront. Formerly St. Louis excursion boat.

Jefferson National Expansion Memorial-Gateway Arch and Old Courthourse—St. Louis. There are river displays and dioramas. Also a large mural (under the Arch at the tram loading dock) of St. Louis's river inheritance. Gateway Arch phone: 314-655-1700. The Gateway Arch is open Labor Day to Memorial Day, 9 a.m. to 6 p.m. Old Courthouse address: 10 South Broadway, St. Louis, MO 63102. Phone 314-655-1700. Open 8 a.m. to 4:30 p.m.

History Museum—Missouri Historical Society, 5700 Lindell Blvd., Forest Park, St. Louis. River displays. Phone: 314-746-4599. Open Tuesday, 9:30 a.m. to 8:30 p.m. Wednesday-Sunday, 9:30 a.m. to 5 p.m. Mailing address: P.O. Box 11940, St. Louis, MO 63112. (The archives and library are at 225 South Skinker Blvd.)

Golden Eagle River Museum—Bee Tree Park, South St. Louis County, Missouri (in greater St. Louis area). Museum is in Nims Mansion overlooking the Mississippi River. Has models, pictures, steamer Betsy Ann pilot wheel, replica of pilothouse for kids. The museum was founded by the Golden Eagle River Club, made up of riders of the steamer Golden Eagle, February 2, 1942. The museum opened in 1964. Address: 2401 Finestown Rd., St. Louis, MO 63129. Off I-255 to Telegraph Road, left on Becker Road, left on Finestown Road. Phones: 314-725-9467 and 846-9073. For tours: 314-832-0974. For information on joining museum, write James V. Swift at 7330 Colgate Ave, St. Louis, MO 63130. Museum open 1 to 5 p.m. Wednesday through Sunday, May 1 through Labor Day; 1 to 5 p.m. Saturday and Sunday, Labor Day-October 31. Museum meetings are on the fourth Sunday of the month when the museum is open.

Museum of Transportation, 3015 Barrett Station Road, St. Louis County, Missouri. Take Dougherty Ferry Road from I-270. Open 9 a.m. to 5 p.m. Phone 314-965-7998. Mailing address is 3015 Barrett Station Road, St. Louis, MO 63122. Displays towboat Herman T. Pott, steamboat bell and pilotwheel. Mostly railroad material.

Cape River Heritage Museum—538 Independence, Cape Girardeau, Missouri. Models, pictures, pilothouse replica. Phone: 314-334-0405. Open Monday-Friday, 10 a.m. to 4 p.m. There are steamboat murals on the Cape Girardeau floodwall and a good view of the Mississippi.

New Madrid Historical Museum—1 Main St., New Madrid, Missouri. Information on the Battle at Island No. 10 during the Civil War and river pictures. Phone 573-748-5944. Open Monday-Saturday, 9 a.m. to 4 p.m.; Sunday, noon to 4 p.m.

Columns-Belmont Civil War Museum—350 Park Road, Columbus, Kentucky. On bluff overlooking the Mississippi is an anchor and chain used to try to stop the Union boats from going south on the Mississippi during the Civil War. Mailing Address: P.O. Box 8, Columbus, OH 42728. Phone: 502-677-2327. Open May-September, 9 a.m. to 5 p.m.; April-October, Saturday and Sunday, 9 a.m. to 5 p.m.

Mud Island Mississippi River Museum—Memphis, Tennessee. Overhead train to island from Adams and 125 Front St. This is probably the best river museum of all. There are full-sized replicas of a steamboat cabin, a Civil War gunboat deck, all with sounds. A Civil War battle is depicted. Life-sized figures are in the dioramas. There is a towboat pilothouse. Many models and pictures are on display. Outside is a riverwalk—the Mississippi is modeled with all its islands and towns. There is a river music room. Mail address: 125 North Front St., Memphis, TN 38103. Phone: 901-576-7241. Open mid-April to October 31, 10 a.m. to 5 p.m. Last train leaves mainland at 4 p.m.

Coors Brewery Visitors Center—Memphis. Center is shaped like a steamboat cabin. It contains a sternwheel, gingerbread and river artifacts. Brewery tour available. Mail to 5151 East Raines Rd., Memphis, TN 38018. Phone: 901-375-2000. Open Thursday-Saturday, noon to 5 p.m.

P. T. Boat Museum and Library—at 1344 Corova Rd, Suite 2, Germantown, Tennessee. Museum at Battleship Cove. PT boats and Japanese midget submarine. Library. Mail to: P.O. Box 18070, Germantown, TN 38183-0070. Phone: 901-755-8440. Fax: 901-751-0522. House at Battleship Cove, September-June, 9 a.m. to 5 p.m.; July-August, 9 a.m. to 5 p.m. Closed on major holidays.

Vicksburg National Military Park-Cairo Museum—Vicksburg, Mississippi. 3201 Clay St. Site of Civil War battle. Visitors center, many monuments and maps of action during siege. The Cairo Museum displays the remains of the famous gunboat Cairo under a canopy and artifacts in the museum. Open days and hours: October 27-April 5 and October 26-April 4, 8:30 a.m. to 5 p.m.; April 6 to October 26, 9:30 a.m. to 6 p.m. Mail to 3201 Clay St., Vicksburg, MS 39180. Phone: 601-636-2199, fax: 601-638-7329.

Old Courthouse Museum—Court Square, Vicksburg. Civil War relics. Mack Moore glass negatives and prints of steamboats. Open Monday-Saturday, 8:30 a.m. to 4:30 p.m.; Sunday, 1:30 to 4:30 p.m. Closed on major holidays. Mail address: 1008 Cherry St., Vicksburg, MS 39180. Phone: 601-636-0741. (When I visited the Old Courthouse some years ago, I opened the door and a phonograph started playing "Dixie.")

Gray and Blue Naval Museum—Vicksburg. The museum has more than 84 models of Union and Confederate Civil War boats and is getting more. Dioramas of the siege of Vicksburg and Battle At Big

287

Black Hawk River. Paintings. Mail to: 1101 Washington Ave., Vicksburg, MS 39180. Phone: 601-638-6500.

Mississippi River Commission History Center—1413 Walnut St., Vicksburg. Corps of Engineers material on flood control, Mississippi River channel work, etc. Models of U.S. Engineers vessels. Maps, drawings, newspaper clippings. Mail to: P.O. 60, Vicksburg, MS 39181-0080. Phone: 601-634-7023. Open Monday-Friday, 8 a.m. to 3:30 p.m.

Historic Warship & Nautical Center—Government Street and Mississippi River, Baton Rouge, Louisiana. Centered on World War II items, including the destroyer Kidd, it has many models, and it is said there is a replica of a steamboat pilothouse. Mail: 305 South River Rd., Baton Rouge, LA 70802-6220. Phone: 504-342-1942. Open 9 a.m. to 5 p.m., seven days a week. Closed Thanksgiving and Christmas.

Ohio River

River Museum—Wellsville, Ohio. River, railroad, Civil War, pottery items on display. Mail to: 1003 Riverside Ave., Wellsville, OH 43968 or P.O. Box 13. Open June-September, Sunday, 1-5 p.m., last two weeks in November and first two weekends in December.

Ohio River Museum—Marietta, Ohio. This is one of the most extensive river museums. Based on artifacts collected by the Sons & Daughters of Pioneer Rivermen. Displays models, pictures, whistles and artifacts. Small vessels. Has pilothouse of the Tell City. The towboat W. P. Snyder, Jr., is tied up in the Muskingum River below the museum. Good example of a working Ohio River towboat. Mail to: 601 Second St., Marietta, OH 45750-2122. Phone: 614-373-3750. Open Wednesday-Saturday, 9:30 a.m. to 5 p.m. and Sunday noon to 5 p.m. in March, April, October and November; Monday-Saturday 9:30 a.m. to 5 p.m., Sunday and holidays noon to 5 p.m. May through September. Closed December, January and February. (The Snyder is open from April 15 to the last weekend in October with the same hours as the museum.)

Becky Thatcher Restaurant and Theatre—237 Front St., Marietta, Ohio. The former U.S. Engineer towboat Mississippi is now an eating establishment with a theatre. It was in St. Louis for many years. Mail to: P.O. Box 572, Marietta, OH 45750. Phone: 740-373-6033.

Majestic Showboat—Foot of Broadway, Public Landing, Cincinnati, Ohio. One of two existing showboats. Various programs. Phone: 573-334-5138.

Howard Steamboat Museum—1101 East Market St., Jeffersonville, Indiana. In the mansion of the Howard family of boat-building fame. The house has original furnishings, and the museum displays many steamboat models, pictures and artifacts.

Special programs through the years. Exhibits and material on LSTs, many of which were built at Jeffersonville. The Carriage House, behind the museum, is being developed for use as a river museum. Newsletter is entitled *Bitts and Pieces.* Mailing address: P.O. Box 606, Jeffersonville, IN 47130. Phone: 812-2283-3728.

River Heritage Museum—Paducah, Kentucky. The old Federal Bank Building is being developed into a museum. It will be part of the Center for Maritime Education at Paducah and is an initiative of The Seaman's Church Institute of New York City. It is adjacent to a building with classes for rivermen and simulators of towboat pilot-houses for training. There will be models, pictures and artifacts. Mail to: 117 South Water St., Paducah, KY 42001. Phone: 502-575-9958. There are river murals on Paducah's flood wall.

Cairo Custom House Museum—Cairo, Illinois. Civil War items, including flag pole from steamer Tigress, model of the gunboat Cairo, and anchor. Mail to: 1400 Washington, Cairo, IL 62914. Phone: 618-734-1019. Open 10 a.m. to noon and 1 to 3 p.m., Monday through Friday.

Other Museums

American Merchant Marine Museum—Kings Point, New York. Adjacent to the U.S. Merchant Marine Academy. Many models and pictures, mainly of deep sea vessels, but it's Hall of Fame in years gone by inducted western rivers boats and people, including the steamer Golden Eagle and Capt. William H. "Buck" Leyhe. Mail to U.S. Merchant Marine Academy, Kings Point, NY 11024-1699. Phone 516-773-5515, fax 516-482-5340.

Arkansas River Historical Society Museum—Catoosa, Oklahoma. (Tulsa Port of Catoosa) Pictures and artifacts of the McClellan-Kerr Arkansas River Navigation System. Address 5350 Cimarron Road, Catoosa, OK 74015. Phone: 918-266-2291, fax 918-266-7678. Open Monday-Friday, 8 a.m. to 4:30 p.m.

Mariners' Museum—Newport News, Virginia. This is one of the best marine museums of all. There is a river connection—the roof bell of the steamer Kate Adams is outside the entrance. Many artifacts, books, paintings and drawings. Address: 100 Museum Dr., Newport News, VA 23606. Phone 757-596-2222 or 800-581-7245, fax 757-591-7311. E-mail, info@mariner.org. Web: www.mariner.org. Open 10 a.m. to 5 p.m. Closed Thanksgiving and Christmas.

Monongahela River Museum—Monongahela, Pennsylvania. Models, pictures, artifacts. Address 175 Second St., Monongahela, PA 15063. Phone 724-938-7856 or 258-6231. Open Tuesday-Thursday, 6-8 p.m. and Sunday 1-3 p.m.

Tennessee River Museum—Savannah, Tennessee. St. Louis and Tennessee Packet Company exhibit, with artifacts from steamer City of Florence, which sank nearby. Civil War and musseling exhibits as well. Address: 507 Main St., Savannah, TN 38372. Phone 901-925-2364. Open Monday-Saturday, 9 a.m. to 5 p.m.; Sunday, 1-5 p.m.

Texas Maritime Museum—Rockport, Texas. Models, shipbuilding tools and pictures. Address: 1202 Navigation Circle, Rockport, TX 78382-2773. Phone 512-729-1271, fax 512-729-9938. Open Tuesday-Saturday, 10 a.m. to 4 p.m.; Sunday, 1-4 p.m.; closed major holidays.

Clifton Steamboat Museum, 7777 Fannett Road, Beaumont, Texas. Tug Hercules is outside the museum. Displays include 40 ships and models and a replica of the walking beam of the Clifton, a vessel involved in the Civil War in Texas waters. Mailing address is P.O. Box 20115, Beaumont, TX 77720. Phone: 409-842-3162 and 842-3326. Fax: 409-842-4049. Open by appointment.

National Museum of American History, the Smithsonian Institution, Washington, D.C. 14th and Constitution Avenue, NW. Phone: 202-357-2700. The marine or maritime section has a towboat pilothouse and models of river vessels. Open 10 a.m. to 5:30 p.m.

Corps of Engineers Museum, Fort Leonard Wood, Missouri. Near St. Robert, Missouri, off I-44. South Dakota and Nebraska Streets in fort. Replica of river snagboat pilothouse and Corps of Engineers items. Open 9 a.m. to 4 p.m.

One thing we tend to note is that many museums seem to end their collections with the end of the steamboat era. But, the river is still very much alive, and I would hope they would give more attention to the towboat era.

In addition to these public collections, there are some private ones I know of that are exceptional. They are at the homes of Keith Norrington, 629 Roseview Terrace, New Albany, IN 47150; Judy Patsch, 921 21st Ave., Rock Island, IL 61201; and Dave Thomson, 10531 Roycroft St., #16, Sun Valley, CA 91342.

Please Do Not Throw Away Any River Material! Let these museums or libraries know about it. I believe they will be interested and that every bit of river history should be preserved.*

Note: I am aware this is not my first mention of this request, but if we are not dedicated to preserving it, much river material can be lost.

Chapter 32——

Sounds of The River

We have had calls at the *Journal* from people doing documentaries and other similar projects; they want to know what music was played on the steamboats. Well, if we are talking about in the cabins, it would just the same as that on the land. The boats weren't that far away from civilization.

Many boats had orchestras or groups of musicians who played during dinner and for dancing after the tables were cleared away. The Golden Eagle, for instance, had three players—on piano, drums and saxaphone.

Some boats were even immortalized in songs being written for them and their captains. There was, for instance, the "City of Alton Schottische" and the "Martha Jewett Polka," the latter dedicated to the boat and Capt.W. C. Jewett by Max Zorer.

Other boats are known in song. People have been "Waitin' For The Robt. E. Lee" for years, but even the famous American song writer Stephen Foster wrote "When The Glendy Burke Comes Down." (This was a real boat, built by the Howard Shipyard at Jeffersonville, Indiana, in 1851. It was a sidewheeler that ran between Louisville and New Orleans.) Then there was the "Jasper Schottisch" done by R. Frank Cardella in honor of the steamer Tom Jasper of the St. Louis and Quincy

Packet Company and dedicated to the officers of that vessel. "The Steamer Saint Louis March" was written for the St. Louis and Tennessee River Packet Company packet of that name.

Today, the Delta Queen has been honored by at least two compositions. A waltz-song, "Steamboat Delta Queen" was written for piano, organ or steam calliope by E. J. Quinby (I'm not sure of the date.) but the DQ was still a Greene Line boat. Today one of favorite tunes at John Hartford's concerts is his "Delta Queen Waltz."

The music down on deck is a different matter. It is one of America's world-known types of music, sung by the roustabouts in their work. Fortunately, Mary Wheeler, of Paducah, collected these songs, and she used them for her master's thesis in musicology at the Cincinnati Conservatory of Music. The stories and information gathered with the songs were used for the book *Steamboatin' Days*, published by the Louisiana State University Press. Later they were sung by Bertha Wenzel for an LP record called "Folk Songs Of The River."

Some boats are featured in these songs, such as the Stacker Lee, John Gilbert, Kate Adams and Joe Fowler. And then there is "Bayou Sara Burned Down," this being about the night at New Madrid, Missouri, when the Anchor Line's City of Bayou Sara caught fire and was consumed. Eight people died.

There also are the haunting tunes like "Alberta, Let Yo' Hair Hang Low" and "Ohio River, She's So Deep and Wide."

We could classify the calling of the lead line a work song, and so it has been done on many records. In those days before depth recorders, the water had to be measured with a lead line, made of rawhide or rope, upon which was placed strips of cloth or leather, and a heavy lead weight on the end. As it slipped through the fingers of the man who threw it from the bow of the boat, he would call back to the man on the roof the depth of the water. Each man had his own particular tone or tune, and some of them are captured by Bertha Wenzel. Others are on a record of *Negro Work Songs and Calls* (done by the Library of Congress) as edited by B. A. Botkin; and sung by three men at Greenville, Mississippi. The Corps of Engineers—I believe it was the Memphis District—did a great recording on the steamer Mississippi one year; it featured calling the lead at a shoal crossing and passing the word back to the pilothouse.

The Calls

Quarter Less Twain	10 ½ feet	Mark Twain	12 feet
Quarter Twain	13 ½ feet	Half Twain	15 feet
Quarter Less Tyree	16 ½ feet	Mark Tyree	18 feet
Quarter Tyree	19 ½ feet	Half Tyree	21 feet
Quarter Less Four	22 ½ feet	Mark Four	24 feet
		No Bottom	

The most famous, of course, is the one for 12 feet, for it was used by writer Samual Clemens as his *nom de plume*.

The other unusual sound from steamboats and showboats came from the steam calliope, or steam piano as it was sometimes called. The music could be heard from a long way off, and it was most beneficial to passenger and excursion boats (particularly the latter) to get people down to the river. Needing so much steam to operate, it would be natural to have them on a steamboat or something coupled to a steam line on a towboat. Now, calliope music is not everybody's cup of tea, so to speak, but it was spectacular to those people in river towns in the days before radio, television, cassettes, video tapes and VCRs.

There were and are some great calliope players such as Homer Denny, Capt. Clarke "Doc" Hawley, E. J. Quinby and Vic Tooker. Capt. C. W. Stoll and Keith Norrington have performed on the calliope on the Avalon-Belle of Louisville. The Belle's regular calliope players have been Eileen Donavan and Joshua Caplinger. Another calliope player was Travis Vasconcelos.

The instrument was invented by one Joshua Stoddard of Vermont. It was used on a steamboat (actually a tug) in New York in 1856. The first calliope into St. Louis was on the Amazon on November 28, 1856. It could be heard when the boat was a mile downriver; by the time the boat had reached the levee, the townspeople had all turned out to see this new thing. (Capt. William Carroll found the account in a St. Louis newspaper.) Capt. Vern Streckfus recalled that a boat would approach what appeared to be an abandoned landing with its calliope playing, and people would appear like magic.

And what is a calliope? A number of steam whistles, 32 or so, mounted together and connected to a keyboard by wires. When a key is pressed, a wire raises a valve, allowing steam to blow a whistle. It is hard work pressing the keys, and players frequently wear a raincoat to keep dry.

The sounds of the calliope have been preserved on records and tapes. My music shelf has these:

> *The Delta Queen Calliope*, with Vic Tooker, pianist Dan Foreman and organist Pete Eveland. It is an LP record by the Delta Queen Steamboat Company.

> *Here Comes The Showboat*! With "Doc" Hawley (pictured with the Avalon and showboats and W. R. Markle). It is an LP produced by Golden Crest Records.

> *Steamboat 'Round The Bend*, with "Doc" Hawley and Vic Tooker and combo on the steamer Natchez. It is an LP produced by Tad Records, Inc.

> *Calliope Selections*, Belle of Louisville (player not named). It's a cassette.

> *The Twilight*, with some calliope by Elizabeth Trone, and other music. It's a cassette.

> There is also a Calliaphone made by Tangley and operated by air. There is a cassette of one called *Brass Whistle Ballyhoo*, made by Marvin Kelley.

For most people river music would mean the tunes heard on the dance floor of an excursion boat, and there were some great bands on the boats over the years.

The most famous, perhaps, is Fate Marable and his jazz ensemble on the Streckfus boats, notably the Capitol. In his group was a young man named Louis Armstrong, who was, as everyone knows, to become a world-renowned musician. There is a story that he was so shy that he wouldn't do a solo. Capt. John Streckfus threatened to put him off the boat unless he did.

Jazz came up the river from New Orleans on the boats; it was played on them in the South, and the bands, like Fate Marable, stayed aboard when the season started up the river. Others in Marable's group included Baby Dodds, Bebe Ridgely, Joe Howard, Louis Armstrong, David Jones, Johnny Dodds, John St. Cyr and Pops Foster, many of whom also became noted jazz men.

The Streckfus brothers were particular about the music on their boats, and it is said that John Streckfus would stand by the band with his watch out, counting the beat. Another Streckfus story is that one band played the new "Turkey Trot," which the captain considered so lewd that he stopped it and said if the band did it again, he would throw them off the boat.

In 1976 Jules Buffano and his Montmartre Orchestra, from Chicago, were on the J.S. at night; Max Newby's Melody Makers were on the J.S. for day trips; the New Orleans Harmony Serenaders were on the Saint Paul at night; Pol Syncopating Artists were on the Saint Paul by day; Tony's Iowa Band was on the Capitol; and Schaefer's Melody Kings were on the Washington.

Later, day bands that were popular on the Admiral were Johnny Polzin and Bob Kuban. Today on Gateway Riverboat Cruises' Tom Sawyer and Becky Thatcher is the Don Scherrer Banjo Band. (It has a couple of cassettes available.) Also on the Admiral were Hal Havard and Dick Renna.

There were on other excursion boats, of course, bands of note with which I am not acquainted. It is interesting to remember that these boats had the biggest dance floors in the country, especially the Admiral's.

When you think of river music today the name that comes to mind is John Hartford. No one has been a better ambassador for the river. "Gentle On My Mind" is his trademark, but his river songs are just as important. He was a student of Ruth Ferris, and to her he says he owes his love of the river; he does a song about her, "Miss Ferris," at nearly every concert. They are almost always sold out. John has several albums and tapes, but the one I enjoy most is called "Headin' Down Into The Mystery Below." A sketch of the Julia Belle Swain is on the front of the jacket, and sketches of golden eagles on the back. Mississippi Queen and Ruth Ferris are on the back along with some nice poetry. One of the songs on the album is "Beatty's

Navy," which was recorded, a note says, in the pilothouse of the Julia Belle Swain at Massengale Rock, Mile 446.0, Tennessee River. In addition to this one, John does a couple of my favorites, "Kentucky Pool" and "In Plain View Of The Town." (This is a Flying Fish record from 1978.) One of his more recent songs, "Old Time River Man," can bring a tear to one's eyes. And there also is his rendition of "Lorena." He now lives in Madison, Tennessee, on the bank of the Cumberland River near Nashville, Tennessee. (A river light has been named after him.)

Up at La Crosse, there is Eddie Allen, who sings river songs. He did an album in 1985 called *The Trempealeau Hotel,* which is a landmark on the Upper Mississippi. He has some delightful songs on the album, which is divided into "Songs of Love" and "Songs of The River." In the former there is one dedicated to, and named for Captain Walter Karnath, and in the latter are those entitled "The Sprague Song" and "The Trempealeau Hotel." Weary Wolf Records put it out; Eddie may have done others of which I am unaware. He lived in Trempealeau.

In St. Louis, Guy Louis Selbert and Maryann Hamer have a show called "On The River," which they have done on the Julia Belle Swain and the Belle of Louisville.

Tapes have been made on the Julia Belle Swain both at LeClaire, Iowa, and LaCrosse. The first included songs by John Hartford, songs on the hammered dulcimer by Ace and Libby Trone, and vocals and violin by Amanda Trone. Also, Jamie Hartford is heard on the violin, guitar and bass; Van Pedigo on the banjo and guitar and Scott Stoke on the guitar. A new one from the Julia Belle is entitled "Light Off, Warm Up, Throw Lines." It features Keith "Beau" Inman, Lee Mavik, and John Bernhardt.

There is also a Twilight tape. It has Elizabeth Trone and Amanda Trone Serra on the dulcimer, and vocals by Amanda Serra. Elizabeth plays the calliope.

Going through my music shelf I also found these:

Jazzou Jones Riverboat Ragtime—two cassettes and an LP record. He plays often on the boats, including the P. A. Denny. The Mike Fink's paddlewheel is on the jacket.

Take Me To The River—a tape by Mike Gentry and Ray Leake contains familiar river songs.

Riverboat Shuffle—a tape by Mike Gentry and Tom Hook.

Riverboat Shuffle—a CD, river songs from the Memphis Archives.

The Back Porch Majority: Riverboat Days!—an LP record with the group in front of the Delta Queen. Contains some original river songs.

The New Christy Minstrels: Ramblin'—some river songs, even though the Minstrels are shown leaning on a freight car.

Steamboat's A Comin'—an LP record from the National Geographic Society. The Idlewild is on the cover, and a two sheet picture of the Lee-Natchez race is included inside (Dean Cornwell). And George Caleb Bingham's *The Jolly Flatboatmen*, sketch of the steamer Buckeye State and a picture of a Pittsburgh steamboat parade with the replica of the New Orleans. Music includes sounding calls and the Glendy Burke.

Jazz and steamboats are loved internationally. I have had the pleasure of corresponding for many years with Zbynek Macha (in what is now the Czech Republic) who loves both. He arranged for three albums of blues, jazz and river songs called "Pisne Otce Vod" 1, 2 and 3. With 1 and 2 come booklets with steamboat pictures and descriptions of the songs. (I guess that's what they are; I can't read a word of them.) He has also done a tape, *Steamboat Salon*.

Some classical music has come from the river, too. The most famous, of course, is Ferde Grofe's "Mississippi Suite," with inspiring parts. Also inspiring is the music Virgil Thomson did for the documentary film, *The River*. Then William Perry did music for the film *Life On The Mississippi*, with sections for *Adventures of Huckleberry Finn* and *Life On The Mississippi*. (I have a CD of it.)

There have been musicals about the river, too. *Big River* is based on the adventures of Huck Finn. The show includes the song "Muddy Water." The show's music won a Tony Award for best musical.

Who can forget *Showboat*, with the great song of all time—"Old Man River"?

From *Pajama Game*, from a book written by a real riverman, Richard Bissel, there is the lively "Something's Always Happening On The River."

River enthusiasts had great expectations for the television series *River of Song*, labeled by the Public Broadcasting System as a "musical journey down the Mississippi," but it was all land music except for John Hartford's segment, which was cut short.

A song that has been a favorite for years, and probably inspired the first Mickey Mouse cartoon, is "Steamboat Bill," written by Ren Shields.

Conway Twitty, the popular country singer, worked on his father's ferry at Helena, Arkansas. One of his hits is "Louisiana Woman, Mississippi Man."

Before we leave this subject, I'd like to mention one other song that doesn't really fit into any of the categories mentioned: The "Ohio River Song" by A. J. P. Vandermyn. He did it to commemorate the completion of the canalization of the Ohio River in 1929, and it was played on the flagship of the steamboat parade that went from Pittsburgh to Cairo—the Cincinnati. Chuck Parrish, public relations chief for the Louisville Engineer District, found a copy for me.

Back to the river and the boats. What beautiful music was that of the big roof bells, with their deep tones. They called the passengers back to the boats and gave the final warning of departure. These bells are prized possessions, and some have gone to churches; St. John's Lutheran in Ellisville, Missouri, has the one from Capt. Ben F. Hutchison's Commonwealth, Continental or Sovereign (it could have been on all three); and the First Christian Church in Paducah has the Kentucky's bell.

There were other bells on the boats, those in the enginerooms. Their various rings called the engineers to handle the throttles, and so moved the engines and the vessels.

What was more satisfying than lying in your bed, listening to those steamboats? The real music of the river was the steady wheeze of the exhaust in the stacks, the jingle of the engine-room bells, and the peal of the whistle.

Indeed, the whistle is the soul of the boat, they say. They came in many varieties from the wildcat ones, which farmers on the Gasconade River took to be real wild animals, to the deep-throated boom of such big boats as the Sprague.

They could bring tears to your eyes. William A. Percy, in *Lanterns On The Levee*, said it well: "And there is no sound in the world so filled with mystery and longing and unease as the sound at night of a river-boat blowing for the landing—one long, two shorts, one long, two shorts. Over the somber levels of the water pours that great voice, so long prolonged it is joined by echoes from the willowed shore, a chorus of ghosts, and, roused from sleep, wide-eyed and still, you are oppressed by vanished glories, the last trump, the calling of the ends of the earth, the current, ceaselessly moving out into the dark, of the eternal dying." *

Many of these steamboat whistles have been preserved; the biggest collection being in the Ohio River Museum at Marietta. They were collected originally by Dan Heekin.

There have been several "Whistle Blows." The first two were arranged by Fred Way, and J. Mack Gamble narrated them, or at least took part in the proceedings. The sounds were recorded on LP records.

Nelson Jones, president of Madison Coal and Supply Company, has built a blowing apparatus, complete with boiler, on a barge towed by the Lady Lois, and he has taken it to S&D meetings, Tall Stacks, and Jack Custer's steamboat conference in Louisville a few years back.

Note: For this beautiful piece we are indebted to Capt. Paul Striegel, who sent it after the death of Capt. George Reid in Greenville, Mississippi. This piece from Lanterns On The Levee was read at the funeral and then Howard Brent blew the landing whistle—adding a very nice touch to the end of the service.

EXTRA

One of the busiest people I know is William J. Shrive, Belleville, Illinois. A member of old mill, canal, covered bridge and river societies, he is an officer and director of the Golden Eagle River Museum—besides being a regular volunteer at the museum. Shive was president of the Sterling Steel Casting Company, which made deck fittings for boats and barges—cavals, bitts, buttons, etc. He is interested in history of all kinds and has done a lot of work on the Shive family history. I am happy to say that he is not one of a kind.

Jim

Chapter 33——

Climbing The Family Tree

*T*he *Waterways Journal* gets letters like this:

"There is a family tradition that my grandfather was a steamboat captain. Send me all you know about him."

Well, now, if any of the readers of this book get the urge to climb their family tree on a river limb, please:

- Tell us the years he was on the river
- What rivers he worked on
- And above all, what boats he was on

It will pinpoint facts that are important to know in doing research on river-related subjects—boats and rivermen. I do enjoy doing research, although I have a backlog from which I am trying to extricate myself.

There is a big interest in genealogy these days, and we suspect most of the *Journal* readers know about checking the newspapers for obituaries and offices for vital statistics for death certificates; but there are some sources that may not be so well known.

For instance, *The Waterways Journal* has a list of those whose notices of death had appeared in the Annual Review Issue between 1938 and 1973. The list shows the dates on which obituaries appeared in the *Journal's* previous 12 months, date of death and other information.

For other information on the spelling of names and company affiliations during the towboat era, a good source would be the list of registrants at the big conventions—Mississippi Valley Association, Ohio Valley Improvement Association, and the Gulf Intracoastal Canal Association. The MVA-WRC lists appeared between 1959 and 1971.

Names of men and boats can also be checked out with the indexes of Capt. Frederick Way, Jr.'s, important directories of steamboats and towboats. Two important indexes of river publications are those for the *S&D Reflector*, the newsletter of the Sons and Daughters of Pioneer Rivermen; and *River Ripples*, from the Midwest Riverboat Buffs.

An invaluable source is the series of books the Herman T. Pott National Inland Waterways Library is doing on the contents of *The Waterways Journal*. The first one is for *Journals* from 1891 to 1900. Work is underway at the Pott Library on later issues.

If your ancestor was involved in the Civil War, he might be listed in the *Official Records of the Union and Confederate Navies*, a many-volume set of books with a good index of both people and boat names.

Then there is the National Archives and Records Administration in Washington, D.C. They have millions of files on just about everything; so it is important, when contacting them, to know exactly what you want. The material is kept in Record Groups. Those interested in river history would most likely want information on boat documentation and licenses in Record Group 26, the Coast Guard, or Record Group 41, Bureau of Marine Inspection and Navigation. (Office of the Chief of Engineers is in Record Group 79.)

Regarding the original licenses of rivermen, our information is that they are no longer in existence; but the National Archives do have some information on them, if not the documents themselves. (Many people do not know that carpenters on the river had to have licenses.)

Documents of the vessels come in several forms, according to tonnage, 20 tons and over and under, and certificates of tonnage admeasurements. There is a lot of information of not only the vessels but also their owners and operators.

Contact Reference Services, National Archives and Records Administration, 700 Pennsylvania Ave., NW, Washington, DC, 20408-0001; phone 202-501-5400; E-mail, inquire@nara.gov. My contact has been Richard Peuser, at 202-501-5385.

The Archives has been breaking up its records and sending them to their regional offices to provide easier access to people away from Washington. The marine records have been included. The breakdown is given here to help interested parties find their information quicker.

Great Lakes Region
7358 South Pulaski Road
Chicago, IL 60629
Phone: 773-581-7816
E-mail: archives@chicago.nara.gov
Fax: 312-353-1294

All of the categories of records may be held for the years to be given; the years shown are the limits for each port.

Burlington, Iowa—1867-1914
Chicago—1865-1966
Des Moines, Iowa—1913-1939

Dubuque, Iowa—1865-1939
Evansville, Indiana—1865-1968
Galena, Illinois—1871-1914

La Crosse, Wisconsin—1874-1921
Louisville, Kentucky—1857-1924
Paducah, Kentucky—1883-1940

Peoria, Illinois—1891-1925
Rock Island, Illinois—1891-1915
Sioux City, Iowa—1901-1931

Southeast Region
1557 St. Joseph Ave.
East Point, GA (Atlanta) 30344-2593
Phone: 404-763-7477

Mobile, Alabama—1887-1964
Memphis, Tennessee—1939-1961
(Inventory available on microfiche.)

Southwest Region
501 West Felix St.
P.O. Box 6216
Fort Worth, TX 76115-0216
Phone: 817-334-5515

New Orleans, Louisiana—1853-1942
Baytown, Texas—1922-1944
Beaumont, Texas—1934-1943

Brownsville, Texas—1875-1922
Galveston, Texas—1860-1942
Houston, Texas—1908-1942

Port Arthur, Texas—1933-1942
Vicksburg, Mississippi—1906-1924
(Inventory available on microfiche.)

Central Plains Region
2312 E. Bannister Road
Kansas City, MO 64131-3011
Phone: 816-926-6920

Cairo, Illinois—1870-1916
Dubuque, Iowa/Galena, Illinois—1856-1942
Duluth, Minnesota—1871-1919
St. Paul, Minnesota—1871-1942
Kansas City, Missouri—1886-1914
St. Louis, Missouri—1835-1942

They also have records from the Red River of the North at Pembina, North Dakota.

Microfilm records of the Kansas City records are in the Herman T. Pott National Inland Waterways Library; they were donated by Herman Radloff.

Mid-Atlantic Region
900 Market St.
Philadelphia, PA 19107-4292
Phone: 215-597-3000

Pittsburgh, Pennsylvania—1892-1946
Wheeling, West Virginia 1901-1913
(Inventory available on microfiche.)

I haven't seen mention of the records for Madison, Indiana, or Cincinnati, Ohio, so hopefully they are safe in Washington, as are the years not listed for the regional offices.

Early river material can be found in reports to Congress called *Report on the Finances* (1852); these were, at that time, in the yearly reports of the Steamboat Inspection Service. These give the changes in rules for machinery and boiler inspections, accidents in some detail, a list of licenses issued, and vessels inspected and on what date. The date of a first inspection might lead to the description of a boat in the local newspapers. *The Waterways Journal* has them to 1911.

The list of merchant vessels lists all documented boats with their official numbers (good for tracing); dimensions are given beginning in 1885 (before this just the tonnage is shown), and in 1906 vessels lost (but no details of the accidents). The last issue of *Merchant Vessels of the United States* was 1994; they were published irregularly in the 1970s and '80s by the Coast Guard.

Happy climbing!

305

EXTRA

Though the WJ was converting to offset printing, we kept file cabinets full of heavy zincs—Old Boat pictures, etc. When we moved to the Security Building in 1978, a two-wheeler was used to push the cabinets onto the elevator. The goal was the fourth floor. After one or more cabinets full, the elevator went down about a foot. Operators held their breaths as they pushed the button and the car slowly crawled up to its destination.
Jim

Chapter 34——

Kept on an Even Keel

(Some Loose Ends)

H. N. "Ray" Spencer, Jr., who had retired as publisher of *The Waterways Journal* was listed in the masthead as chairman in July 1995. He died that year. It was in 1980 that Nelson Spencer III, a son, became publisher—only the fifth in the long history of the newspaper.

Nelson was with Crounse Corporation from 1966-1968, before joining the *WJ* staff in advertising sales in St. Louis in 1968. In 1970, he opened the *Journal*'s New Orleans office, then returned to St. Louis in 1972 and continued in sales until being named advertising sales manager in 1975. He continued in that post until being named publisher.

Another son, John, in advertising sales since 1977, moved to advertising sales manger in 1980.

Ray had been able to talk easily with leaders in industry, for he had been an advertising agency executive and knew top echelon people. The big move he made was to take the *Journal* from the Chemical Building in the 700 block of Olive Street, due east to the Security Building on North Fourth Street, from which the staff could actually see the river.

This is a classic *Waterways Journal* picture that shows two publishers and staff members that cover many years of the publication's history. It may have been taken in late 1964 or early 1965 in Donald T. Wright's office. The model of the steamer Mary Morton is in the background. In the front row, left to right, are Wright, publisher; Catherine Courtney, secretary; Claire Beatty, circulation manager; Mary Ann Gifford, ICC editor and long-time secretary. In the back row, left to right, Fred Hume, Jr., assistant to the publisher; Arthur Hirsch, news editor; James V. Swift, advertising and business manager; Joyce Favier, circulation; H. N. "Ray" Spencer, associate publisher; and Capt. Roy N. Barkhau, administrative assistant. (These were their 1965 titles.)

Nelson has held offices in the river organizations and has expanded the scope of the *Journal* organization to include recreational as well as commercial boating. *Heartland Boating* and *Quimby's Cruising Guide* are now in the stable at the Security Building.

In taking a look back at the paper's history, it is interesting to note how many people got their start in river history notoriety through the *Journal* at an early age.

Capt. Frederick Way, Jr., did his own biography for the April 19, 1919, *Journal*, telling the readers that for three years he had been the youngest subscriber to the paper, which would have made him 15. He had taken his first river trip in 1911 on the steamer Queen City. He started collecting steamboat pictures in 1914. When Fred began to write, his first efforts were published in the *Journal* and were well received. The readers know what happened after that—he bought the steamer Betsy Ann; wrote many books, including *The Log of the Betsy Ann* and the great packet directory and, with J. W. Rutter, the towboat directory. He was for years president of the Sons and Daughters of Pioneer Rivermen.

Charles W. "C. W." Stoll, also began writing for the *Journal* at the age of 15; he took his first steamboat trip on the Southland that year. He didn't sign his articles to the paper because, as he explained, who would believe a 15-year-old kid. C. W. was third clerk on the steamer Gordon C. Greene in 1933, her first season for the Greene family. He went to Carlton College at Northfield, Minnesota, and continued to do articles for the *Journal* while in school. When World War II came along, he went into the Coast Guard; as a steersman and assistant pilot he helped take 57 LSTs downriver. C. W. became chairman of the operating board for the Belle of Louisville when Jefferson County, Kentucky, bought her in 1962. He had earned his pilots and masters license. When Fred Way died, he (C. W.) became president of Sons and Daughters.

J. Mack Gamble started his "Notes From the Upper Ohio River" on July 6, 1916. He was also 15 when he began writing for the paper. Mack did his column for 52 years and also wrote the "Annual Review" for the Christmas issue for a long time. Included among his efforts was the book *Steamboats On The Muskingum*. Mack was very active in the S&D, and one year he gave a memorable speech titled "That's Progress." He died February 13, 1973.

Just as *The Waterways Journal* had few publishers, it also didn't have many news editors. Donald Wright decided in 1941 that he needed more help with the news. When I returned from the Army, I found Irwin McDonald Uring in the news editor's slot. A native of Baden, Pennsylvania, he had been with the *Ambridge* (Pa.) *Daily Citizen* and the Carnegie Hero Fund Foundation before joining the WJ. Although an Urling, he really favored the McDonald name, because that family had river connections. And, he liked the Scottish part of it. He would buy a whole box of neckties (with the McDonald clan tartan) at a time. Irwin was also one of the most dedicated of our new editors; each Sunday he would go down to St. Louis Fuel and Supply Company to wait for a towboat that was going to take on fuel. He'd hitch a ride up to Locks and Dam 26 and ride another boat back down.

One of Irwin's big scoops developed when he was on the steamer Golden Eagle on May 18, 1947. (He had been in my wedding party earlier that day.) When the boat sank on Grand Tower Island early the next morning, Irwin helped row a yawl to Grand Tower, Illinois, to tell the sad news. Actually, the current stopped them and two fishermen in an outboard towed them in. He also got a good news break on another river tragedy; his father was taking a shower in the YMCA in Pittsburgh when the excursion steamer Island Queen blew up there on September 9, 1947. So *The Waterways Journal* was the first to get the news.

Irwin and Donald Wright did not have a pleasant relationship, which leads to another humorous *Journal* story. One day Donald was "all over" Irwin for a misplaced comma or something of that nature. I looked in and saw Irwin's wastebasket on fire—from a cigarette, I guess. I filled a cup with water, ran in, and threw it on the fire. While this was going on, Donald never stopped talking.

After seven and a half years Irwin retired as news editor and went back to the Carnegie Hero Fund. He died February 27, 1988. He was last in the masthead on January 13, 1951.

There was no news editor during most of 1951. In fact, after Andy Franz died on June 29, 1951, Donald and I were the only names in the masthead.

James H. Lavely came aboard as news editor for the December 22, 1951, issue. From Joliet, Illinois, he had been writing news from the Illinois River for some time. Jim had been with the Ohio River Company and Central Barge Company. During dinner at a Propeller Club meeting in 1952 he disappeared; we later learned that he was being lured away from the *Journal* by a competitor. His name came out of the masthead after April 12, 1952.

Again the paper had no news editor. Then, on December 20, 1952, Capt. Roy L. Barkhau's name appeared in that capacity. Roy was a riverman from way back, having been with the Greene Line since 1933. He became general passenger agent for the Greene Line and later was purser on the steamer Gordon C. Greene. While on one of her trips, he met Capt. S. S. Yeandle, head of the Second Coast Guard District, who was recruiting rivermen for what was to be called the "Cat Fish Navy"; the purpose was to take war vessels downriver to New Orleans. Roy was in that service until 1945. He returned to the Greene Line and was again purser on the Gordon C. Greene and later on the Delta Queen.

We can attribute to Roy's river orientation his move in 1955 to start Mid-West Navigation, Inc., with the excursion barge Thunderbird and a towboat. It didn't work out, and he came back to the *Journal*. I've always thought it was a low point in his life to have to ask Donald Wright for his job back. He held the titles of administrative assistant and circulation manager. Roy retired from the *Journal* on February 1, 1969.

He wrote two books, *History of the Eagle Packet Company* and *Great Steamboat Race Between The Natchez And The Robt. E. Lee.* Roy and I were good friends, and on important holidays he joined us for dinner. He came back to St. Louis one year, and late one night I received a call from St. Louis City Hospital; they had picked Roy up on the street after a heart attack or stroke. He was in the hospital several weeks, and when he was able to travel, we took him to the airport. C. W. Stoll met him at the other end and took him to a home owned by C. W.'s father.

When Roy left for his river business, the paper was again without a news editor until Richard Armfield took over on December 7, 1955. A large and amiable person, his claim to fame in *Waterways Journal* history is that he talked Donald Wright into closing the office on Saturdays. We had been work-ing a half day on Saturdays at the time. (I don't think Donald ever forgave him.) Dick was interested in dramatics; he belonged to little theater groups. He served until 1963; his name was last seen in the October 19 mast-head.

Publisher Donald T. Wright, the author, and Richard Armfield, news editor.

This picture was posed in 1960 but for what reason, I cannot recall. It was probably to show my "little corner of the world."

Almost immediately Arthur Hirsch took over. He had been editor of *WorkBoat* magazine, published in the Greater New Orleans area. When he arrived, he was still driving a unique British-made car that he had acquired from Harry Peace, the magazine's publisher. Art didn't like New Orleans much, and he liked to tell the story about how, during a Mardi Gras parade, he had reached out to catch some beads thrown from a float, and someone pulled his wrist watch off his arm. He was a quiet man but most efficient. Art retired June 30, 1974.

Jack R. Simpson took over right away. A newspaper man, he was also a photographer, having operated his own photo studio at one time. Due to his frequent contact with authors during his 22 years with the *Journal*, he developed an interest in publishing—happily, I might add, or this book may never have reached the press. He has written WJ editorials for more than 20 years. Since he retired on June 3, 1996, Jack's company, J. R. Simpson & Associates, Inc., has produced for his customers more than a dozen river-related books, including manuals on subjects such radar, safety, rules and regulations. *Backing Hard Into River History* marks the introduction of a new book series being published by his Little River Books Division. In addition to the series, the company has plans to publish its first river-related historic novel. Its author is Dean Gabbert, who authored *The Log Of The Jessie Bill* (about raft boats on the Upper Mississippi) and who is presently completing a book that will follow this one in the Little River Books series.

Upon Jack's retirement, John S. Shoulberg, who had been assistant editor since 1991, stepped up to the plate as editor. John had been employed by St. Louis-area newspapers for years and possessed good writing and editing skills.

Each of the editors put his or her (remember Kathleen Smith?) mark on the style and production of the newspaper, making it more businesslike.

Other news department staff members who covered the waterfront included former employees Donald Grot, Randy Walleck, Dan Layton and Bill Morrison, in addition to a fluctuating list of correspondents.

Donald Wright and Ray Spencer had men on their staffs that the Army might have called chiefs-of-staff; they helped with the general business of the publication. Fred Hume, Jr., came aboard about the same time that Roy Barkhau did, December 20, 1952. He had been an aide to St. Louis Mayor Aloys Kaufmann, and was good at public relations. His name last appeared in the masthead on March 2, 1968.

J. Benton "Ben" Wilkins came to the *Journal* in mid-March 1969. He was good at handling production and advertising matters. In 1974, upon the arrival of a new editor and departure of Art Hirsch, it was decided to appoint Ben to serve as associate publisher in addition to his other duties. Due to Ben's health problems, John Spencer (Nelson's brother) became advertising sales manager in 1980 and served to August 2, 1991. Then came Rick M. Bensinger, whose term lasted through the end of June 1999.

Journal Publisher H. Nelson Spencer, right, presents to Guy Jester, vice president of J. S. Alberici Company, a painting of the Becky Thatcher by James Godwin Scott. Jester, former St. Louis District engineer, was being honored for his work for the Corps and his contributions to the Association for the Improvement of the Mississippi River.

A new development took place upon Rick's departure. Edward H. Rahe, who had joined the *Journal* news staff in June 1996, became director of business development, a responsibility that includes advertising and work with the various *Journal* publications.

I remind readers that my work with the *Journal* has covered six decades. Unfortunately there are employees I don't remember. But in any case, my intention has not been to list them all—just the ones with whom readers and advertisers may have had contact.

During the early days, the *Journal* had advertising agents—Don Dennett in Chicago and Robert U. Kayser in New York City.

The *Journal* has always been fortunate to have on staff over its many years some efficient, pleasant and faithful women who had a knack for soothing the waters when things got rough. Mary Ann Boschert (who became Mary Ann Gifford) was secretary and held other positions for many years. She even did some reporting. Alice Hammann followed, and then Martha Kranefuss, who was also assistant business manager at one time. Claire Beatty was active for 30 years before she retired in July 1974. Also putting in 30 years of faithful service before her retirement was Cathy Courtney. All of these women possessed a variety of office skills and were were crucial to the operation. Presently serving in that capacity is Joyce Cassidy, a most pleasant, efficient secretary.

I mentioned the establishment of the New Orleans office earlier. Serving there at different times were H. E. Falboum, Wade McIntyre, and Jeff Yates. Later, William A. Evans, Jr., took over the office, and Jeff established an office at Paducah, Kentucky. The New Orleans office has subsequently been moved to Mandeville, Louisiana. Operating satellite offices is more difficult than working in the home office. The managers not only had to handle advertising matters but write news stories and features as well. Each office was responsible for a sizable geographical area.

With the addition of other publications, the order of things has changed, with new titles and responsibilities at the *Journal*. The masthead from the 1999 Annual Review Issue reflect this:

It lists: H. Nelson Spencer, publisher; John S. Shoulberg, editor; Daniel C. Owen, associate editor; Matthew W. Sorrell, staff writer; James V. Swift, contributing editor—Old Boat Column; Jack R. Simpson, contributing editor—editorials; Edward H. Rahe, director of business development; Damien Yank, advertising sales assistant; Cyndi Wiley, production artist; Victoria Flint, classified advertising; Laura E. Schindler, circulation; Linda L. Deutschlander, accounts receivable; Joyce A. Cassidy, secretary; and William A. Evans, Jr., who manages the Mandeville office. (Weekly mastheads also list e-mail addresses.)

A word is in order about Dan Owen's multi-purpose role for the *Journal*. He served as editor and compiled the *Inland River Guide* right from its conception. Early on, he assisted Capt. Fred Way with work on the *Inland River Record* and then became its editor. He continued holding three editor titles under this unique arrangement—he even shipped the IRGs and IRRs— until his retirement in August 2000. River people he talked to about stories for the *Journal* could expect to be quizzed about boat name changes, repowerings, boat sales, company takeovers, etc. For every phone call he made there was the potential for gaining valuable information for each of the three publications, and he did. His avocation, collecting boat pictures, also provided an invaluable service to the *Journal*.

A word about Robert H. Kennedy, who wrote the Upper Ohio News and the "Annual Review" for several years. He worked at Merdie Boggs boat store at Catlettsburg, Kentucky, where he was in touch with the boats.

Finally I got a fleet of my own.

When Bob died, I went to the funeral. While standing on the porch of the funeral parlor while the rain fell outside, I told a man standing next to me that it was going to be hard to find someone to replace Bob as writer of the "Upper

Ohio River News" column. He replied that he would like to try. That man was Capt. David Smith, who has done a great job. Susan Eastman stopped writing the "Annual Review" in 1999. It may now be staff written. Also appearing is "Texas Gulf News," by Roy Durrenberger. "Columbia River Watch, by Rick Rubin, has been discontinued. John R. Miller now writes the "Keokuk News" column previously authored by his father, Robert.

The latest news from the Nation's capitol has come to the *Journal* for seven years from Carlo J. Salzano, who knows his way around from working with *Traffic World*. Carlo was editor of the popular magazine until it relocated, and he decided not to move with it. He now covers the Washington scene for several publications.

Some former columns were relatively regular but not weekly. They included "Cook's Corner," written first by Rose M. Stauffer, a riverboat cook and resident of Illinois. Rose published the cook book, *Galley Favorites*. The column was later written by Sharon Runsick of Arkansas, who compiled a cook book called *Cookin' & Towin' On The River with Sharon Runsick*. Joe M. Dee of Cincinnati spent years in law enforcement and provided various investigative services for towing companies; he submitted an occasional column called "Rocks and Shoals." It involved maritime legal matters. Finally, Denny Kundert, formerly of the St. Louis, Missouri, area, now of Louisiana, provided columns dealing with towboat safety. They ran under the heading "Focus on Safety."

Another *Journal* feature, though not a column, was a cartoon strip, *Tommy Towboater,* produced by Capt. Luke A. Moore, now port captain for Western Kentucky Navigation, Inc. Some may have raised their eyebrows when Moore had an ancient sternwheeler, fueled by aviation gas, flying down the river at warp speed, but a *Journal* survey inquiring into reader interest had *Tommy Towboater* listed among the first features read by subscribers.

A last note about the *Journal*. As a bonus to advertisers, I once compiled a little booklet of historical material called *River Drift* from 1952-1969. Also, a *Journal* insert called *From The Pilothouse* appeared in some issues; it, too, focused on marine issues.

Chapter 35——

Full Ahead

W^e have been backing long enough. A new century is here, so let's go full ahead to close out this book.

It is really a new world in communications now, with the Internet beginning to dominate everything. You can find about anything on the net—if you have the right key!

There are, for instance, "Capt. Randy's River Pages," coded for Netscape Navigator 3.0 under http//members.com/randi-ward/river.htm. The pages we are working with are updated to January 6, 1999; they have the following leads to Internet listings: Wabash Queen. River Boat Cruising (Jerry has done some interesting things with an old houseboat); Shantyboats; Mississippi Riverboat Pilot; Tugboat Willie's pages, into Columbia River traffic, tug photos, works on the boats; Life on the River With Towboater Poncho Villa, David Estrada's site, dedicated to a towboater's way of living, he is a deck-hand/tankerman in Texas; Mississippi River Home Page; Upper Mississippi; Henry Bosse's River Photos; Murphy Library; John Hartford's Steamboat Photo Page; Illinois Valley River Project; American Heritage Rivers Initiative; Modeling Towboats; and Plans For a River Ntrak Module.

Randy Ward is interested in modeling, and the address of the Inland River Workboat Modelers is on his web page. He has tips on getting more information on the river, including *The Waterways Journal, Inland River Record*, and the Sons and Daughters of Pioneer Rivermen.

The Waterways Journal index can be found by going to: St. Louis Mercantile Library at www.umsledu/services/library. On the left side of the page there is a list of libraries. Click on Mercantile. For canal and parks restoration, go to www.aarp.org/bulletin.

John Hartford's new web site has examples of some of the steamboat pictures he offers, and one of Ruth Ferris.

Other categories are riverboats, steamboats, paddlewheelers, sternwheelers, individual rivers and names of boats, such as the Golden Eagle and Arabia.

People have been finding river items on Internet auctions, under eBay.

The Coast Guard is on the Internet, too. Dan Owen gave me these:

Port State Information exchange:
http.//psik.uscg.mil/vesselsearch.asp

For Documentation Number Search:
http.//www.st.nmfs.gov/commercial/landings/cg_vessels.html

For name search use the same as for the documentations search except change the "s" at the end of "vessels" to a "2", i.e. "vessel2."

The National Waterways Conference did a real service to the river industry by publishing the web addresses of marine-oriented organizations, including:

American Association of Port Authorities: www.aapa-ports.org
American Heritage Rivers Initiative: www.epa.gov/rivers
American Waterways Operators, Inc.: www.americanwaterways.com

Army Corps of Engineers: www.usace.army.mil
Eno Transportation Foundation: www.enotrans.com
Inland Rivers Ports and Terminals, Inc.: www.irpt.com

Lake Carriers Association: www.lcaships.com
Marine Transportation System Initiative:
marad.dot.gov/reading_room/MTS/index.htm

Backing Hard Into River History

MARC 2000: www.ribb.com/marc2k.html

Mermaid Marine Resource Directory: maritime.tamu.edu
National Industrial Transportation League: www.nitl.org
National Waterways Conference, Inc.: www.waterways.org
Propeller Club of the United States: www.propellerclubhq.com
River Industry Bulletin Board: www.ribb.com

Navigation Information Connection:
www.mvr.usace.army.mil/navdata/nic.htm

Tennessee-Tombigbee Waterway Authority: www.tenntom.org
U.S.. Congress information: thomas.loc.gov

USDA Agricultural Transportation Summit:
www.ams.usda.gov/tmd/summit

U.S. Section, PIANC: www.wrsc.usace.armr,mil/pianc/
Waterways Association of Pittsburgh: www.ribb.com/wap/wap.html

NWC also listed the web addresses of other associated organizations and subjects, such as:

Agricultural barge and rail links:
www.agribiz.com/agInfo/.resTrans.html

Hurricane information, on-line tracking:
www.nws.noaa.gov/om/hurricane/index.html

International Work Boat Show: www.workboatshow.com

IRPT education program: frontpage.webzone.net/irpteducation
Marine Transportation System Initiative:
www.uscg.mil/hq/g-m/mts/index.htm

Ohio River Navigation Outreach: f7784.lrh.usace.army.mil

Recreational Boating (Boat U.S.): www.boatus.com
Storm Prediction Center, Norman, Oklahoma: www.spc.noaa.gov

Southeast rivers water supply study:
www.sam.usace.army.mil/sam/pd/actacfeis

Texas waterways industry: www.texaswaterways.com

Upper Mississippi/Illinois modernization:
   www.mvr.usace.army.mil/pdw/nav_study.htm

You can reach *The Waterways Journal* site at: www.waterwaysjournal.net. (E-mail address for some *Journal* employees appear weekly in the publication's masthead.)

The web site for Little River Books, a division of J. R. Simpson & Associates (where river-related books can be found) is www.littleriverbooks.com.

Many Internet users are finding www.ebay.com a productive web site for discoving steamboat memorabilia that is for sale. The *Journal's* enterprising Ed Rahe passed along to me some information about the amount of interesting material being auctioned. Visitors to the site can type the word steamboat into the eBay search engine and be whisked to a list of interesting items. Recent listings included such things as a March 23, 1907 *Waterways Journal*, engraving of steamboats on the St. Louis levee, postcards, pictures and a brass boiler gauge. The site lists items and bids. A word of caution. In June it was reported that some buyers and sellers have been "stiffed." Steps are being taken to set up free arbitration on the Internet. It is, however, a popular site, and a great deal of business is transacted.

As we go into the new millenium, to use a favorite phrase of Harry Cook and the National Waterways Conference, "SPREAD THE WORD" about the importance of inland waterways transportation. (As long as I can remember, we have been warned that we are just speaking to the choir, and we still are!) There are helpful signs: Inland Rivers Ports & Terminals is setting up an educational program that will include school district programs and field trips to help get the word out about the waterways. The National Waterways Conference is giving annual awards for waterways literature and promotional materials.

For *The Waterways Journal*, remember its longtime slogan: HELP US GROW!

Finally, "Thank you" to all those who have helped the "Old Boat" run for such a long time. And best wishes to all who have read this book.

–30–

Appendices

Vessels and Other Structures Constructed on the Mississippi River System for War Purposes and Moved by Water to New Orleans and Beyond Between January 1, 1942, and September 30, 1945 (See legend at end if section.)

Type of Vessel or Structure	Where Constructed	Number Built	Total
Description			
Ice breaker tug (USSR)	U.M.V.D.*	15	15
Motor torpedo boat tender	Illinois River	5	10
	Great Lakes	5	
Auxiliary net tender	Illinois River	6	11
	Great Lakes	1	
	Ohio River	4	
Assault, personnel, dispatch	Great Lakes	10	10
Coastal transport	Great Lakes	1	8
	Ohio River	7	
Auxiliary repair ship	Illinois River	6	12
	Great Lakes	6	
Auxiliary repair ship, landing	Illinois River	22	22

*There once was an Upper Mississippi Valley Division of the U.S. Engineers, we're told. We believe U.M.V.D. was used as a general description of where construction took place so that sensitive, site-specific information would not be revealed.

Type of Vessel or Structure	Where Constructed	Number Built	Total
Description			
Aircraft rescue vessel	Great Lakes	23	23
Destroyer escorts	Great Lakes Ohio River	17 18	35
Aircraft repair vessel	New Orleans Ohio River	18 17	35
Barge, steel, dry, cargo	New Orleans	34	34
Barge, Army, cargo	Cumberland River Tennessee River	55 27	82
Barge, oil, Army	Cumberland River Tennessee River New Orleans	10 6 29	45
Barge, steel, utility	New Orleans	109	109
Barge water, Army	Cumberland River New Orleans	4 5	9

Type of Vessel or Structure	Where Constructed	Number Built	Total
Description			
Barge, water	Great Lakes	28	28
Barge, steel, F.D., balloon	New Orleans	44	44
Barge, tanker, steel, (x standard)	New Orleans	20	20
Barge, tank	Tennessee River	9	9
Barge, tank, wood-steel	New Orleans	61	61
Barge, tank, steel	New Orleans	6	6
Barge (x)	Illinois River	12	
	Great Lakes	12	
	Ohio River	39	63
Barge, wood, oil (6000 bbl.) (a)	Memphis	18	18
Barge, NOIBN (b)*	Missouri River	3	3
Barge, NOIBN	Missouri River	5	5
Barracks, Navy	Cumberland River	7	7

*NOIBN is a military acronym meaning: not otherwise identified by name.

Type of Vessel or Structure		Where Constructed	Number Built	Total
Description				
Cargo, vessel (c)		New Orleans	9	9
Cargo, vessel, LIBERTY		New Orleans	132	132
Cargo, vessel, steel		New Orleans	6	6
Cargo, vessel		New Orleans Great Lakes	98 107	205
Coaster, Maritime Comm.		Tennessee River	7	7
Colliers		New Orleans	24	24
Cranes		Missouri River	5	5
Crash boats		Great Lakes	30	30
Cutter, Coast Guard		U.M.V.D. Missouri	5 5	10
Derrick barge		Great Lakes Tennessee River	1 8	9

Type of Vessel or Structure	Where Constructed	Number Built	Total
Description			
Distribution box boat (QM)	U.M.V.D.	2	
	Great Lakes	4	6
Bridge tender	Missouri River	5	
	New Orleans	1	6
Landing craft, infantry (light)	Great Lakes	188	188
Landing craft, tank (f)	U.M.V.D.	154	
	Ohio River	57	
	Memphis	(d)192	
	Missouri River	221	
	New Orleans	15	639
Landing ship, medium	Great Lakes	42	
	Illinois River	124	
	Ohio River	580	746
Freighter, small	Great Lakes	1	1
Freighters	Great Lakes	18	18
Freight and passenger	Great Lakes	11	11

Type of Vessel or Structure	Where Constructed	Number Built	Total
Description			
Freight and supply	Great Lakes	15	15
Launches	Great Lakes Missouri River	16 8	24
Mine planters	Ohio River	16	16
Mine sweeper	U.M.V.D. Great Lakes Ohio River Cumberland River	2 50 5 2	59
Motor torpedo, tank	New Orleans	167	167
Net tender	New Orleans	6	6
Patrol craft	Great Lakes	20	20
Patrol boat	New Orleans	200	200
Patrol corvette escort	Great Lakes	6	6
Patrol craft escorts	Great Lakes	20	20

Type of Vessel or Structure	Where Constructed	Number Built	Total
Description			
Patrol frigates	Great Lakes	45	45
Patrol gunboat	Great Lakes	3	3
Scow, Navy Y&D	Great Lakes	8	8
Subchaser, Navy	Great Lakes Cumberland River U.M.V.D.	107 14 3	124
Retrievers	Great Lakes	10	10
Supply vessel, Army	Tennessee River	13	13
Tanker, Navy	U.M.V.D.	13	13
Tankers, steel	Great Lakes New Orleans	14 5	19
Tanker	New Orleans	32	32
Q-boats	Great Lakes	17	17

Type of Vessel or Structure (Description)	Where Constructed	Number Built	Total
Rescue boat	Great Lakes	16	16
Tug, harbor	New Orleans	5	5
Tug, steel, harbor	New Orleans	9	9
Tug, sea going	New Orleans	21	21
Tug, steel	New Orleans	41	41
Towboat	Missouri River	4	4
Tug, Army	Tennessee River	37	37
Tug, large	Great Lakes Ohio River	42 47	89
Towboats	Ohio River	4	4
Tugboat, (Army-water transport)	U.M.V.D.	4	4
Towboat (Army Engineers)	U.M.V.D.	1	1

Type of Vessel or Structure — Description	Where Constructed	Number Built	Total
Submarine	Great Lakes	27	27
Lighter, self-propelled	Ohio River	13	13
Lighter, towed	Great Lakes Ohio River	3 27	30
Lighter, barge, Navy	U.M.V.D. Illinois River Cumberland River	4 1 8	13
Fuel oil barge	Great Lakes Ohio River	10 25	35
Yard salvage	Great Lakes	1	1

Total Number of Vessels Built = 3,943

Total Vessels Built by: U.M.V.D. = 203   Illinois River = 176   Great Lakes = 927   Ohio River = 859
Cumberland River = 100   Tennessee River = 115   Missouri River = 256   Memphis = 210   New Orleans = 1,097

Other Construction

Description	Where Constructed	Number Built	Total
Dry Dock, floating, (Navy)	U.M.V.D.	6	6
Dry Dock, standard	New Orleans	3	3
Dry Dock, sections	Ohio River	6	6
Dry Docks, sectional (e)	New Orleans	14	14
Stern, bow and hull sections (D.E.) Destroyer Escorts (j)	New Orleans	117	117
Ship, sections (g)	Ohio River	43,744 tons	
Sectional bulkheads (h)	New Orleans	500 tons	
Structural steel, Monongahela River 50,546 tons (i)			

These tables are based on compilations by the Statistical Division, Board of Engineers for Rivers and Harbors, December 10, 1945. See Legend on next page.

Legend

(a) For use on Inland waterway

(b) For use of U.S.E.D. (U.S. Engineer District) Rock Island, Ill.

(c) Partially constructed elsewhere, towed to and completed at New Orleans

(d) Sixteen from Memphis to Great Lakes

(e) To New Orleans via Gulf and Gulf Intracoastal Waterway for additional work and outfitting

(f) 38 Upbound on Illinois Waterway through Welland Canal to ocean

(g) Shipped to various shipyards for assembly

(h) To Mobile

(i) Shipped by rail to Glassport and McKeesport for river shipments to shipyards

(j) To Orange, Texas, via Intracoastal Waterway

Keeping Track Of Tonnage

Keeping track of tonnage of goods carried on the inland waterways is done by the U.S. Army Corps of Engineers. Each boat that passes through a lock must give the lock crew a report specifying what cargo is being moved. This information is compiled by the Water Resources Support Center of the Corps at Fort Belvoir, Virginia. It is published annually in a set of books called *Waterborne Commerce Of The United States,* by the New Orleans Engineer Office, P.O. Box 60267, New Orleans, LA 70160.

The following figures show how the tonnage has increased for selected waterways through the years. An interesting contrast can be made by comparing these figures with those for tonnage carried by barge and steamboat in 1889, as given by Louis Hunter in his book *Steamboats On The Western Rivers*—21,744,707 tons.

Table of Tonnage and Ton-Mile Totals
for
Selected Waterways

Year	Gulf Intracoastal Waterway Between Apalachee Bay, Fla., and the Mexican Border		Mississippi River System (Internal Traffic)	
	tons * 1000	ton miles * 1000	tons * 1000	ton miles * 1000
1998	113,376	18,474,610	488,387	284,355,189
1997	118,112	19,788,625	488,876	286,654,016
1996	118,027	19,515,691	482,791	296,092,437
1995	117,963	19,603,745	479,421	301,037,796
1994	117,620	20,033,201	478,673	274,707,788
1993	115,002	19,344,638	451,731	243,853,421
1992	112,272	19,591,876	465,434	291,688,177
1991	110,989	12,983,177	445,149	249,862,234
1990	115,386	13,577,132	457,497	284,808,956
1989	112,739	20,786,364	431,463	268,089,320
1988	117,712	20,939,710	423,025	257,802,545
1987	107,032	19,189,498	414,176	251,571,979
1986	106,961	19,394,523	402,802	239,293,452
1985	102,464	17,436,298	378,852	224,714,120

Continued Next Page

Year	Gulf Intracoastal Waterway Between Apalachee Bay, Fla., and the Mexican Border		Mississippi River System (Internal Traffic)	
	tons * 1000	ton miles * 1000	tons * 1000	ton miles * 1000
1986	106,961	19,394,523	402,802	239,293,452
1985	102,464	17,436,298	378,852	224,714,120
1984	93,439	17,246,885	386,568	234,629,261
1983	85,093	15,521,444	351,953	223,064,745
1982	82,980	15,015,219	347,474	217,990,680
1981	91,577	16,248,290	362,930	234,426,986
1980	94,512	16,512,229	365,569	193,492,234
1979	97,272	17,286,3221	370,758	184,436,341
1978	102,333	7,506,123	355,365	176,483,643
1977	104,934	18,277,332	351,544	166,923,758
1976	99,085	16,511,686	345,511	164,839,947
1975	96,951	15,594,606	330,087	151,283,215
1974	103,076	17,078,856	330,090	150,888,689
1973	100,767	16,578,105	317,597	139,788,892
1972	108,999	17,879,308	326,631	144,432,270
1971	105,975	17,767,479	303,246	129,782,686
1970	100,149	16,401,377	297,290	125,880,420
1969	100,077	16,895,517	286,804	114,032,045
1968	93,063	15,949,168	270,557	109,164,714
1967	87,850	13,925,882	258,367	103,474,600
1966	81,279	12,720,408	247,200	95,870,451
1965	78,537		237,631	87,407,020
1964	71,595		226,475	80,087,305
1963	67,320		211,540	73,520,069
1962	60,424		200,041	70,999,266
1961	58,867		190,968	64,839,942
1960	54,948		188,098	62,366,714
1959	51,306		183,909	62,366,714*
1958	46,008		172,582	59,565,053
1957	48,104		188,214	53,442,610
1956	45,354		179,257	54,768,579
1955	41,379		163,760	51,733,286
1954	36,982		136,392	47,417,668
1953	41,727		142,569	38,703,034

* *1959 Ton-mile figure (same as shown for 1960) is identical to that shown in the Corps table.*

Source: Waterborne Commerce Statistics Center

Domestic Barge Traffic by Type of Traffic and Commodity

Comparative Statement of Traffic (thousand short tons)

Year	Total	Year	Total	Year	Total	Year	Total
1988	740,893	1991	749,654	1994	782,014	1997	820,432
1989	743,196	1992	762,540	1995	786,560		
1990	776,146	1993	753,287	1996	802,275		

Freight Traffic, 1997
(thousand short tons)

Commodity	Total	Barge Traffic					Domestic	
		Coastwise	Lakewise	Internal	Intraport	Intra-Territory	%-Barge	Traffic
Total all commodities	820,432	113,766	10,770	605,797	85,198	4,901	73.7	1,112,527
Total coal	206,957	12,683	251	175,989	18,033	-----	89.1	232,336
100 coal lignite	203,275	12.573	240	172,477	17,985	----	89.0	228,286
1200 coal coke	3,682	111	12	3,512	48	----	90.9	4,050
Total petroleum and petroleum products	260,872	63,521	1,889	149,235	41,340	4,887	65.8	396,693
Subtotal crude petroleum	39,329	1,294	----	36,581	1,454	-----	32.7	120,402
2100 crude petroleum	39,329	1,294	----	36,581	1,454	----	32.7	120,402

Continued from preceding page—

Commodity	Total	Coastwise	Lakewise	Internal	Intraport	Intra-Territory	%-Barge	Traffic
Subtotal petroleum products	**221,543**	**62,227**	**1,889**	**112,654**	**38,886**	**4,887**	**80.2**	**276,292**
2211 gasoline	61,586	23,391	306	29,860	6,686	1,343	68.8	89,475
2221 kerosene	2,041	582	---	841	499	119	92.5	2,206
2330 distillate fuel oil	50,900	15,745	287	24,018	9,656	1,195	77.4	65,727
2340 residual fuel oil	67,535	17,711	163	29,074	18,386	2,201	88.1	76,672
2350 lube oil and greases	3,987	155	---	3,272	560	---	71.0	5,619
2410. jelly & waxes	144	54	---	90	---	---	84.6	171
2429 naptha & solvents	5,363	219	---	3,728	1,387	28	92.3	5,812
2430 asphalt, tar & pitch	14,389	3,362	1,013	9,087	927	---	98.4	14,620
2540 petroleum coke	9,302	366	120	7,693	1,123	---	98.4	9,448
2640 liquid natural gas	2,521	280	---	2,170	71	---	99.8	2,525
2990 petro. products nec.	3,775	362	---	2,821	591	---	94.0	4,016
Total chemicals and related products	**68,084**	**6,339**	**131**	**51,391**	**10,223**	---	**84.0**	**81,029**
Subtotal fertilizers	**13,133**	**1,583**	---	**11,424**	**126**	---	**97.4**	**13,478**
3110 nitrogenous fert.	6,228	390	---	5,739	99	---	99.9	6,233
3120 phosphatic fert.	1,930	200	---	1,728	2	---	95.9	2,013
3130 potassic fert.	1,275	35	---	1,236	4	---	99.9	1,276
3190 fert. & mixes nec.	3,699	958	---	2,720	21	---	93.5	3,956
Subtotal other chemicals and related products	**54,951**	**4,756**	**131**	**39,967**	**10,097**	---	**81.3**	**67,551**
3211 acyclic hydrocarbons	2,453	0	---	2,261	191	---	99.0	2,478
3212 benzene & toluene	6,141	23	---	4,055	2,063	---	95.5	6,431
3219 other hydrocarbons	11,886	787	---	9,059	2,040	---	85.2	13,954
3220 alcohols	7,165	122	---	5,557	1,487	---	92.1	7,776
3230 carboxylic acids	1,785	11	---	1,071	703	---	92.1	1,939
3240 nitrogen func. comp.	1,651	0	---	1,631	20	---	99.3	1,663

Continued from preceding page— Commodity	Total	Coastwise	Lakewise	Internal	Intraport	Intra-Territory	%-Barge	Traffic
3250 organo-inorganic comp.	41	0	---	38	2	---	90.3	45
3260 organic comp. nec.	1,175	1	---	1,134	40	---	85.9	1,367
3271 sulphur (liquid)	3,863	1,323	---	2,411	129	---	43.8	8,820
3272 sulphuric acid	1,791	16	---	1,422	353	---	99.9	1,793
3273 ammonia	2,577	91	---	2,463	23	---	91.5	2,815
3274 sodium hydroxide	7,010	1,610	---	4,757	643	---	93.6	7,488
3275 inorg. elem., oxides, & halogen salts	1,491	21	---	973	497	---	98.0	1,521
3276 metallic salts	1,211	51	131	947	83	---	98.5	1,229
3279 inorgan chem. nec.	231	1	---	230	---	---	99.8	231
3281 radioactive material	0	0	---	---	---	---	5.4	1
3282 pigments & paints	13	9	---	3	---	---	27.8	46
3283 coloring mat. nec.	1	1	---	---	---	---	36.0	2
3284 medicines	2	2	---	0	0	---	1.9	124
3285 perfumes & cleansers	26	24	---	2	---	---	16.2	163
3286 plastics	29	22	---	7	---	---	29.1	101
3291 pesticides	7	6	---	---	1	---	22.7	30
3292 starches, gluten, glue	4	4	---	---	---	---	25.5	16
3293 explosives	2	1	---	1	---	---	50.4	3
3297 chemical additives	3,811	517	---	1,589	1,705	---	57.2	6,666
3298 wood & resin chem.	120	23	---	97	---	---	54.5	220
3299 chem. products nec.	465	90	---	258	117	---	74.0	628
Total crude materials, inedible except fuels	**150,143**	**17,503**	**6,947**	**115,655**	**10,028**	**9**	**60.9**	**246,504**
Subtotal forest products, wood and chips	**11,461**	**1,383**	**0**	**10,018**	**59**	---	**58.1**	**19,731**
4110 rubber & gums	8	6	---	2	---	---	91.8	9
4150 fuel wood	101	1	---	100	0	---	98.6	102

Continued from preceding page—

Commodity	Total	Coastwise	Lakewise	Internal	Intraport	Intra-Territory	%-Barge	Traffic
4161 wood chips	7,432	510	---	6,912	10	---	100.0	7,432
4170 wood in the rough	3,261	363	---	2,849	50	---	28.9	11,290
4189 lumber	610	492	0	118	0	---	81.9	745
4190 forest products nec.	48	11	---	37	---	---	31.6	153
Subtotal pulp and waste paper	**199**	**37**	---	**161**	---	---	**81.9**	**242**
4225 pulp & waste paper	199	37	---	161	---	---	81.9	242
Subtotal soil, sand, gravel, rock and stone	**106,508**	**14,474**	**3,139**	**79,366**	**9,524**	**4**	**78.7**	**135,384**
4310 building stone	120	---	---	120	---	---	99.9	120
4322 limestone	30,126	786	2,993	26,327	21	---	52.6	57,230
4323 gypsum	712	6	---	706	---	---	40.3	1,766
4327 phosphate rock	6,262	6,103	---	159	---	---	100.0	6,262
4331 sand & gravel	69,244	7,572	146	52,019	9,502	4	99.0	69,956
4338 soil & fill dirt	43	8	---	35	1	---	89.8	48
Subtotal iron ore and scrap	**14,215**	**956**	**3,451**	**9,422**	**386**	---	**20.0**	**71,058**
4410 iron ore	7,803	7	3,449	4,336	11	---	12.1	64,391
4420 iron & steel scrap	6,412	949	2	5,086	375	---	96.2	6,667
Subtotal marine shells	**546**	**0**	---	**546**	---	---	**94.0**	**581**
4515 marine shells	546	0	---	546	---	---	94.0	581
Subtotal non-ferrous ores and scrap	**5,246**	**40**	---	**5,195**	**10**	---	**99.9**	**5,252**
4630 copper ore	16	0	---	16	---	---	99.1	16
4650 aluminum ore	3,274	18	---	3,255	---	---	100.0	3,274
4670 manganese ore	578	---	---	568	10	---	100.0	578
4680 non-ferrous scrap	28	0	---	27	---	---	82.6	33
4690 non-ferrous ores nec.	1,351	22	---	1,329	---	---	100.0	1,351
Subtotal sulphur, clay and salt	**796**	**134**	---	**654**	**4**	**4**	**53.9**	**1,477**

Continued from preceding page—Commodity	Total	Coastwise	Lakewise	Internal	Intraport	Intra-Territory	%-Barge	Traffic
4741 sulphur, (dry)	4	0	---	---	---	4	100.0	4
4782 clay & refrac. mat.	792	134	---	654	4	---	53.8	1,473
Subtotal slag	**1,429**	**65**	**358**	**1,007**	**—**	**—**	**79.4**	**1,800**
4860 ALAG	1,429	65	358	1,007	---	---	79.4	1,800
Subtotal other non-metal	**9,744**	**414**	**—**	**9,286**	**44**	**—**	**88.7**	**10,979**
4900 non-metal. min. nec.	9,744	414	---	9,286	44	---	88.7	10,979
Total primary manufactured goods	**33,883**	**6,549**	**1,550**	**24,928**	**855**	**—**	**91.1**	**37,178**
Subtotal paper products	**953**	**124**	**—**	**825**	**4**	**—**	**66.9**	**1,425**
5110 newsprint	62	2	---	60	---	---	87.0	71
5120 paper & paperboard	683	13	---	666	4	---	65.7	1,040
5190 paper products nec.	208	108	---	100	---	---	66.2	314
Subtotal lime, cement and glass	**13,368**	**2,642**	**1,180**	**8,841**	**705**	**—**	**85.2**	**15,686**
5210 lime	2,456	0	---	2,456	---	---	100.0	2,456
5220 cement & concrete	10,548	2,545	1,179	6,119	705	---	82.9	12,721
5240 glass & glass products	86	28	---	59	---	---	70.8	122
5290 misc. mineral prod.	278	70	0	207	1	---	71.9	386
Subtotal primary iron and steel products	**14,204**	**104**	**371**	**13,590**	**138**	**—**	**98.6**	**14,409**
5312 pig iron	3,288	---	10	3,269	8	---	100.0	3,288
5315 ferro alloys	1,012	---	---	985	27	---	100.0	1,012
5320 i&s primary forms	1,589	32	---	1,552	4	---	99.9	1,591
5330 i&s plates & sheets	5,026	1	360	4,624	40	---	99.9	5,030
5360 i&s bars & shapes	1,011	13	---	995	3	---	96.3	1,050
5370 i&s pipe & tube	1,081	20	0	1,022	39	---	87.7	1,233
5390 primary i&s nec.	1,197	38	---	1,142	16	---	99.4	1,204

Continued from preceding page— Commodity	Total	Coastwise	Lakewise	Internal	Intraport	Intra-Territory	%-Barge	Traffic
Subtotal primary non-ferrous metal products	**5,143**	**3,603**	**0**	**1,532**	**8**	**----**	**95.2**	**5,404**
5421 copper	14	1	---	12	2	---	69.5	20
5422 aluminum	191	3	---	187	---	---	92.8	205
5429 smelted prod. nec.	124	6	---	118	---	---	95.6	130
5480 fab. metal products	4,815	3,593	0	1,215	6	---	95.4	5,049
Subtotal primary wood products	**215**	**75**	**---**	**140**	**---**	**---**	**84.4**	**254**
5540 primary wood prod.	215	75	---	140	---	---	84.4	254
Total good and farm products	**88,036**	**3,402**	**---**	**84,326**	**307**	**---**	**94.0**	**93,654**
Subtotal fish	**9**	**9**	**---**	**---**	**---**	**---**	**8.0**	**118**
6134 fish (not shellfish)	9	9	---	---	---	---	10.1	93
6136 shellfish	0	0	---	---	---	---	0.4	25
Subtotal grain	**48,536**	**593**	**---**	**47,887**	**56**	**---**	**98.9**	**49,063**
6241 wheat	11,992	224	---	11,755	13	---	96.4	12,438
6344 corn	33,095	297	---	32,768	30	---	100.0	33,096
6442 rice	1,271	70	---	1,201	---	---	95.5	1,331
6443 barley & rye	553	1	---	549	3	---	100.0	553
6445 oats	154	1	---	149	3	---	88.5	174
6447 sorghum grains	1,472	---	---	1,465	7	---	100.0	1,472
Subtotal oilseeds	**25,811**	**67**	**---**	**25,712**	**33**	**---**	**99.9**	**25,828**
6521 peanuts	0	0	---	---	---	---	2.4	6
6522 soybeans	21,495	20	---	21,450	25	---	100.0	21,495
6590 oilseeds nec.	4,316	47	---	4,262	8	---	99.8	4,327
Subtotal vegetable products	**1,331**	**97**	**---**	**1,219**	**14**	**---**	**81.6**	**1,630**
6653 vegetable oils	1,243	49	---	1,180	14	---	99.4	1,251
6654 vegetables & prod.	88	49	---	39	---	---	23.1	379

Continued from preceding page—

Commodity	Total	Coastwise	Lakewise	Internal	Intraport	Intra-Territory	%-Barge	Traffic
Subtotal processed grain and animal feed	**8,566**	**495**	---	**7,958**	**113**	---	**98.0**	**8,738**
6746 wheat flour	48	8	---	41	---	---	57.4	85
6747 grain mill products	666	300	---	356	10	---	95.0	701
6781 hay & fodder	40	8	---	32	---	---	85.8	47
6782 animal feed, prep.	7,811	179	---	7,529	103	---	98.8	7,905
Subtotal other agricultural product	**3,783**	**2,141**	---	**1,550**	**92**	---	**45.7**	**8,278**
6811 meat, fresh, frozen	70	69	---	0	---	---	28.4	245
6817 meat, prepared	7	7	---	---	---	---	9.0	74
6822 dairy products	47	47	---	---	---	---	46.7	100
6835 fish, prepared	26	7	---	20	---	---	64.3	41
6838 tallow, animal oils	17	4	---	12	1	---	94.6	18
6839 animals & prod. nec.	53	35	---	18	---	---	7.3	723
6856 bananas & plantains	0	0	---	---	---	---	1.3	13
6857 fruit & nuts nec.	4	4	---	---	---	---	1.1	386
6858 fruit juices	109	109	---	0	---	---	39.3	276
6861 sugar	1,582	1,004	---	578	---	---	83.3	1,900
6865 molasses	560	112	---	391	58	---	81.5	687
6871 coffee	3	3	---	---	---	---	16.8	17
6885 alcoholic beverages	274	76	---	197	---	---	35.6	768
6887 groceries	315	293	---	21	1	---	40.9	771
6888 water & ice	108	3	---	82	23	---	10.4	1,030
6889 food products nec.	564	344	---	211	9	---	53.0	1,065
6891 tobacco & products	12	12	---	---	---	---	39.6	31
6893 cotton	2	1	---	1	---	---	79.6	3
6899 farm products nec.	29	10	---	19	---	---	25.9	112
Total alll manufactured equipment, machinery & products	**6,928**	**3,765**	**1**	**2,979**	**178**	**6**	**35.5**	**19,503**

Continued from preceding page—

Commodity	Total	Coastwise	Lakewise	Internal	Intraport	Intra-Territory	%-Barge	Traffic
7110 machinery (not elec)	329	92	1	227	9	---	3.5	9,270
7120 electrical machinery	78	65	---	13	---	---	39.7	195
7210 vehicles & parts	796	771	0	19	0	6	69.3	1,149
7220 aircraft & parts	0	0	---	0	---	---	15.3	2
7230 ships & boats	7	3	---	3	2	---	69.4	11
7300 ordnance & access.	1	1	---	---	---	---	33.2	3
7400 manufac. wood prod.	102	45	---	56	0	---	60.1	170
7500 textile products	72	27	---	45	---	---	30.6	234
7600 rubber & plastic pr.	134	28	---	106	---	---	66.7	201
7800 empty containers	411	5	---	406	0	---	99.9	412
7900 manufac. prod. nec.	4,998	2,727	0	2,104	167	---	63.6	7,857
Total waste & scrap nec.	**5,528**	**1**	**0**	**1,294**	**4,234**	**---**	**99.7**	**5,545**
8900 waste & scrap nec.	5,528	1	0	1,294	4,234	---	99.7	5,545
Total unknown or not elsewhere classified	**2**	**2**	**---**	**---**	**---**	**---**	**2.3**	**83**
9900 unknown or nec.	2	2	---	---	---	---	2.3	83

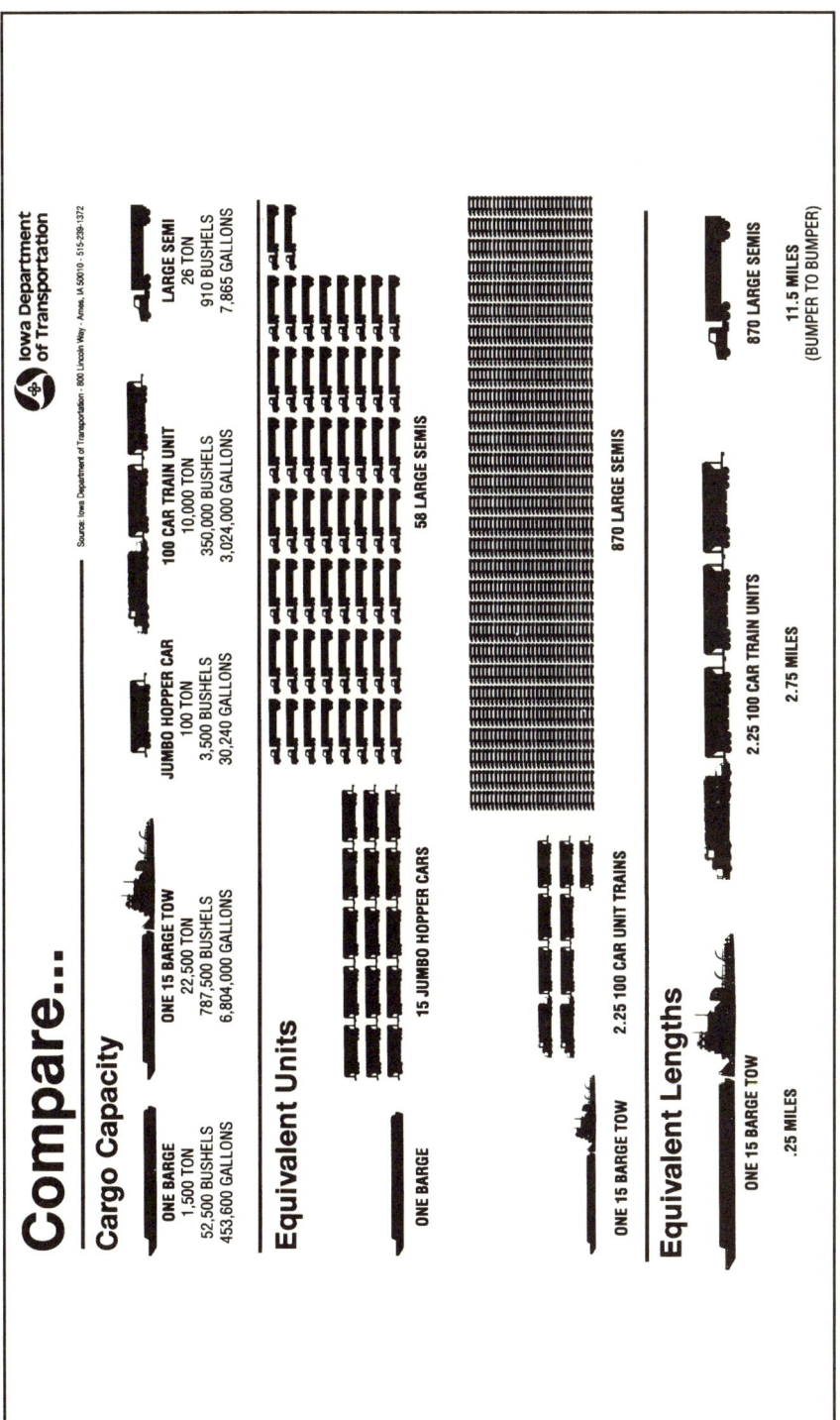

Compare...

Cargo Capacity

ONE BARGE
1,500 TON
52,500 BUSHELS
453,600 GALLONS

ONE 15 BARGE TOW
22,500 TON
787,500 BUSHELS
6,804,000 GALLONS

JUMBO HOPPER CAR
100 TON
3,500 BUSHELS
30,240 GALLONS

100 CAR TRAIN UNIT
10,000 TON
350,000 BUSHELS
3,024,000 GALLONS

LARGE SEMI
26 TON
910 BUSHELS
7,865 GALLONS

Equivalent Units

ONE BARGE

15 JUMBO HOPPER CARS

2.25 100 CAR UNIT TRAINS

58 LARGE SEMIS

870 LARGE SEMIS

Equivalent Lengths

ONE 15 BARGE TOW
.25 MILES

2.25 100 CAR TRAIN UNITS
2.75 MILES

870 LARGE SEMIS
11.5 MILES
(BUMPER TO BUMPER)

Iowa Department of Transportation

Source: Iowa Department of Transportation - 800 Lincoln Way - Ames, IA 50010 - 515-239-1372

345

Honors And Activities

One doesn't spend nearly 60 years at any pursuit without being serious about it. Being serious, it was incombent upon me to hold membership in various organizations, serve as an officer when colleagues selected me to do so, and eventually end up being honored by those who believe that participation was worth while. Along the way, much to my surprise and pleasure, I picked up a room of my own at the Ruebel Hotel, Grafton, Illinois.

Honors

The author received the Distinguished Service Award from St. Louis Mercantile Library in 1986; Certificate of Merit from the U.S. Coast Guard on October 2, 1986; the Commander's Award for Civilian Service from the U.S. Department of the Army; a Certificate of Appreciation from the National Association of Passenger Vessel Owners on March 18, 1987; the Achievement Award, National Rivers Hall of Fame, September 21, 1989; and the Donald T. Wright Award for Maritime Journalism, Herman T. Pott National Inland Waterways Library, September 1989.

Offices

He served as president of the Propeller Club, Port of St. Louis, 1977-1979; president of the Inland Rivers Ports and Terminals, Inc., 1978-1979; and president of the Golden Eagle River Museum at St. Louis.

Committees

The author served on the Transportation Task Force of the East-West Gateway Coordinating Council in St. Louis; on the Selection Committee of the National Rivers Hall of Fame, Dubuque, Iowa; the Selection Committee of the American Merchant Marine Hall of Fame, Kings Point, New York; and on the Board of Pilots, Midwest Riverboat Buffs, Keokuk, Iowa.

Memberships

His memberships have included,the Sons and Daughters of Pioneer Rivermen, Marietta, Ohio; Middle Ohio Chapter of the Sons and Daughters, Cincinnati; Mississippi River Chapter, Sons and Daughters, St. Louis; Missouri River Rats, Brownville, Nebraska; and Midwest Riverboat Buffs.

Certificate of Merit

James V. Swift is cited for exceptional public service and contribution to the missions of the United States Coast Guard. Mr. Swift was a frequent reporter of Coast Guard activities spanning a career of forty-five years in journalism. He has seen and reported on hundreds of river closures, collisions, groundings, changes in licensing requirements for Rivermen and changes in aids to navigation, not to mention green versus black buoys. He faithfully reported who was renewing and upgrading their license as well as keeping the industry informed of which Coast Guard people were being transferred into and out of the Western River System. Jim Swift never missed an important gathering of river people at a meeting or conference. He not only reported the news but also defined the issues with an insight and perspective that few others have and which will be missed in the months and years ahead. Mr. Swift's gathering and dissemination of information impacted greatly on the ability of government and industry to understand each other and to thus work more closely together toward a common goal of ensuring the continued safe and efficient use of the nation's inland waterway system. The development of our river resources was a cause he never tired of advocating. His comments to regulatory officials and congressmen were discerning and based upon a historical outlook that few can provide. His wealth of historical information was a valuable asset frequently called upon and he never failed to answer a request for assistance. Mr. Swift's services and accomplishments have enhanced the Coast Guard's ability to perform its missions and for that he is most heartily commended.

The certificate was presented on October 2, 1986, by Rear Adm. R. T. Nelson, Second Coast Guard District Commander.

The author
poses
with copies of
The Waterways Journal
at the door
of the
James V. Swift Room
at the
Ruebel Hotel
in Grafton, Illinois.

The author presents the Captain Donald T. Wright Award in Maritime Journalism to John Hartford on February 25, 2000, during a river symposium at the University of Missouri-St. Louis Campus.

River Person of the Century

It seems only fitting, as a postscript to *Backing hard Into River History*, that I once again take advantage of *Waterways Journal* stories to honor Capt. Jesse Brent, who was selected as River Person of The Century (WJ April 3, 2000), and others who were nominated for the award.

"It was a wrenching decision," said the *Journal*, "but in the long run an extraordinary outpouring of public support propelled Capt. Jesse Brent, 1912-1982, to be selected as *The Waterways Journal*'s 'River Person of the Century.'"

Journal editor John Shoulberg compiled the following account of Jesse's career:

Capt. Jesse Brent

Brent began his career as a deckhand in 1939 with the U.S. Engineers in Vicksburg, Miss. He quickly rose to the position of captain, and left the Corps to establish his own company. With his father, he began Brent Towing in the mid-1940's. At the time of Jesse Brent's death, Brent Towing had 20 towboats and 55 barges, and employed more than 600 workers. He also owned Brent Marine Supply Company and Brent Shipbuilding & Repair, Inc., and was a director of Superior Boat Works in Greenville.

As hard as he worked at his own ventures, however, Brent spent much of his time promoting the industry, said many of the people who nominated him for the award. He was one of the founding members and served as chairman of the board of the American Waterways Operators, and chaired the association's budget/finance committee and political action committee, and was a longtime member of its legislative committee. He was also highly active in the National Waterways Conference and the Water Resources Congress.

In addition, he was a civic leader in his hometown of Greenville, Miss., and the state of Mississippi. He was an officer of the Delta Council, chairman of the Radio Free Europe Fund for 1969 in the Mississippi

Delta, member of the Mississippi Economic Council Committee, president of the Rivers and Harbors Association of Mississippi and a member of the Greenville Port Commission.

His obituary in the WJ said,'With all his awards and honors, Capt. Brent may best be known in the river industry for the most talked-of and enjoyed social event on the waterways—the famous "Brent Fish Fry" held at the Region 4 meeting of The American Waterways Operators every other year in Greenville.

Other Finalists

Space does not allow for a lengthy account for each of the other nominees, and I leave it to readers to refer to the April 3 *Journal* for details. Pictures of the other four finalists follow:

Capt. Fred Way—(1909-1992) river captain, author, editor, pulisher, president of Sons & Daughters of Pioneer Rivermen, founder of the River Museum in Marietta, Ohio.

Marshall and Rouaud Dravo—were the original founders of F. R. Dravo & Company, which spawned a number of other companies that designed and built boats, barges, bridges and waterway facilities; towed goods throughout the inland waterways system; and supplied raw materials for construction.

Herman Pott—(1897-1982) began St. Louis Shipbuilding & Steel Company in 1933 with two partners, Everett Enslin and R. C. Bradshaw. Ultimately bought out Paducah Marine Ways, added another yard at Caruthersville, Missouri, and purchased

Capt. Fred Way   **Marshall Dravo**   **Rouaud Dravo**   **Herman Pott**

Federal Barge Lines.

Other Nominees

Other nominees—Harry N. Cook, president, National Waterways Conference; George P. Crounse, formed Crounse Corporation; Raymond A. Eckstein, builder of Wisconsin Barge Line and Marquette Transportation; Clancy Horton, chief engineer for Dravo Corporation; Lachlan Macleay, industry leader and president of the Mississippi Valley Association (an officer of the association 30 years); Charles and Charles Edwin Ward, father and son, founded Ward Engineering Works, Charleston, West Virginia, in late 1800s; and Charles C. Webber, principal founder of the Upper Mississippi Barge Line Company and promoter of the nine-foot channel on the Upper Mississippi River.

From The Author's Bookshelf

Here is a list of books I frequently use in writing the "Old Boat Column" or just for pleasure. I am sure I have left some out, but these are the ones most used. (On the following page I have taken the liberty of using illustrations and additional information for the three publications with which I have been associated during my journalistic career.)

Of course, always at my elbow are:

Way's Packet Directory, 1948-1994, Ohio University Press, 1983, Capt. Frederick Way, Jr.

Way's Steam Towboat Directory, with J. W. Rutter, Ohio University Press, 1990.

Merchant Vessels of the United States, 1790-1868.

The Lytle-Holdcamper List, The Steamship Historical Society of America, 1975.

Books of fiction are not shown, for the most part, but the readers are alerted to the series of books by Ben Lucian Burman, who had a lot to do with bringing the rivers to the Nation's attention with *Mississippi, Steamboat 'Round the Bend, Blow for a Landing*, and *Big River To Cross*. He also did the "Catfish Bend" series for children.

Also not listed is the series of books on southern rivers by Bert Neville, such as the Apalachicola-Chattahoochee-Flint, Coosa River, and Tennessee River. He also did a book on towboats on the Mobile, Alabama, Tombigbee and Warrior rivers.

The Books

The Allegheny, Frederick Way, Jr., Farrar & Rinehart, Inc., 1941.

Perilous Journeys: A History of Steamboating on the Chattahoochee, Apalachicola, and Flint Rivers, 1828-1928, Edward A. Mueller, Historic Chattachoochee Commission, 1990.

Steamboatin' on the Cumberland, Byrd Douglas, Tennessee Book Company, 1961.

Steamboats on The Green: And The Colorful Men Who Operated Them, Agnes S. Harralson, Kentucky Imprints, 1981.

Sternwheelers on the Great Kanawha River, Gerald E. Sutphin, Pictorial History Publishing Company, 1991.

MISSISSIPPI, LOWER
The Mississippi Steamboat Era in Historic Photographs, Joan W. and Thomas H. Gandy, Dover Publications, 1987.

Rising Tide, Mississippi Flood in 1927, John M. Barry.

Father Mississippi, Lyle Saxon, The Century Co., 1927.

Lanterns on the Levee, Recollections of a Planter's Son, William Alexander Percy, Alfreds A. Knopf, 1945.

MISSISSIPPI, UPPER
Between the Saints: Louis and Paul, Kathy Flippo, Little River Books Division, J. R. Simpson & Associates, 1998.

Upper Mississippi River History, Capt. Ron Larson, U.S.M.M. Ret., Steamboat Press. Two editions, second 1998.

A-Rafting on the Mississip', Charles Edward Russell, The Century Co. 1928.

Upper Mississippi River Rafting Steamboats, Edward A. Mueller, Ohio University Press, 1995.

Steamboating on the Upper Mississippi, William J. Petersen, The State Historical Society of Iowa, 1968.

Lore and Lure of the Upper Mississippi River, Capt. Frank J. Fugina, self-published, 1945.

A Raft Pilot's Log, A History of the Great Rafting Industry on the Upper Mississippi 1840-1915, Walter A. Blair, The Arthur H. Clark Company, 1930.

From Canoe to Steel Barge on the Upper Mississippi, Mildred L. Hartsough, The University of Minnesota Press (for the Upper Mississippi Waterway Association), 1934.

MISSOURI RIVER

Steamboat Legacy, The Heckmann Family, Hermann, Mo., Dorothy Heckmann Shrader, The Wein Press, 1993.

Steamboat Treasure, Capt. William H. Heckman, Dorothy Heckmann Shrader, The Wein Press, 1997.

Steamboating Sixty-Five Years on Missouri's Rivers, Capt. William H. Heckman, Burton Publishing Co., 1950.

History of the Missouri River, Phil E. Chappell, Bryant-Douglas, 1903.

The River And I, John G. Neihardt, The MacMillan Company, 1927.

Old Man River, The Memories of Captain Louis Rosché, Pioneer Steamboatman, Robert A. Hereford, The Caxton Printers, Ltd., 1943.

A History of Steamboating on the Upper Missouri River, William E. Lass, University of Nebraska Press, 1962.

The Conquest of the Missouri, Being the Story of the Life and Exploits of Captain Grant Marsh, Joseph Mills Hanson, A. C. McClurg & Co., 1916.

Towboat Pilot, Elston J. Melton, The Caxton Printers, Ltd., 1948.

The Steamboat Bertrand, History, Excavation and Architecture, Jerome E. Petsche, National Park Service, U.S. Department of the Interior, 1974.

History of Early Steamboat Navigation on the Missouri River of Joseph La Barge, Hiram Martin Chittenden, in two volumes, Francis P. Harper, 1903.

MONONGAHELA AND MUSKINGUM
The Monongahela River: River of Dreams, and Sweat, Arthur Parker, State University of Pennsylvania Press, 1999.

The Monongahela, Richard Bissell, Rinehart & Co., Inc., 1949.

Monongahela, The River and Its Region, Richard T. Wiley, 1937.

Steamboats on the Muskingum, Jay Mack Gamble, The Steamship Historical Society of America, 1971.

OHIO RIVER
Thrills of the Historic Ohio River, Frank Y. Granson, Cincinnati Times-Star, 1929; edited by Barbara Fluegeman and republished by Spancil Hill Publishing Co., 1999.

Who's Who on the Ohio River and its Tributaries, Ethel C. Leahy, The E. C. Leahy Publishing Co., 1931.

The Ohio River Handbook and Picture Album, fourth edition, Young & Klein, 1954.

Towboat on the Ohio, James E. Casto, The University Press of Kentucky, 1995.

The Ohio River, A Course of Empire, Arthur Butler Hulbert, G. P. Putnam's Sons, The Knickerbocker Press, 1906.

A History of Transportation in the Ohio Valley, Charles Henry Ambler, the Arthur H. Clark Company, 1932.

On The Ohio, H. Bennett Abdy, Dodd, Mead and Company, 1919.

OTHER RIVERS
The Great Red River Raft, Peter Zachary Cohen, Albert Whitman & Company, 1984.

Steamboats on the St. Croix, Anita Albrecht Buck, North Star Press, 1990.

A History of Navigation on the Tennessee River System, An Interpretation of the Economic Influence of this River System on the Tennessee Valley, A message from the President of the United States, transmitting a survey entitled "A History of Navigation on the Tennessee River and Its Tributaries," U.S. Government Printing Office, 1937. *The Upper Tennessee,* Comprehending desultory records of river operations in the Tennessee Valley, covering a period of 150 years, T. J. Campbell, self-published, 1932.

Texas Riverman, The Life and Times of Captain Andrew Smyth, William Seale, University of Texas Press, 1966.

Sandbars and Sternwheelers, Steam Navigation on the Brazos, Pamela Ashworth Puryear and Nath Winfield, Jr., Texas A&M University Press, 1976.

Steamboats and Ferries on White River, Duane Huddleston, Sammie Rose and Pat Wood, University of Central Arkansas Press, 1995.

GENERAL
Steamboats on the Western Rivers, Louis C. Hunter, Harvard University Press, 1949, has been reprinted.

King and Queen of the River, Delta King and Delta Queen, Stan Garvey, River Heritage Press, 1995 (hardbound) and 1999 (softbound).

From Paddle Wheels to Propeller, Howard Shipyard, Charles Preston Fishbaugh, Indiana Historical Society, 1970.

That Splendid Little Steamer Hartford, Sonie Liebler, 1989.

Showboats: The History of an American Institution, Philip Graham, University of Texas Press.

Moonlight at 8:30, Alan A. Bates and Capt. Clarke C. Hawley. 1994.

The Western Rivers Steamboat Cyclopoedium, Alan L. Bates, Cyclopoedium Press, 1996.

The Western Rivers Engineroom Cyclopoedium, Bates, Cyclopoedium Press, 1996.

Master of the Mississippi, about Henry M. Shreve, Florence L. Dorsey, Pelican Publishing Co., paperback edition, 1998.

Hardluck Ironclad, The Sinking and Salvage of the Cairo, Edwin C. Bearss, Louisiana State University Press, 1966.

Transport to Disaster, about the Sultana, James W. Elliott, Holt, Rinehart and Winston, 1962.

Road to The Sea, The Story of James B. Eads and the Mississippi River, Florence Dorsey, Rinehart & Company, Inc., 1947.

Mississippi River Panorama, The Henry Lewis Great National Work, William J. Petersen, Clio Press, 1979.

She Takes the Horns, Steamboat Racing on the Western Waters, Frederick Way, Jr., 1953.

Towboat River, Edwin and Louise Rosskam, Duell, Sloan and Pearce, 1948.

Steamboat in a Cornfield, John Hartford, Crown Publishing Co., 1986.

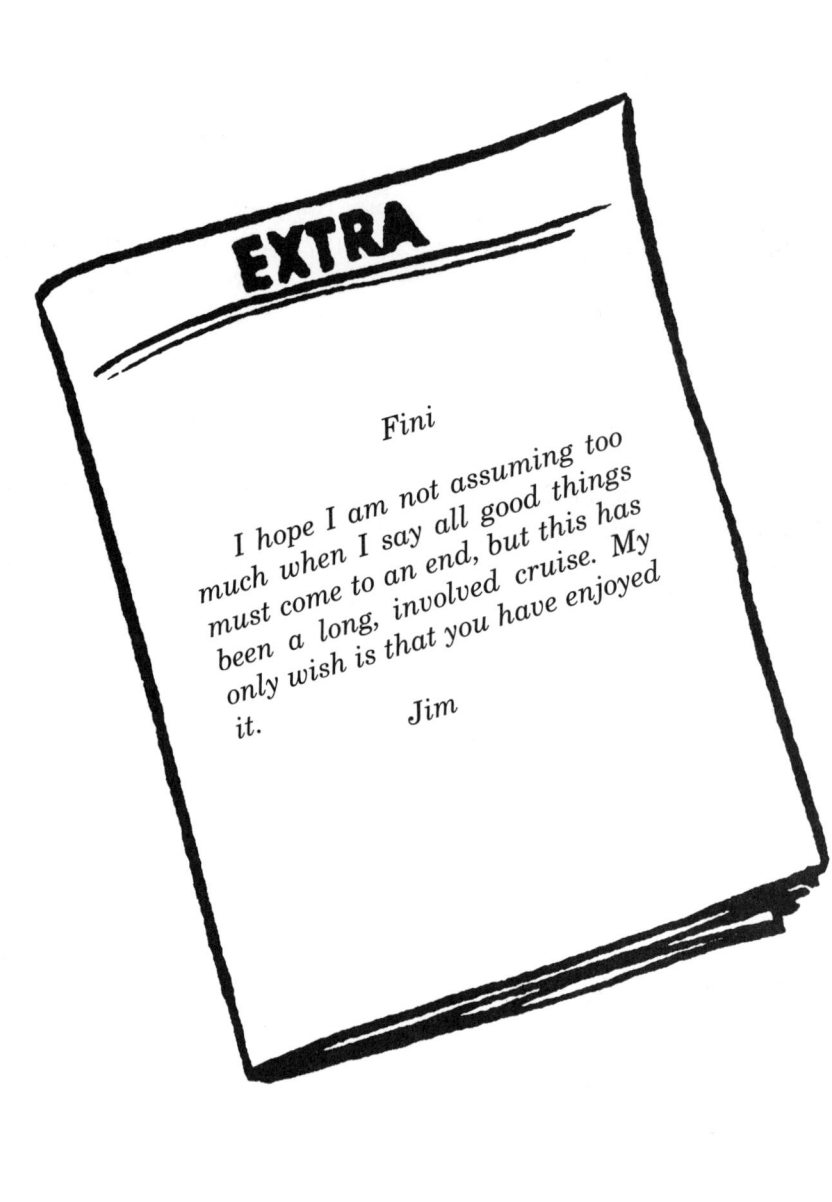

EXTRA

Fini

I hope I am not assuming too much when I say all good things must come to an end, but this has been a long, involved cruise. My only wish is that you have enjoyed it.

Jim

Towing Industry Leaders

American Waterways Operators Officers and Offices

Looking back at the AWO, its presidents following Chester C. Thompson and Braxton Carr were James Smith, 1972-1977; Anthony Kucera (acting president), 1977-1979; James B. Potter, Jr., 1979-1980; Kucera, 1980-1983; Joseph A. Farrell, 1983-1993; and Thomas A. Allegretti, 1994 to present.

In the beginning AWO had a Chicago office; it was closed November 1, 1945. There was also one in Pittsburgh, in charge of W. W. Partkow. This office was shifted to Cincinnati on April 1, 1946, and was closed March 15, 1947. What was considered the organization's first national office opened first in St. Louis, then moved soon to Washington. Because it was first in St. Louis, the AWO chose to celebrate their 50th anniversary in St. Louis in April 1, 1994.

An office to cover the Midwest was set up in St. Louis in 1977, with Lonnie P. Jacobs in charge. Robert G. Goodwin, Jr., took over in 1978, and it, too, was closed in 1983. Paul J. Werner was in charge when the office reopened in 1993.

The AWO New Orleans office for the Southern Region has been a vital one for years. A number of people have maintained it, including R. D. Brown, Jr., N. L. Caruthers, Harry W. Parsons, James P. Kenny, David Brown, McVey Ward, Merle L. Harbourt, Cornel Martin, John Duke, and Ken Wells.

Dave Brown was later moved to the Washington office. Handling publicity for AWO was Yates Catlin and Homer Hendrickson.

Board Chairmen

1944-1947—Henry F. DeBardeleben, Coyle Lines Incorporated

1948-1950—Alex W. Dann, Union Barge Line Corporation.

1951-1952—Manger T. Ball, Sabine Towing Company

1953-1954—A. M. Thompson, Central Barge Company

1955-1957—V. A. Kogge, Marquette Cement Manufacturing Co.

1958— A.C. Ingersoll, Jr., Federal Barge Lines Company

1959— David A. Wright, Lake Tankers Corporation

1960— Robert L. Gray, Ashland Oil & Refining Company

1961— Bailey T. DeBardeleben, Coyle Lines

1962— Jesse E. Brent, Brent Towing Company

1963— M. F. Spellacy, Humboldt Oil & Refining Co.

1964— F. A. Mechling, A. L. Mechling Barge Lines

1965— Gresham Hougland, Hougland Barge Line

1966— Robert L. Bryant, Dow Chemical Co.

1967— Neville Stone, Crounse Corporation

1968— G. W. Gladders, G. W. Gladders Towing Co.

1969— George H. Blohm, Dow Chemical Company

1970— Peter J. Brix, Knappton Towboat Company

1971— William C. McNeal, Oil Transport Company

1972— Harley G. Noland, Union Carbide Corporation

1973— Robert J. Hughes, James Hughes

1974— Harold G. Williams, Gulf Atlantic Transport Corporation

1975— Louis P. Struble, Jr., Dravo Corporation

1976— John D. Geary, Midland Enterprises

1977— Frank T. Stegbauer, Southern Towing Company

1978— Ralph W. Hooper, Interstate & Ocean Transport Co.

1979— William A. Creelman, National Marine Service

1980— John M. Donnelly, Jr., Ingram Barge Co.

1981— Ralph E. Van der Naillen, Cargo Carriers

1982— Thomas A. Gladders, G. W. Gladders Towing Company

1983— Archie L. Wilson, Dixie Carriers, Inc.

1984— William A. Creelman, National Marine Service

1985— James H. Sanborn, Sonat Marine, Inc.

1986— Berdon Lawrence, Hollywood, Marine, Inc.

1987— Capt. Arthur M. Knight, Reinauer Companies

1988— Arthur M. Knight, Reinauer Companies
1989— Jerry A. Tinkey, Mid-America Transportation Company

1990— Robert A. Guthans, Tennessee-Tombigbee Towing Company

1991— Alois Luhr, Luhr Bros., Inc.

1992— Don Duffy, Foss Maritime Company

1993— Donald Duffy Foss Maritime Company

1994— Clint Odell, Cargo Carriers

1995— Michael Hagen, American Commercial Barge Lines

1996— Greg McGinty, Turecamo Maritime

1997— Ronald C. Dansby, Kirby Inland Marine, Inc.

1998— Charles Nalen, Marine Services, Inc.

1999— Fred Raskin, Eastern Enterprises

National Waterways Conference

1960-1961—Paul G. Blazer, Ashland Oil & Refining Co., president
and chairman of the board
1961-1962—Paul G. Blazer, chairman
Wade W. Holowell, first National Bank, Greenville,
Mississippi, president
1962-1963—Wade W. Hollowell, chairman
Joseph M. Jones, Canal Barge Company, president
1963-1964—William E. Kemp, attorney, Kansas City, Missouri,
chairman
Gilbert M. Dorland, Nashville Bridge Company, president
1964-1965—Tom Adams, Secretary of State, Tallahassee, Florida,
chairman
Gilbert M. Dorland, president
1965-1966—John C. Kelly, Journal-Tribune Publishing Company,
Sioux City, Iowa, chairman
Tom Adams, president
1966-1967—Same as 1965-1966
1967-1968—C. H. Vescelius, Olin Matheson, chairman
John C. Kelly, president
1968-1969—Same as 1967-1968
1969-1970—Calvin T. Watts, Louisiana Department of Public Works,
chairman
Louis C. Purdy, Toledo-Lucas County Port Authority,
president

1970-1971—Same as 1969-1970
1971-1972—Same as 1970-1971
1972-1973—L. P. Struble, Jr., Dravo Corporation, chairman
William J. Hull, Ashland Oil, Inc., president
1973-1974—Same as 1972-1973
1974-1975—Herbert R. Haar, Jr., Port of New Orleans, chairman
Houston Adams, F&M Bank and Trust Co.,
Tulsa, Oklahoma, president
1975-1976—Same as 1974-1975
1976-1977—Glover Wilkins, Tennessee-Tombigbee Waterway
Development Authority,chairman
1977-1978—Same as 1976-1977
1978-1979—Lloyd E. Anderson, Port of Portland Commission,
chairman
Robert S. Kerr, Jr., Oklahoma Water, Inc., vice
chairman
1979-1980—Same as 1978-1979
1980-1981—James A. Skinner, Jr., T. L. Herbert & Sons, Inc.,
chairman
Robert S. Kerr, vice chairman
1981-1982—Same as 1980-1981
1982-1983—Richard A. Wilson, Agri-Trans Corporation, chairman
L. E. "Les" Sutton, Dravo Mechling Corporation,
chairman
1983-1984—L. E. Sutton, chairman
George R. French, Jr., Atlantic Cement Company, vice
chairman
1984-1985—Same as 1983-1984
1985-1986—Rodman Kober, Continental Grain Company, chairman
Sheldon Morgan, First Alabama Bank, Mobile, vice
chairman
1986-1987—Same as 1985-1986
1987-1988—Sheldon Morgan, chairman
Berdon Lawrence, Hollywood Marine, Inc., vice
chairman
1988-1989—same as 1987-1988
1989-1990—Berdon Lawrence, chairman
1990-1991—Berdon Lawrence, chairman
J. D. Laman, Dow Chemical, vice chairman
1991-1992—J. D. Laman, chairman
W. Richard Christensen, Ashland Petroleum Co.,
vice chairman
1992-1993—Same as 1991-1992
1993-1994—W. Richard Christensen, chairman

> Robert W. Portiss, Tulsa Port of Catoosa, vice chairman

1994-1995—Same as 1993-1994

1995-1996—Robert W. Portiss, chairman
> Dennis L. Kirwin, Midland Marine Corporation, vice chairman

1996-1997—Same as 1995-1996

1997-1998—Dennis L. Kirwin, chairman
> Craig E. Philip, Ingram Barge Company, vice chairman

1998-1999—Same as 1997-1998

1999-2000—Craig E. Philip, chairman
> Fred C. Raskin, Eastern Enterprises, Inc., vice chairman

Inland Rivers, Ports and Terminals

Presidents

1998-2000—John Bennett, JIT Terminal, Chattanooga, Tennessee

1995-1998—Glen Cheatham, Jr., Oklahoma Department of Transportation

1994-1995—John F. Hines Missouri Department of Transportation

1993-1994—Ron Coles, W. R. Coles & Associates

1992-1993—Richard Cirre, Kentucky Port and Rivers Development Commission

1991-1992—Pat Ross, Tennessee-Tombigbee Waterway Development Authority

1990-1991—Thomas Cooley, Loriment Development Corporation, Cape Girardeau, Missouri

1989-1990—Brian Frennea, Logistic Services, Inc.

1988-1989—Cliff Mitchener, Yellow Creek State Inland Port Authority

1987-1988—Chris Kennett, Indiana Port commissioin

1986-1987—T. J. Stevens, Pemiscot County Port Authority

1985-1986—David Work, Rosedale-Bolivar County Port Commission

1984-1985—Mark Allen-Carl Ranft, Southwind Maritime Centre

1983-11984—Carl Ranft, Tri-City Regional Port District

1982-1983—Howard Margraff, St. Louis Terminals

1981-1982—N. M. "Buck" Shell, Fort Smith Port Terminal
1980-1981—Col. Paul Sheffield, Memphis-Shelby County Port
    Authority
1979-1980—James Swift, The Waterways Journal
1978-1979—Wally Gieringer, Pine Bluff Port Authority
1973-1978—Col. Milton Barschdorf, Greenville Port
    Commission.

MARC 2000
(Midwest Area River Coalition)

Chairmen

1992-1993—Mike Hagen, American Commercial Lines
1994-1995—Fred Schrodt, Farmland Industries
1996-1998—Al Anderson, Cenex/Harvest States
1999-2000—Stephen Sheridan, Peavey Barge Line

DINAMO
(Association for the Development of Inland Navigation in America's Ohio Valley)

Chairmen

1981-1984—Dan Galbreath, John W. Galbreath & Company
1984-1986—Eugene Cattabiani, Westinghouse
1986-1989—Bobby Brown, ConsolEnergy
1989-1992—Neil N. Diehl, Ingram Barge Company
1992-1997—Joe R. Irwin, PNC Corporation
1997-2000—George Weber, Jr., U.S. Steel Minning LLC
2000—   —J. Brett Harvey, ConsolEnergy